D0287562

AMERICAN AID TO GREECE

AMERICAN AID TO GREECE

A REPORT ON THE FIRST TEN YEARS

by C. A. Munkman

FREDERICK A. PRAEGER · *Publisher* · New York.

BOOKS THAT MATTER

First published in the United States of America in 1958
by Frederick A. Praeger, Inc., Publishers
15 West 47th Street, New York 36, N. Y.

© 1958 in the United States of America
by Frederick A. Praeger, Inc.

Library of Congress catalog card number 58-9694

Printed in the United States of America

ACKNOWLEDGMENT

As a whole, references to individuals have been excluded from the text. It is therefore only right to acknowledge here those who had a large part in the original work on which this book is based. If this book has any value, major credit must be given to my former colleagues and friends of the American Economic Mission to Greece, who gave so much advice and help, especially to Messrs. White, Mace, Packard, Bishop, Miller, Liccado, and Mattingley; to my former staff, who did the main investigation work, especially Messrs. Christodoulates, Houlis, Saliaris, Zeis, Theologis, and our driver, "Yanny"; to the Greek Government employees, who so freely provided information and facilities, especially Messrs. Kalinsky, Samarras, Christodoulou, and Palaeologus, and to foreign technical experts, especially Messrs. Foan and Hopkins.

Very kind assistance in preparing the text, and in proofreading, by the Misses Jean H. Macdonald, M. L. Brice, and M. N. Waterman is most gratefully acknowledged.

I am indebted for certain statistical information contained in the text to the "Greek Statistical Yearbook."

PREFACE

The purpose of this book is to tell the ordinary taxpayer something of what happens to the dollars and pounds provided for foreign aid programs. The author has been associated with various aid agencies for ten years, and, as a public accountant, has had the opportunity of obtaining reliable information on the use of aid funds.

Much of the matter contained in this book is based on extensive reports of investigations undertaken when the author was Chief of Audits and Surveys of the United States Economic Mission to Greece. These investigations, initiated by the Mission to secure better use of United States aid to Greece, included within their scope evaluation and criticism of projects concerned. They have covered a very large part of the progress of United States economic aid to Greece, the largest individual program to an underdeveloped country. It is the only program of reconstruction and development that continued throughout the period from 1944 to 1956. No other country's program has yet been the subject of reports and investigations of this type.

It is generally recognized that the postwar foreign aid programs have involved very considerable waste and extravagance. Nevertheless we are committed, in America and Britain especially, to the continuation and expansion of a policy of financial and technical assistance to underdeveloped countries. This is a matter of enlightened self-interest as well as neighborliness. Under modern conditions the backward dweller in distant places follows world affairs with a far greater intensity of interest than do the majority of Americans or Britons. He knows about New York, London, and Hollywood; about our food, clothes, and amenities. He and his wife and children want the same economic benefits. He knows that generations of unaided efforts will be required to reach this goal, but with our help he may attain it in a few years. His test of friendship is our willingness to give him a helping hand.

Four years ago this was brought home to me during a visit to a Cretan village on a high mountain plateau. An UNRRA bulldozer had just chewed a rough road through twenty miles of mountains over which even mules formerly traveled with difficulty. The president of the village said, "During the war the British agents promised us help for a better life. For six hundred people of this community, I thank our British and American allies for keeping this promise. Previously we produced to live only, because it was virtually impossible to carry our goods to market. Yesterday the first truck arrived to transport our grapes to the cities. We are increasing our cultivated acreage by 50 per cent this year. Next year our wives will go shopping in town by bus."

Two months later another village president said, "We are unable to understand these radio stories that America has given two billion dollars to Greece. That would be $125 for every man, woman, and child in Greece, or $200,000 for this village. Two years ago we wrote to ask the Greek government and the American Mission to lend us $25,000 to drain the swamp below our village to reclaim a thousand acres of new land. No one has replied. We wish you to tell the American Mission that someone must have stolen the aid money. We know no one who has benefited, and we are sure that so large a sum properly used should have made a new Greece."

This simple logic may explain to readers why so vast an expenditure of aid has attracted so little gratitude from its recipients. In the author's considered opinion, the blunt and unpleasant truth is that in Greece and in other countries the aid investment has not been applied in a manner that would yield the best possible results. Nor has its administration been entirely free from graft, corruption, and incompetence.

If we are to compete effectively in the development of the huge potential markets of the backward countries, we must learn from past mistakes how to make much better use of aid program funds and investments in the future. The new era of "competitive coexistence" will inevitably strain our resources to the utmost, and careful management is therefore imperative.

This books consists of three parts. The first two chapters explain the postwar aid programs. The succeeding part follows a particular program—Greece—from the planning stage to the present day. The final chapters reveal the problems in the light of the lessons learned from this case study.

—C.A.M.

Khorramshahr, Iran
September, 1957

CONTENTS

AMERICAN AID TO GREECE

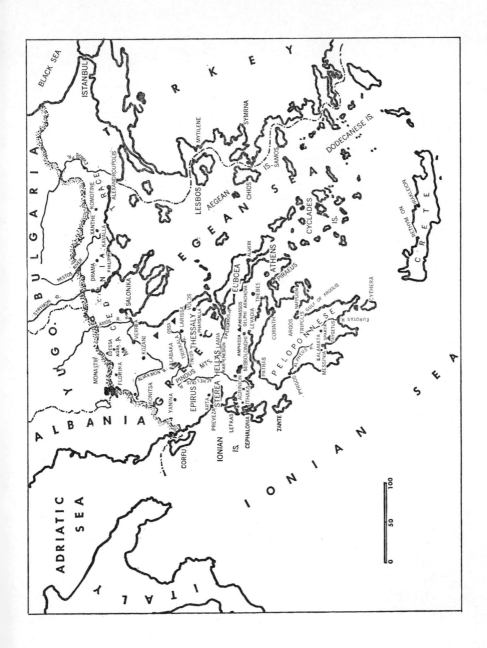

CHAPTER 1.

The Story of Aid Programs

FOREIGN AID AND INVESTMENT PRIOR TO 1939

Records of diplomatic and commercial relations between independent states cover a period of at least five thousand years, and, consequently, contemporary experiences are rarely novel or unique.

There are in fact many precedents for policies of direct financial assistance between allied states in peace or war. King Solomon and Hiram of Tyre had a mutual agreement for financial and technical assistance in building the Temple at Jerusalem. The Roman Empire regularly subsidized neighboring nations that had suffered bad harvests or other calamities in order to avoid the unpleasantness of border raids. Granting subsidies to allies to provide arms and maintain armies has always been a regular practice. Likewise, schemes of capital development in backward countries have precedents. The Roman Empire was notable for substantial reclamation works as well as major programs of road construction. In past eras mutual assistance was on a restricted scale between near neighbors. The tremendous advance in communications during the 130 years that followed the advent of the steam locomotive has extended the concept of "neighbor" to include the entire world.

Practical businessmen and theoretical economists of the last century early recognized the inevitable impact of industrial progress on the development of backward countries. Throughout the hundred years preceding the 1914 war the theory of mobility of capital implied that, with the inevitable evolution of a free and stable world economy, the more advanced countries would automatically provide from their own export surpluses the necessary investments in productive development. Through this period of expansion the outward flow of private capital, pouring from Britain, France, and Germany into overseas investments in railways, new industry, land development, and innumerable other enterprises, did in fact spread progress all over the world.

The United States was the most outstanding beneficiary; colonial territories and South America were also developed; but investment was not limited to politically controlled areas or to countries with close ties. Russia and China, despite political insecurity, were major fields of investment. The private investor rested in a serene confidence that he was behaving rightly and properly (for a suitable interest rate) and that his rights would, in the last resort, be supported by the guns of a warship or the bayonets of his country's army.

World War I effectively eliminated France and Germany as foreign investors and severely curtailed British capacity, but the gap was temporarily filled by the United States. The reckless nature of early American adventures in the field partly contributed toward the Wall Street collapse of 1929, and appears to have acted as a deterrent to private United States investors. New American capital has tended to confine itself within its own political boundaries and to a few "stable areas," or to types of specialized investment such as oil, where risks and returns are commensurate.

Prior to 1939, therefore, foreign investment of private capital had slowed down very considerably, and it is certain that even without the effects of World War II some measures would have had to be taken to encourage or replace the flow of private capital into underdeveloped countries. Perhaps an expansion of League of Nations loans or of "guaranteed loans" might have been considered. However, no one conceived of direct state intervention on the scale that has actually occurred between 1945 and the present time and that has now become a permanent feature of international affairs.

FOREIGN INVESTMENT AND INTERNATIONAL TRADE

Before considering postwar conditions it is necessary to review some of the fundamentals underlying the operation of our modern economic system. We all live by production and exchange of goods and services. During the last century of free economies, political boundaries were not regarded as seriously affecting trade relations, but over the last thirty years state intervention through customs duties, currency controls, and trade restrictions has increasingly tended to build a trade wall on the political foundations, and to manage, control, and direct the economic policy within the political unit. As a consequence states have become loose types of joint-stock corporations, so that coterminous with the boundaries of their political influence we have an economic unity, which we may conveniently call "G.B. Inc." or "U.S.A. Inc." to distinguish the economic from the political activity. Dependent from these major corporations are a number of subsidiary undertakings wholly or partially controlled, such as Cuba Inc., Australia Inc., and a whole complex of commercial associations throughout the world, but for clarity it is better to take the simple example.

U.S.A. Inc., like any major trading corporation, has a complex of departments of which the end product of one constitutes the primary product of another. It also has an elaborate pattern of internal services and trading departments to meet the needs of its staff and members and the maintenance and extension of its plant and equipment. In this analysis we are concerned only with its external customers and suppliers. As with any other trading organization external sales are conditioned by demand, and within certain policy decisions external purchases are dependent on its sales. The principal selling lines are primary products such as wheat, maize, cotton, and tobacco, and manufactured items such as heavy machinery, tractors, and other farm equipment, and transport equipment such as motor vehicles and airplanes. Its outside purchases are mainly raw materials such as rubber, metals, etc., and amenity or luxury items such as Scotch whisky, French champagne, Spanish olives, Japanese silks, and English textile specialities.

Like any great corporation, U.S.A. Inc. could reduce its external trade to a minimum and live largely off itself, but this policy has certain unpleasant consequences. First, a considerable amount of interdepartmental dislocation would occur; second, in certain departments substantial cost increases would result as a consequence of the reduction in the volume of output; third, ultimately due to technical changes or to the deliberate policy of other traders the basic exports would be excluded from world markets, and essential imports would become unobtainable. The whole of man's historical experience proves that expanding international trade involves increasing prosperity, whereas its contraction appears to result inevitably in stagnation and poverty. It is therefore established policy to achieve the maximum external sales.

This, of course, raises the problem of the medium of exchange. A great deal of confusion in economic thought arises through a belief in the separate, independent existence of "money." We forget that if millionaire X, through a ship or plane wreck, is precipitated like Robinson Crusoe on a desert island with ten million dollars in bank notes, checks, or other such paper, their only value to him is to kindle a fire, and not the slightest difference is made to the world's real wealth whether he does so or not. Wealth is represented by production goods: natural raw materials worked on by human hands. These goods exist at any time in three forms: in inventories, processed or partly processed, as wheat at all stages between the germinating seed and the loaf of bread; in process of consumption to satisfy human needs, as the loaf in the kitchen, the refrigerator in which it is stored, or the tiles on the kitchen floor; or incorporated in capital assets to facilitate production and processing of more goods, as the water gates in an irrigation dam, the plant of a textile mill, or the locomotives, track, and crossties of a railway line.

International trade by sale of goods simply means the exchange of inventory goods for a token that represents a right to buy some other goods. U.S.A. Inc. therefore sells its inventory wheat, tractors, machine tools, etc. for acknowledgments of debt from the buyer. This "debt paper" may be subject to many conditions and qualifications, depending on the terms of sale and the creditworthiness of the buyer. Like a dollar bill it may be immediately salable in exchange for goods of any kind, anywhere; or like a sterling credit it may be a voucher to buy goods only from G.B. Inc. and its numerous subsidiary and associated corporations known as the "sterling area." The debt may be payable in installments over twenty years, or it may be payable in two months. As in any commercial transaction, the conditions of sale depend on the state of the market and the type of goods. U.S.A. Inc., with rising inventories of wheat, will offer the buyer inducements in longer credit or greater restrictions on the salability of the debt paper. With falling inventories sales will be for immediate cash. Generating plants, locomotives, and farm tractors will tend to be on deferred payment terms. It is this "deferred debt paper" that makes up the portfolio of foreign investment held by U.S.A. Inc.

It may consist of stocks and bonds of foreign states, public bodies, or private corporations, loans or book debts

to foreign business houses, bankers' balances, term bills, installment contracts, clearing account balances, or any conceivable
form of property entitlement. The debt paper may be held
by the government or by individual citizens of U.S.A. Inc.
Two qualities of all debt paper must be considered: transfer-
ability and realizability. With regard to the first, one has to
recall that a buyer often pays a seller by handing him a debt
paper on another trader; so Greece Inc. may pay U.S.A. Inc.
for wheat purchased with debt paper on G.B. Inc. for currants
supplied. The value of any debt paper depends on the good
standing of the debtor. Certain losses are almost inevitable,
and it may be necessary to scale down the debt.

Another factor to be considered in connection with
debt paper is the disposition the holders may wish to make of
it. Human relations, individual and international, are not
governed solely by commercial criteria. U.S.A. Inc. and other
holders of international debt paper may settle, waive, cancel,
or give away part of the portfolio. Typical examples in individual human relations are remittances by American citizens to
aged parents in Eire, Italy, Greece, etc., and gifts to missionary
societies, relief funds, charities, and the like. Or United States
citizens may expend funds on sight-seeing tours in Rome, or
on Scotch in London bars.

Every nation strives to hold a balance of debt paper,
both short- and long-term, to meet special emergencies or to
tide over hard times. This is usually described as "foreign
exchange balances." A moment's thought will indicate that
this is impossible, since every debtor must be balanced by a
corresponding creditor. There must always be "debtor" and
"creditor" nations, and it is evident that normally the stronger
and more advanced, such as U.S.A. Inc. and G.B. Inc., will be
creditors and the poorer and less developed will be debtors.
However, a nation may be a long-term debtor and a short-
term creditor or vice versa. A creditor position normally arises

through providing more goods and services to the debtors than are received from them. It is quite obvious that if this debt is ever to be discharged, the productive capacity of the debtor must be increased, so that in years to come the debt may be liquidated by a reverse flow of goods. Normally, then, the debt paper of a less developed country should be contracted in respect of capital asset goods such as heavy machinery, land or mineral development, railways, and similar "productive capital investments."

Debt paper and foreign investment are obviously affected by the political relations between the various national economic corporations. Part of the debt paper acquired by U.S.A. Inc. and G.B. Inc in commercial transactions is utilized to support the poorer military allies of the United States and Great Britain in NATO, SEATO, etc., in their arms and defense establishments. This has been recognized for fifty centuries as an essential cost of trade relations, since it is self-evident that levels of material production, trade expansion, and especially long-term capital development, depend on internal and external security. All great trading nations have consequently been committed to maintaining substantial defense establishments and to subsidizing the establishments of allies.

Another type of international assistance also has a parallel in individual human relations. Blood ties, friendship, and moral duties enter into economic relations to a far greater degree than is generally realized. It is therefore by no means uncommon for individual trade debtors to receive special assistance from associates or creditors when some unfortunate loss has made it difficult for them to meet their commitments. This assistance may be in the form of postponement, partial waiver or cancellation of debts, direct loans, guarantees, or even gifts. These concessions may be based on nothing more than past trade contacts.

This type of assistance is equally applicable between national economies, and it is a long-standing tradition that when some state has been smitten by economic disaster such as crop failure or physical destruction, friendly nations should extend a helping hand by long-term loans, outright gifts of goods, credit, or services, and moratoria or extinction of debt claims. Innumerable cases are recorded in history of emergency shipments of grain and similar basic supplies to meet famine conditions after national catastrophes or as a consequence of war devastation.

Precedents therefore existed for the steps to be taken to meet the economic consequences of World War II, but never had devastation occurred on such an astronomic scale. It was quite clear, even in 1943, that many ravaged countries would be in desperate need of the most essential supplies, and that large-scale destruction of major capital assets had occurred. It was also clear that the countries most severely hit were without any of the reserve holdings of foreign exchange, and therefore had to be provided with essential supplies either as gifts or on long-term credit. The position was further complicated by the acute shortages among potential suppliers. Neither private nor independent national initiative could meet this situation, and the only possible solution lay in coordinated international action.

UNITED NATIONS RELIEF AND REHABILITATION
ADMINISTRATION (UNRRA)

Under the guidance of President Roosevelt the allies established in 1943 the organization commonly known as UNRRA to meet the immediate postwar needs of the liberated allies. In theory the allied countries that had never been occupied by the enemy were to raise a levy, based on their national incomes, to provide the funds to place their allies who had suffered military occupation back on a "working basis." The occupied countries of the British Commonwealth were excluded from benefits as being a concern of their immediate partners.

According to original plans the immediate responsibility for maintaining essential supplies and services rested with the liberating armies. Immediately after military operations were concluded in a region, responsibility passed to UNRRA. It was planned that the UNRRA operation would be divided into two stages. The first, relief, would be concerned with the necessity of meeting basic human needs until the national economy could be revived. The second, rehabilitation, would be concerned with the restoration of the economy by importation of essential supplies and capital goods.

As it was appreciated that aid requirements would exceed available funds, assistance was to be restricted to those countries whose exiled governments did not have available resources in foreign exchange to take initial steps on their own account. Under this provision France, Belgium, Netherlands, Luxembourg, Norway, and Denmark waived any claims to UNRRA assistance. Aid was in fact given primarily to China, Yugoslavia, Greece, Albania, Czechoslovakia, and Poland. It was later extended to certain countries that technically had been enemy (Italy, Austria, Finland, and Hungary), and to the Ukraine, Byelorussia, and Ethiopia in a limited field.

UNRRA, to perform its responsibilities, was given the status of a sovereign state, and was commissioned to act on a humanitarian basis without regard to political alignments. Total funds placed at its disposal finally aggregated four billion dollars, of which Britain provided six hundred million. Levies from smaller countries, including certain voluntary donations by invaded countries such as Norway and Denmark and by friendly nonmember states (Eire, Portugal, Argentina) somewhat exceeded the British share. The balance was found by the United States.

Many criticisms have been made of UNRRA and of its personnel. The tally of "UNRRA scandals" is almost past counting. In the eyes of many people, to have been associated with UNRRA implies a dubious moral and political background. Many UNRRA scandals arise through mistaken identity. The line of demarcation between military and civil responsibilities was not readily comprehensible to the informed outsider, and UNRRA has often been blamed for the activities of the civil government sections of the allied armies and other similar bodies. Planning was difficult due to lack of reliable informants; decisions had to be immediate, and in the absence of regular economic and administrative organization in the beneficiary countries they were inevitably based on inadequate information. All types of civilian supplies were short, and alternative selections often raised difficulties. In such circumstances blunders and waste were inevitable.

Recruitment of competent staff was virtually impossible in 1944 and 1945, and inevitably a number of incompetents and dubious characters squeezed in. The author held a position (deputy director of accounting for the European Region) that necessarily placed in his possession the bulk of the information about financial scandals, whether proved or unproved. It was, and still is, his considered opinion that despite many errors, much waste, and more than a little misuse, the vast bulk of the UNRRA funds were properly used. The faults have to be weighed against the benefits. In the ordered society of London or Washington human failings exist in the best of times. Where the very lives of men, women, and children are at stake, the precautions and safeguards that limit waste and loss must be sacrificed to speedy action. The margin of fraud and error automatically expands. Against these increased losses we must weigh the saving in human lives, health, and happiness. This is the criterion by which UNRRA must be judged.

Before proceeding to later events a particular circumstance that affected the UNRRA program must be mentioned, since it has important bearings on later events. The original UNRRA conception had envisaged a comparatively short relief period, with the consequence that the bulk of funds would be committed to rehabilitation, i.e. the restoration of capital assets. In actual fact, the reverse occurred. The significant causes varied between country and country, and require complicated and detailed explanations. In general, however, it may be said that the destruction and disorganization were much more widespread than anticipated. Inevitably, basic production fell far below anticipated levels, with the result that funds intended for capital goods had to be diverted to the procurement of essential food supplies and so on. Political changes and instability necessarily had their effects, and shortages in American and British economies delayed deliveries of capital goods, which inevitably checked the expansion of production in the "beneficiary countries."

As the end of UNRRA aid approached, it was generally recognized that the work was far from completed. However, changes in political alignment and public opinion made a new approach necessary.

POST-UNRRA AID

By the summer of 1947, Poland, Hungary, and Yugoslavia (to be followed by Czechoslovakia) had fallen within the Russian sphere of influence. Austria was divided. Italy was recuperating. Attention was particularly concentrated on China and Greece, where revolutionary movements were making headway. Under special legislation military aid programs were developed for these countries and Turkey. These military aid programs included a strong element of economic assistance.

In addition, various other techniques were used. Greece, for example, received a loan from the Export-Import Bank, which was used for capital equipment, etc. The military assistance program ("AMAG program," as it is known in Greece) was a stopgap which was shortly to be absorbed in a larger concept.

THE MARSHALL PLAN

The Marshall Plan, administered by the Economic Cooperation Administration, was on vastly greater scale. It included within its scope the UNRRA beneficiaries—Austria, Greece, and Italy—but extended its protection to the entire group of Western nations—Britain, France, Benelux, etc. An explanation of this extension of aid is necessary. The essence of our modern economy is the division of labor, resulting in a highly developed system of exchange of goods within the national economy and with other nations.

Any trading corporation in normal conditions has four characteristics essential to this system: an inventory of marketable goods, a substantial number of debts due at varying dates from customers who have bought goods, a substantial number of debts payable to suppliers, and either a cash reserve or the equivalent in loan facilities from a bank. Refusal of credit by suppliers and bankers will force any corporation out of business. A national economy is only a sum of individuals. In normal circumstances, the developed national economy has its working capital, involving debit and credit balances with other nations and a reserve in gold, foreign exchange, or credit facilities, as well as inventories available for international trade.

Let us explain this by an example. A nation earns its foreign income by exporting wheat, but must import fertilizers, pesticides, and petroleum products. It is obvious that it must obtain credit for its imports, to be liquidated from sales of wheat after harvest. Normally speaking, international trade is a well-oiled machine in which such arrangements follow long-established lines. From 1939 to 1945 it was virtually suspended. The foreign exchange and credit facilities of the nations were exhausted by war demands. The objective of each country was to expand its inventories and short-term foreign exchange. With short supplies, transactions were on an immediate basis, with every nation counting its pennies and rejecting any requests for longer credit. Some of the more substantial nations could get some credit, but the less wealthy were obviously thrust aside. "Immediate terms" meant dollars, since these were the only freely exchangeable debt paper.

[The primary objective of Marshall Plan aid to the Western countries was therefore to supply the working capital to get international trade moving.] One of the requirements of the Marshall Plan aid was the establishment of the Organization for European Economic Cooperation (OEEC) and the European Payments Union (EPU), whose objectives were to re-establish the old trade and credit system. Marshall Plan aid was given to recipient countries in the form of procurement authorizations, which could either be expended in the United States or be used to settle their liabilities to other countries through EPU or other clearing machinery. Ultimately, there was, of course, no difference between the two processes. A dollar credit was an authority to buy in the United States. It could be exercised directly or could be given to someone else to exercise in exchange for his goods or services.

The objective of Marshall Plan aid was substantially achieved by 1951. At this point, with the opening of the Korean war, Congress limited future aid by military conditions;

certain types of credits were no longer forthcoming, and Economic Cooperation Administration became Mutual Security Agency. The European countries, with one or two exceptions, had been placed on a sound trading basis, and international credit had been re-established, so that goods were once more being sold on deferred-payment terms.

POINT 4 PROGRAM (TCA)

In the interim President Truman had announced a new type of aid, to be administered through the State Department, known as the Technical Cooperation Administration. This type of assistance was to be given to countries whose standards of living were far below those subsisting in the Western world. In general, this program laid more emphasis on technical assistance and educational projects. In the Marshall Plan programs for the European nations some provision had been made for exchange of technical information, for provision of experts, and for training of technicians, but these projects were small in relation to total aid. In less developed countries technical training and expert advice are sometimes more important than financial assistance. In most instances provision of capital goods and development of natural resources must be associated with technical guidance.

LATER PROGRAM CHANGES

In July, 1953, the Technical Cooperation Administration, the Mutual Security Agency, and the Escapee Program, together with certain functions in relation to UN programs, were merged under the title of Foreign Operations Agency, which functioned under Stassen as an entity separate from the State Department.

On July 1, 1955, the functions were absorbed by a new agency, the International Cooperation Administration, subordinate to the State Department. This ended, for the time being at least, the independence of the economic aid functions. The merits and demerits of the change have been heatedly discussed. Some comments are forthcoming at a later stage in this book.

Fundamentally, the issue turns on whether economic aid and cooperation are regarded as a weapon to be directly used for enforcing the day-to-day political relations between the United States and its allies or friends, or whether they are to be regarded as being administered in accord with the higher ideals of enlarging human prosperity and happiness, regardless of casual differences. As a policy instrument, economic aid loses the dignity given it by former United States declarations and becomes a payment for conformity with a certain line of thought or action, which may be accepted or rejected by the consciences of its recipients.

DISGUISED FORMS OF AID

So far, reference has been made to the aid programs so described. However, certain other measures have been taken that have a double motive. The most outstanding examples are "offshore procurements" and "stockpiling of strategic materials."

These techniques are applied mainly in conjunction with the military aid with which this book does not profess to deal. The supply departments of the United States government might contract with British factories to supply war materials to Italy. Chromium might be bought from Greece or Turkey for stockpiling in the United States. More elaborately, bauxite might be bought in Greece, refined in Germany, and manufactured into airplanes in France. Such activities benefit the economies of the countries concerned without adversely affecting the United States, since the dollar credits provided are used to procure, say, machine tools in United States. In fact it is an interesting example of the circulation of credit and division of labor. The American government could buy airplanes in the United States and supply them to its allies. This would expand American aircraft production but depress machine tool production. By permitting its allies, in effect, to make airplanes against payment in machine tools, the United States balances its own economy and simultaneously expands the productive capacities of its allies.

AGRICULTURAL SURPLUS DISPOSAL

A less constructive form of economic aid is embodied in the recent schemes for disposing of agricultural surpluses in the United States. Increased production at home and in the recipient countries and the cutbacks in aid have left the United States government with large inventories of agricultural products procured under price stabilization legislation.

Recent congressional legislation empowers the executive to dispose of these surpluses by gift to certain defined groups in economic distress at home and abroad. Legislation also empowers the sale on deferred terms of repayment extending to forty years. The recipient countries, of course, are the former beneficiaries of the aid program, although it is now proposed to extend the field.

To clarify this operation, the way this program works in Greece may be cited. Greece receives its regular program allocation from FOA (now ICA), which is currently in the form of procurements of wheat, sugar, and other items. Greece also procures wheat on long-term repayment from agricultural surpluses. In addition, through American voluntary agencies, Greece was allocated around thirteen million dollars in 1956 from the "giveaway" agricultural surpluses, which may be taken in wheat, sugar, dairy products, etc. This giveaway program is at present operated in the form of meals for school children, food parcels for the unemployed and destitute, and bulk food supplies for old peoples' homes, hospitals, orphanages, and earthquake victims.

No comment is necessary on the effects of this competition in aid between various agencies. It is a new feature and apparently arises through internal pressures on Congress to reduce aid but maintain purchase of the commodities.

CHAPTER 2.

The Mechanics of Aid Programs

PUBLIC MISCONCEPTIONS OF THE AID PROGRAM

Since returning from my last assignment with the United States government I have been astonished at the general lack of knowledge of the fundamentals of the aid programs. Most people assume that aid is a form of charity in which thousands of hungry and naked are fed and clothed. Quite understandably they are puzzled as to why this condition should exist now. This type of operation, properly known as relief, was largely completed in 1946, although, the poor being always with us and life providing a regular quota of disasters, some relief will always be necessary.

The intelligent businessman who appreciated the purpose of Marshall Plan aid in lubricating the machinery of international exchange regards this operation, too, as completed and is unable to understand why further economic aid is needed. Another, again, can understand why credits are provided to Greece for a power-generating station or for technical assistance or earthquake relief, but cannot understand why United States aid credits include the procurement of wheat, sugar, coal, coffee, oil, and typewriters.

The explanation of this puzzle is provided in the previous chapter. No national economy can buy from others goods to a greater value than it sells without issuing debt paper. Most economies have established an equilibrium that enables them to meet current import needs over a period out of current exports. Most countries exercise controls of various types to limit imports to the level that they can afford to pay for with exports. A poor or underdeveloped country has little to offer the world, and consequently its imports will be scaled down to such absolute necessities as grain. The process of development involves the importation of heavy capital equipment such as railroad materials, machinery, bulldozers, reinforcing steel, etc. This importation must occur before any increased supplies of exportable goods can be available to pay for them, often ten or twenty or more years before. This excess importation can be made only if one of the prosperous economies is prepared to supply this need against deferred debt paper. Now we come to another problem. Our creditor economy has supplied the capital goods to build, say, a large dam that will provide power and irrigation water. Construction may take five to ten years. Full benefits may not be felt for fifteen or twenty years or even more, because factories must be built after the power and the irrigation canals. New crops or herds of cattle have been provided, and a host of new techniques must be learned. During the construction period labor must be withdrawn from productive processes, but it still requires food and clothes. If the project is to be carried out quickly and efficiently, then, deferred debt paper must be also provided to cover the cost of importing grain and textiles, to feed and clothe the construction gangs, and to pay off the fees and salaries of foreign contractors and technicians to supervise and advise. When the project is finished some exportable goods will be available to pay off the old deferred debt paper. However, rising living standards have generated new needs, and presumably they will force the lifting of austerity import controls. New capital will be required to supplement the original investment, and the old deferred debt will simply continue under the same or another name. The precedents of the United States, Canada, and Australia, which successfully liquidated their debts to Great Britain over two world wars by selling strategic materials and war munitions at exceptionally inflated prices, cannot be taken as generally applicable. Without this exceptional stroke these economies would perhaps still be in the debtor nations category as they were in 1914.

Of course, a nation lucky enough to strike oil, uranium, or some other vital commodity may soon emerge from the debt stage, but the majority of underdeveloped countries will have to come up the hard way. The immediate need is for investments that will increase the production of basic necessities to lift their populations from substandard conditions to a more endurable life. Private capital flows readily to develop the oil fields of Saudi Arabia, but no enthusiastic foreign investor is prepared to give the same financial support to nearby Jordan or to Turkey and Greece. Yet if such investments are not made, the world is going to consist of an incredible checkerboard of "haves" and "have nots," of starvation and luxury, which can result only in continuous disturbance and unrest.

In practical terms, investment in the less developed countries is an inevitable insurance premium to safeguard more profitable investments elsewhere, and an investment in future goodwill; for even if the original investment is not repaid the creditor nation may expect to benefit from future increased purchasing power of the debtor. Any good businessman recognizes that new markets cannot be gained without expenditure of market build-up, advertising, and initial losses. It is the purpose of this book to consider whether this type of investment should be loan or grant, private or public, conditional or unconditional. The following sections consider the general principles that have applied to the administration of aid funds over the last ten years.

As we know, American aid credits are voted by the United States Congress on an annual basis. These credits include a number of diverse elements. Military aid in the form of military supplies or common-use items for military purposes are not the direct concern of this book. They may, as we have seen, be of economic benefit in developing natural resources or in providing facilities that may be of general economic value. Local construction or the presence of United States military personnel may provide a country with additional foreign exchange, but this is accidental. The balance of the aid voted consists mainly of the economic-aid-to-country programs. In addition there are contributions to various UN agencies that are occupied with the problems of development.

There are also a number of "relief operations," such as agencies for assistance of Palestine Arab refugees, political escapees, and the residual hard core of displaced persons from World War II. These operations may be constructive, such as contributions toward migration and re-establishment. Relief grants may also be made in cases of national catastrophe such as the recent earthquakes in Greece.

ORIGINAL FORM OF UTILIZATION OF DOLLAR CREDITS

The economic aid credits in dollars provided to country programs may be expended in any form approved by United States operating agencies. The state may, on its own account, use the credits to procure consumer goods such as wheat, sugar, or dairy products, or capital goods such as railway engines, power plants, etc. Alternatively private importers may use the credits to procure goods through regular trade channels, including, of course, wheat, sugar, coal, machine tools, and so forth. The private importer is often unaware that he is in fact using aid funds, since the decision to use aid credits rather than free funds is usually made by the central bank or other agency approving the application for foreign exchange.

Formerly aid funds were often given as a deficit payment on a clearing account, thereby covering a group of transactions with a particular country or countries rather than individual items. Currently, under global procurement, certain funds may be expended for imports from many countries. The supplying countries will, of course, spend the aid credits passed to them in payment to finance their own purchases in the United States. A form of control is exercised over aid credits to insure that the procurements are of a serious and not a frivolous nature. The first effect of aid is therefore to ease the foreign exchange position of a country and enable it to buy consumer or capital goods not otherwise available.

COUNTERPART FUNDS

A second effect is achieved within the national economy. Local currency, equivalent in exchange to the dollar credit used, is deposited by any private importer using United States aid credits. This credit is passed to an account with the central bank generally known as "counterpart." The account is also credited normally with the local currency equivalent of the dollar value of goods imported for state account. (In certain circumstances deposit of counterpart may be waived).

The counterpart is divided into two portions. Ten per cent (formerly 5 per cent) is deposited in a United States government account and is available for use within the country at discretion of the United States. It is normally used for mission, State Department, and other governmental local salary costs, rentals, building construction, etc. The balance, under joint control of the national and the United States governments, is used to sponsor projects jointly approved by the two parties for the benefit and assistance of the people of the country. These may be social needs such as hospitals, relief works, or major capital investments in development. In certain exceptional circumstances partial waiver of counterpart deposit is made. If, for example, a government imports wheat for resale, the United States government might approve that proceeds of sale instead of landed value be deposited, thereby giving a subsidy to local living costs.

In Greece the government was authorized to import capital goods such as heavy tractors, rolling stock, industrial machinery, and housing materials on its own account, against a bank loan offset against counterpart. This, in practice, had the consequence of relieving the state not only of the foreign exchange but of the necessity of charging the state budget for these programs.

TECHNICAL ASSISTANCE

Part of the aid program is often given in the form of payment of salaries and expenses to expert advisers and technical specialists directly employed by the beneficiary government, or in the form of costs of training of local nationals in the United States, or elsewhere. The requirement of depositing counterpart applies also to this program, although it may be and often is waived in whole or part.

Originally the economic missions were quite heavily staffed by experts paid from other United States budget funds. But recent economy measures have heavily reduced staffs, either actually or nominally, by transferring personnel to the technical assistance head.

COUNTRY PROGRAM

The actual program of development depends on a merger of the three forms of aid by foreign exchange credits, technical assistance, and advances from counterpart. If we assume the example cited in the first section of this chapter, in which a country contemplates the construction of a hydroelectric power station combined with an irrigation scheme, the form of coordination of assistance will be appreciated.

Technical assistance funds will pay the foreign technicians who make the surveys and plans and supervise the construction. The essential plant, machinery, and construction materials will be procured from part of the dollar credits on state account. Local currency should be deposited by the state in the counterpart account to cover this, but where the state budget does not possess the necessary funds this requirement might be waived.

The local contractors undertaking the construction may import equipment such as draglines, bulldozers, etc. against the aid credit, for which they will deposit local currency as counterpart. Alternatively, the state may import this equipment and later lease or sell it to the contractor by installments. The balance of the aid credit will probably be used by private importers to procure grain, textiles, and other approved imports. The local currency paid to the central bank for these imports will be deposited in the counterpart account. Ten per cent will be transferred to the American Mission to meet its local currency costs, and the balance will be released from time to time, with Mission approval, to meet the labor and other costs of project construction.

This is a simple example. Normally a country program will involve a wide field of activity and many varied projects. In later chapters we shall see something of the complexities and problems. Before we reach this point, however, a few words are necessary on the structure of an economic aid mission.

ECONOMIC AID MISSION

The development of any substantial economic aid program is obviously a complex affair. Initially, some governing

agreement between the United States and the beneficiary country is necessary to set out the general conditions and terms
of aid. This lays down the controls on use of dollar and counterpart funds and provides for the presence of a mission of
appropriate size to supervise implementation and settle day-to-
day problems. The agreement provides that any funds not
used for the approved purposes, or any improperly used, should
be repayable.

The actual build-up of the mission will depend on country and program needs. There are the basic administrative
units; a management or programing unit to coordinate plans,
approve procurements against aid credits, and examine projects; a controller unit to maintain financial records, conduct
financial audits and investigations, and make "end use" checks
of aid imports; and a chief of mission with necessary administrative staff. Much administrative support is provided by
existing State Department units such as personnel, general
administration, budget and fiscal, etc.

Over and above these, operating units of specialists in
agriculture, industry, power, transport, public health, civil
government, and economics may be necessary. Most underdeveloped countries are sparsely equipped with experienced
technicians and administrators. It is obvious that if aid funds
provided by the American taxpayer are to be committed to
various projects, the plans and proposals should be reviewed
by competent specialists. The function of these specialists is
to work with the specialist officials of the national government
in the preparation of plans for aid utilization and in the general development of the various branches of the national economy and the machinery of civil government.

Latterly, many of these specialists have been reclassified
as Technical Assistance to the United States Mission (or country government) in their work as program advisers and super-
visors. The Mission is partly staffed by local employees in

addition to American personnel. These may be administrative workers such as clerks, typists, and interpreters; or they may themselves be program specialists such as engineers, doctors, or agriculturists acting as assistants to the American specialists.

In a number of cases (the writer is an example) "third-nation" nationals have been employed within the missions on specialist assignments. Inevitably, mission personel have close contacts with foreign technical assistance experts working in the country. Such experts may be American, sponsored by the mission and supported by Aid program funds, or they may be sponsored and supported by UN agencies.

WORK OF UN AGENCIES

Some of the funds voted by Congress for economic aid are actually passed to UN agencies to administer. These funds are matched by contributions from other nations, and are principally devoted to technical assistance of underdeveloped countries. The aid agency, now International Cooperation Administration, coordinates activities at headquarters level with the UN programs.

The UN Technical Assistance Committee is the main organization for the administration of the T.A. funds, but a major part is played by such UN agencies as FAO (Food and Agricultural Organization), WHO (World Health Organization) UNESCO (UN Educational, Scientific and Cultural Organization). Fundamentally these agencies are concerned with the exchange of knowledge, information, and experience, so that the less developed countries may have the opportunity to share with the more advanced. Technical Assistance programs are also concerned with sharing experience by making expert services from other nations available to less advanced countries. The monopoly of experts does not rest with, say, the United States or Great Britain. Many smaller nations have special experience or techniques. In some fields better help may be provided by specialists of a nation that has recently met similar problems, and may in fact be only a short distance ahead of the state requesting assistance.

Unfortunately the financial allocations can meet only a fraction of the demand, and United States experts of equal caliber are considerably more expensive than those of Great Britain or other European countries.

EMIGRATION AND REFUGEE ASSISTANCE

The problems of transfer of population and assistance to refugees and displaced persons arc so complex that they merit a book in themselves. Two special agencies, the UN High Commissioner for Refugees and the Intergovernmental Committee for European Migration (ICEM), are partly supported by aid program grants. The former is a UN agency, the latter an association of the United States and other interested governments. They have succeeded to the work of the International Refugeee Organization, which had previously taken over the work of UNRRA and other agencies for displaced persons and political refugees. ICEM has, of course, an interest in the wider field of migration from overpopulated countries.

The Political Escapee Program (now integrated with the present United States aid agency, ICA) administers a program in coordination with these agencies and also has a program of its own to assist postwar political refugees.

GENERAL

The foregoing presents a brief summary of the main divisions of economic aid. No statistics of cost are of real use, since figures over a billion dollars lose significance. Greece, whose program is the subject of this case study, has absorbed at least two billion dollars of combined British and United States aid since 1945. British contributions are mostly to colonies and dominions and are spread over a multiplicity of programs.

The ultimate cost of assisting development cannot be foreseen or estimated. Part will certainly be met by private initiative, and part of any national program may finally be repaid. The problem and possibilities can not be recognized in generalities, but a glimpse of the state of an aided country and of the results of aid planning may help to achieve an understanding of the very complex issues involved.

CHAPTER 3.

Greece

SOUTHEASTERN EUROPE

The corner of Europe commonly known as the Balkans has been a region of instability and disturbance for many centuries. At one time this region between the River Danube and the Mediterranean sea, together with the neighboring coast of Asia Minor, contained the world's richest and most advanced cities. Incoming waves of migrants from the northeast constantly threatened this civilization through the first thirteen centuries of our era. Nevertheless these migrants were progressively integrated, Christianized, and civilized by the Romano-Byzantine Empire.

The Turkish invaders of the fourteenth and fifteenth centuries finally overwhelmed and conquered the provinces of southeastern Europe that we now know as Greece, Yugoslavia, Romania, Bulgaria, and Turkey. The invaders then moved on to attack the Central European powers: Austria, Hungary, Poland, and Czechoslovakia. The bitterness of the seven hundred years of struggle that only ended in 1923 has no historic parallel. The conquered and invaded nations were all Christian states with a common culture and the same Indo-Aryan ethnic origin, and possessed a generally advanced civilization and economic system. The invaders were a primitive nomad people of simple soldierly qualities, but ignorant of the arts, techniques, and culture of civilization, and with entirely different linguistic and ethnic origins.* Moreover they followed a religion that in

* Actually the Hungarians and the Bulgars of similar ethnic origin had been integrated after accepting Christianity and European civilization.

33

their interpretation commanded the extinction of nonbelievers and assured the absolute superiority of its believers.

This unending war of annihilation brought untold miseries to this corner of the civilized world. Millions were slaughtered, and millions were sold into slavery. No one who does not know the Balkans appreciates that the scars are still not healed. Here, villagers will tell you, some heroic guerilla was flayed and roasted to death; there, another suffered inconceivable tortures while his wife and daughters were raped and slaughtered in front of his eyes. One of my staff recently mentioned to me that his grandmother (as a teen-age girl) had been seized and sold as a slave. A friend, a Greek government official of no more than fifty years, remarked to me in casual conversation that, of course, the Turks were not a subtle people. He recalled that when he was a boy the Christians usually knew when another massacre was coming.

Of course, matters were not always one-sided. The last great Turkish invasion laid siege to Vienna in 1683. Broken by Sobieski's Polish lancers, the routed army fled toward home. Few escaped the hands of the vengeful Christian peasants of the conquered and ravaged lands through which they had to pass. Final liberation of the Balkans occupied another 240 years, however, and the Turks, now on the defensive, excelled in repressive measures against their unwilling subjects.

One after another the conquered European nations—Yugoslavia, Romania, Bulgaria, Greece—came to life again, but seven centuries of war and servitude had left little of their civilization. Impoverished and broken, but with pride in recovered honor and a superbly passionate fanaticism for freedom, they started to build again. Over this sorely battered area passed the German invasions in two World Wars, to inflict further destruction and check the hardly won gains.

Romania, possessed of rich grainlands, soon discovered rich oil fields. Prior to its absorption within the Soviet sphere its recovery had been almost complete. Yugoslavia and Greece are rugged, mountainous lands. Their natural beauty hardly compensates for their lesser fertility and lack of obvious natural resources. The way of progress is therefore not easy, since the struggle to live leaves little margin to build up new capital.

The peoples as a whole feel that for seven centuries they suffered in the general cause, and that this record and the further losses suffered in World War II when they fought again to defend liberty give them a moral claim to constructive assistance from the other Western nations. Greeks often express this claim in direct terms. Serbs are less outspoken. Nevertheless one acquaintance summarized Yugoslav policy in a conversation in 1947, before the break with Russia: "Assistance to build our country is badly needed. We welcome it as the assistance that one friend gives another who is in need, and we shall hope some day to repay such friendship. The United States and Russia must both understand that the soul and honor and the sword of Serbia are not for sale. We have broken with America, and we will break with Russia if their economic aid requires that we should be their dogs."

This attitude is common to Greece and to many other underdeveloped countries.

THE LAND OF GREECE

Greece is the most southerly of the Balkan countries, and its northern frontiers, as our map shows, march in turn with Albania, Yugoslavia, Bulgaria, and Turkey.

The country is exceedingly rugged. Of its 51,000 square miles, little more than a quarter is cultivated. Most of the balance is mountain—rangeland, forest, and barren. Olympus rises to nearly 10,000 feet. An enumeration of the lesser peaks from 4000 feet up would be a catalogue. Its inhabitants may claim that, rolled out flat, Texas would encircle the globe. After traveling more than 150,000 miles in Greece I am prepared to accept a statement that the mountains of Greece, piled on end, would reach the moon. The rugged nature of the terrain has another peculiar result: deep indentations give Greece the longest coast line, in proportion to area, in the world.

Geologically, Greece is a Tertiary formation, an extension in a southeasterly curve of the upheaval of the earth's surface that created the Alpine and Balkan mountains. The predominant rock is limestone. Due to destruction of the once extensive forests, which now cover no more than 8000 square miles, the runoff of water from the steep slopes is extremely rapid. Rain at once produces boiling mountain torrents pouring their waters into the river valleys to break the banks and flood the fields. Within hours the torrents can cease and the rivers run dry. The erosion in the mountains and the destruction in the valleys are considerable. The river deltas are clogged with the detritus brought down by the floods.

The climate of Greece is Mediterranean, characterized by a hot, dry summer and a short winter, with rainfall occurring mainly in heavy downpours between November and March. The total population of Greece is rather over eight million, of whom one-fifth are concentrated in the more industrialized capital area of Athens and Piraeus.

The characteristics of the country and of the people vary markedly between the different regions. Conveniently, these can be divided into four: Continental or North Greece, bordering on Yugoslavia, Bulgaria, and Turkey; Peninsular Greece to the south, almost entirely surrounded by sea except where it joins the European continent to border with Albania and North Greece; South Greece or the Peloponnese, virtually an island linked to Peninsular Greece by a ridge of land two miles wide;

and the Islands, scattered to the south, east, and west of Peninsular and South Greece in a broad arc.

North Greece (Macedonia and Thrace), containing 16,500 square miles and two and one half million people, is continental. With Turkish Thrace (to the east) it forms the southeast corner of the main European.land mass. It is a comparatively level coastal strip from thirty to fifty miles wide hemmed in between the sea and the Balkan ranges which mark the frontiers with Yugoslavia and Bulgaria. The Balkan rivers Axios (Vardar), Strymon (Struma), and Evros have cut the valleys that make the entry roads into the hinterland. This is primarily a grain-producing area. Peninsular Greece consists of the provinces known as Sterea Hellas, Thessaly, Epirus, and Euboea, and contains around 18,500 square miles and around three and one-half million people, including, of course, the capital area of Athens-Piraeus. Down the center of the peninsula on a north-south line run the Pindus mountains. To east and west this rocky spine throws out ribs to cut the country up into a series of compartments. Communications over this area have always been a problem. Any traveler between east and west must traverse ranges whose most convenient pass attains six thousand feet above sea level. North-south communications are almost equally difficult, since the mountains must be crossed from one valley to the next. It is this characteristic that has made the Greek the seaman of the world for thirty-five centuries, and that even today places under Greek ownership an ocean-going fleet comparable with that of America or Britain. Until recent times it was easier to transport goods and passengers between the valleys by sea than by land. Peninsular Greece is a region of wide variations in climate and cultivation. Thessaly, bordering North Greece, is a broad grain-growing plain. Epirus is an extremely mountainous area. The remainder of the region includes fertile plains and rugged mountains in a confused pattern. The island of Euboea, heavily forested and joined to the mainland by a fifty-foot bridge, is an island in name only.

By contrast, the Peloponnese (8300 square miles, with a population of nearly one and one-half million) which is linked to Peninsular Greece by the narrow isthmus of Corinth, has definite island characteristics and is clearly distinguished in climate and characteristics from the peninsula. Geologically, the Peloponnese is the continuation of the spinal column of Pindus which some subterranean force split with a deep chasm into which the seas have entered. This chasm is still a line of seismic disturbance, as witness the recent earthquakes that affected the Ionian Islands of its western end and the Corinth area. The Peloponnese is aptly described by its medieval name of Morea (plane tree leaf). The narrow stem of the isthmus suddenly broadens out to east and west to taper away gradually in a number of southward-running capes. The central mountain area is bordered to north and west by a coastal belt of intense cultivation of vines and olives: the regions long known as Corinth, Achaea, and Elis. High central mountain plateaus with forest and rangelands characterize Arcadia. Southward, narrow fertile valleys run down to the sea, rich in olives, fruit, and garden crops: "lovely Laconia and smiling Messinia," as the ancient poets called them.

The fourth region of Greece is an arbitrary classification: the Isles. With a total area of 7700 square miles and a population of one and a half million, they have no homogeneity in size, characteristics, or locations. Scattered to east and west and south of the mainland, they range from almost submerged mountaintops to the great island of Crete (3200 square miles, with 500,000 inhabitants). Some, like Lesbos, Chios, and Rhodes, lie off the coast of Asia Minor. Corfu on the extreme west is the steppingstone to Italy and has many of that land's characteristics. Crete stands on its own, unique, and too big for island characteristics to be sharply defined. Yet nature so endowed it that it became the first home of our Western civilization.

In the west are the Ionian Islands, principally Corfu, Lefkas, Cephalonia, Ithaka, and Zante, with a dense but declining population of 250,000. These are the lands of Odysseus, inhabited and cultivated for 3500 years. On Corfu and on Zante nature is mild; on the others, more rough and rude. Thirty centuries ago Homer wrote of Ithaka that it was a rugged home for goats, but Corfu was a garden of paradise in which fruit trees blossomed and yielded throughout the year.

The Aegean islands on the east consist of two main groups: Chios, Samos, Lesbos, with the Dodecanese belonging to continental Asia rather than Europe. Total population exceeds 400,000. These are the remnants of Greek expansion into Asia. The Cyclades are a collection of mountaintops that scatter the sea between the Aegean isles, Crete, and mainland Greece; they formed the steppingstones of early Greek trade and expansion. Now their total population is 150,000, seamen and fishermen mostly, who form the hard core of the crews of the Greek shipping fleets.

THE BACKGROUND STORY OF GREECE

History is an essential part of the training of anyone in foreign service, since it provides important clues to the present. The first inhabitants of Greece of whom we have certain knowledge were members of the Indo-Aryan race, belonging to the same family as the other Western nations, who moved into the area we have just described around 2000 B.C. They appear to have been among the first members of the Western family to get moving from their place of origin in the central mass where Europe and Asia join.

Having moved, these people have occupied the same area for forty centuries. Pioneers in emigration among the

Western people, they have been pioneers in almost every other field. Reading, writing, and keeping accounts in the same language since 1500 B.C. at least, they laid the foundation of Western techniques of trade, industry, shipping, science, art, literature, politics. First Western people to adopt Christianity, first to grow wheat, first to erect magnificent buildings, first to codify their laws and establish democratic institutions . . . it is almost impossible to enumerate the credits.

Four thousand years of Greek history have known many ups and downs, but the greatest disaster was the fall of Constantinople, in 1453, and the consequent Turkish conquest of the Greek lands. History has known no comparable catastrophe. The following centuries of oppression literally reduced their numbers by 80 per cent. In 1821 a poverty-stricken, broken remnant of this great people in the Peloponnese once more lifted the standard of liberty. In 1453 the last Greek Emperor, Constantine Palaeologos, and the Pope had called on the Western nations for a crusade to help defend Constantinople and Western Civilization. The Great Betrayal, the failure of the sister nations to respond to that call,* has never been forgotten and is in part responsible for the religious schism. In 1827 partial recompense was made, when the combined Western naval squadrons shattered Turkish naval power in the bay of Navarino and brought liberation again to the Peleponnese, the Cyclades, and a small area of "Sterea Hellas" (18,000 square miles with 700,000 people).

Throughout the nineteenth century this little area was expanded in a series of wars and treaties culminating in the Balkan War of 1912. At this time the frontier rested on the Olympus ranges, which separate Peninsular Greece from Continental (Northern) Greece. In a desperate battle the Greek

---

* The Turks were particularly fortunate in that every Western nation was at this time in a state of political and economic upheaval, with civil war in England and France. Otherwise a response would certainly have been made.

army forced the passes in a victorious sweep that liberated Salonika and also Macedonia. The soldiers of Greece, in whom patriotism and love of liberty combine with religious sensitivity, testify that the last charge that cleared the Turks from the pass of Sarandaporo was led by the armored figure of Saint Demetrius, soldier saint and patron of Macedonia, mounted on a great white horse.

Unfortunately this victory was not the end. Greece gained further territory in Europe after the First World War. More dangerous, however, was the acquisition of the coastal cities of Asia Minor. These cities had been Greek since 1000 B.C., and in pre-Turkish times Asia Minor had been entirely Greek. Turkish infiltration, however, had progressively reduced Greek ethnic influence in the hinterland and restricted it largely to coastal pockets. An overexpanded and disorganized Greece was unable to sustain its latest conquests against a rejuvenated Turkish revolt under Kemal Ataturk.

The Treaty of Lausanne in 1923 defined the final frontiers. Greece was to retain Western Thrace to the Evros River, but Eastern Thrace (the strip of Turkey in Europe) and Constantinople were to remain with Turkey. The isles off the Turkish Asiatic coast were to remain Greek (except Imbros and Tenedos guarding the Dardanelles, under Turkey; Dodecanese, under Italy; and Cyprus, under Britain) but the mainland cities were to be surrendered to Turkey. To secure this peace as permanent, the treaty provided for exchange of populations. The Greek ethnics of the Asiatic cities and Eastern Thrace were moved en masse to Greece: Turkish nationals were moved from Macedonia, Crete, and other recently liberated territories to take their places. (The exchange was not absolutely enforced in Western Thrace, where a substantial Turkish minority still lives, in consideration of a similar tolerance to the Greeks of Constantinople.)

FRUITS OF VICTORY

The fruits of victory (for the country had doubled in area and tripled in population in ten years) were embittered by the tragic failure to redeem Constantinople and by the Asia Minor disaster. This left a mark on Greek political unity which only time has healed. The significance of Constantinople to the Greek mind is almost impossible to appreciate. Always important, from the third to the fifteenth centuries it was Europe's, and probably the world's, greatest city. The City, as the Greeks call it, even in decay under Turkish sovereignty, has still an amazing psychological effect, and its loss still rankles and inevitably affects Greco-Turkish relations.

Political and economic stability was essential after 1923. The huge migration of nearly two million foreign-born Greeks had to be established. "Old Greece," liberated in the nineteenth century, so long on a war footing, had neither faced nor solved its own problems of development. The "liberated province" of Macedonia, once one of Europe's most prosperous areas, had sunk into decay. The British and French armies had learned this to their cost in 1914–1918. Endemic malaria from undrained swamps and marshes sapped the health and vitality of the country.

From 1925 onward, major drainage schemes backed by international loans were initiated in Macedonia, Thessaly, and West Greece. Expanded Athens was provided with water and power. The economic crisis severely hit Greece's major exports, the semiluxuries tobacco, and dried fruit. More serious was the catastrophic fall of the shipping on which Greece largely depended. A campaign of self-sufficiency through wheat-growing was initiated.

By 1939, although the Greek position was not by any means satisfactory, progress was being made. The resettlement program had been faced and largely solved; the cities of Athens and Salonika had expanded and improved housing conditions; major productive developments were in progress; health standards had been vastly improved by drainage, sanitation, and better water supplies; and new roads had been built. Most important of all was the greater political and economic stability.

THE SECOND WORLD WAR AND ITS AFTERMATH

On October 28, 1940, the Italian ambassador presented to General Metaxas a demand for free passage of Italian troops through Greece. The laconic negative that ultimately brought almost total destruction to the country was the only reply that the Greek sense of liberty would permit. The repulse of the Italians was followed by a German attack on Macedonia. Total defeat of Greek and British armies swiftly followed.

The four years of privation that followed cannot be fully appreciated without an intimate knowledge of the country's physical structure and economy. Prior to World War II the wages of Greek seamen and the profits of the shipping magnates largely provided the foreign exchange to buy wheat and sugar. Greece has been from time immemorial a wheat importer. The Greek is unquestionably the world's greatest bread-eater. Absorption in a conquered Europe already deficient in grain meant literal starvation. Moreover, communications in the mountainous terrain and between the isles are tenuous at best. Under war conditions, with the restrictions on movement imposed by the occupying powers, they virtually broke down. Wheat might be available in Salonika and olive oil in Mytilene, but one could not be exchanged for the other except by risking death and forfeiture of cargo.

Guerrilla activity, mainly evidenced by blasting of road and rail, intensified the transport problem. In 1944 the retreat

of the occupying armies was accompanied by a mass destruction
of road and rail, by removal or destruction of rolling stock, and
by sabotage of all port installations. Other losses had to be
added. The newly constructed drainage systems in North
Greece were largely wrecked; mass destruction of forests had
occurred at the hands of the enemy or of a civil population
without fuel; draft animals and farm machinery had been
requisitioned by the military, friendly and hostile. Guerilla
activities and punitive raids had destroyed small towns and
villages. Livestock had been stolen or consumed. Agricultural
productivity in such conditions had fallen to fractional levels.

To this confusion was added the Communist insurrection in Athens in December, 1944, and the political instability
that followed. The Communist revolt, checked for a time by
British military intervention, nevertheless continued in various
forms and broke out again in the provincial areas in 1946. It
was not until mid-1949 that the Greek government, with
American and British military assistance, was finally able to
end the insurrection, which had of course been continually
receiving aid from Albania, Yugoslavia, and Bulgaria, along the
whole extent of the northern frontier.

During this period of civil war, not only communications but villages were attacked and razed. In general, the
government forces were able to safeguard the larger towns, but
some smaller cities were captured and sacked. For example
Naoussa, a textile mill center near Salonika, was looted and
its mills and machinery destroyed. Seizure and destruction of
livestock and crops in the mountain areas were inevitable, and
the towns were flooded with over a million homeless refugees.
Much of the destruction seems to have been carried out as part
of a deliberate Communist policy to wreck the economy even
if the revolt were unsuccessful. This is the only explanation for
firing standing timber and poor mountain villages.

ALLIED AID

Outside the military field the earliest allied aid was in the form of essential foodstuffs, medicines, and other basic supplies. Emergency repair work, including the installation of Bailey bridges, was carried out to restore essential communications. On April 1, 1945, UNRRA assumed responsibility for civilian relief and rehabilitation, and from this date until closure of operations in June, 1947, it was assisted by the British forces in Greece.

Food, clothing, and medicine still had priority. Draft animals, fertilizers, tractors, seed were imported to get agricultural production going. Boats for fishing and transport, railway, port, road, and bridge equipment were next essentials, as well as raw materials for industry, lumber, trucks, etc. British and American army surplus equipment was supplied, and equipment was fetched from Germany as reparations.

It was generally admitted, however, that only a fraction of the work involved in restoring the economy had been completed by June, 1947, and at that time the full effects of the Communist war had not been felt.

CONDITION OF GREECE IN 1947

It is impossible to convey a picture of conditions prevailing when an economy is broken down. Even worse than actual material destruction are the effects of deterioration through lack of maintenance. More intense than these are the breakdowns of the elaborate systems of administration, production, and trading that are the basis of our civilization.

A few comparative statistics will indicate the effect.

	Thousands of Tons	
	1938	*1947*
Wheat production	768	578
Currant production	158	76
Meat production	111	88
Milk production	705	441
Industrial production	*1939:* 100	*1947:* 67
	1939	*1947*
Locomotives in service	412	134
Freight cars	6,725	2,036
Number of merchant ships	607	270

Losses of draft animals—horses, mules, and donkeys—had been largely replaced by UNRRA in 1946, but their number was still 250,000 below prewar figures. The relevant data on road transport are not available, but despite UNRRA and the British army the supply was well below prewar levels.

It was obvious that the position in 1947 necessitated considerable further assistance to restore the prewar economy of Greece, in addition to the settling of the Communist war. Greece moreover was the only Western nation with three Iron Curtain neighbors on her borders. It was therefore imperative to give a lesson in the benefits of free economy. American aid therefore, when initiated in late 1947, was quickly concerned not only with the problem of relief and rehabilitation of a war-stricken ally, but also with a further stage of developing her economy. It was therefore necessary to consider the longer-term problems of Greece.

SOCIAL PROBLEMS OF GREECE

Reference has already been made in this chapter to the vast expansion in Greek territory and populations between

1910 and 1920 and to the influx of Asia Minor Greeks. Something must now be said of its social effects.

Through all history Greeks have been traders and shipowners, and it is by these vocations that they are best known. Even under the Turkish Empire these activities were not completely suppressed. The Greek merchants of Constantinople, Chios, and Smyrna, subjected to oppressions and exactions by the Turks, nevertheless managed to maintain a position as the traders of the Turkish Empire. In the nineteenth century many of this group established themselves abroad.

Moreover, the Constantinople Greeks formed a large part of the civil government machinery of the Turkish Empire. Basically, then, the Greeks who were liberated between 1910 and 1920, and the resettled populations, were city dwellers engaged in trade, banking, shipping, and administrative work. This classification is not absolute, of course, since many Cretans, Aegean Islanders, and even Asia Minor Greeks were agriculturists.

"Old Greece" was very different. Long ago Athens, Corinth, and Thebes had lost their trading interests to the cities of Asia, the Black Sea, and Thrace. The people of the Peloponnese and southern Peninsular Greece, liberated in 1833, were predominantly farmers and shepherds of a very low level of subsistence. Many were not ethnic Greeks but had infiltrated from Albania and Bulgaria and the Slav groups to the north. The Cyclades provided traders and shipowners. Only in the present century has Piraeus (the port of Athens) displaced Siros in the Cyclades as the port of Greece. Of fifty towns of over 10,000 population in present day Greece, twenty-five have been Greek since 1912, but of the eighteen over 25,000, only seven belonged to "Old Greece."

A backward rural population, living primitively, with restricted contacts with the world, was suddenly joined by a large, urbanized trading, merchanting, administrative group.

The result may be seen in the following data of urban population:

	1920	1928	1940	1951
Athens (including Piraeus)	453,042	802,000	1,124,109	1,378,586
Salonika	174,390	251,254	278,145	297,164
Volos	30,046	47,892	54,919	65,090
Irakleion	24,848	33,404	39,550	51,144
Drama	15,263	29,339	30,425	29,488
Serrai	14,486	29,640	34,630	36,760
Patras	52,174	61,278	62,275	79,014
Corfu	27,175	32,221	29,988	27,431
Trikkala	20,194	18,682	18,892	24,131
Siros	18,663	21,156	18,922	16,971

The first six, except Athens and Volos, are Greek since 1912. Athens and Volos were especially affected by Asia Minor refugee settlement. The last four are cities of Old Greece unaffected by the population exchanges. At the last census Serrai and Drama showed the effects of the Communist war, in which they were front-line towns.

In this context it may be remarked that the annual birth rate is around twenty per thousand, against a death rate of eight, which tends to cause a drift to the towns. This progressive urbanization is evidenced by census figures:

POPULATION DISTRIBUTION

	Towns under 2,000	Towns 2,000 to 10,000	Communities over 10,000
1928	48.9%	20.6%	30.5%
1940	48.4%	19.8%	31.8%
1951	44.6%	19.1%	36.3%

It is quite clear that an expanding industry is essential to absorb the increasing population. At present an underemployed population has developed in the cities, which is a source of material and political discontent.

In the rural areas the expanding population, lacking new lands, creates a class of underemployed laborers and results in further reduction in size of landholdings. By a process of subdivision under owner cultivation, these have already been reduced to an average size of six acres. As a consequence family incomes, where the land is not irrigated, may be as low as one hundred dollars per year. Apart from seasonal unemployment of workers, the farmers as a whole lack full employment due to limited crops cultivated. Enforced leisure results in social and political instability. Social services are poor. Medical facilities are generally inadequate. Housing generally is of low standard and fairly costly in relation to value.

ECONOMIC PROBLEMS OF GREECE

To maintain her people even on the present subnormal diet, Greece must import in best conditions approximately sixty million dollars' worth per year of basic food, primarily wheat and sugar. Fuel and petroleum products require a further forty million dollars. To these must, of course, be added a wide range of raw materials and manufactured goods that are essential—chemicals, fertilizers, steel and other metals, transport vehicles, machinery, spare parts, rubber, paper pulp, etc.—and that the economy is unable to provide. In 1953 total landed value of imports was $257,000,000, but this was the lowest since the war due to an exceptional harvest.

Against these essential goods Greece in the past has had very little to offer. Tobacco, dried fruits, olive oil were the major exports before the war. Until 1952 Germany, the main tobacco customer, was not importing, and Britain, the principal fruit consumer, was restricting her imports. Olives and olive oil could not be exported as they were required for home consumption. Exports of tobacco and dried fruit in 1953 realized nearly $80,000,000. Comparatively small exports of ores and cement and wine were the only other significant items. The adverse balance of trade ranged from $210,000,000 in 1947 to $320,000,000 in 1951. The deficit was mainly met from American aid payments.

It was evident that the immediate need was to expand agricultural production to provide greater self-sufficiency and exportable surpluses of exchangeable commodities. Over and above this, industrial production had to be developed, with the same objectives.

The educational problem presented in other underdeveloped countries did not exist to the same degree in Greece. The country had a tradition of high culture and civilization; the population was predominantly literate, and at many levels was in contact with Western developments. Labor was in abundant supply, and could presumably be trained in new crafts and techniques. Only capital and political stability appeared to be necessary to its rapid progress.

FINANCIAL PROBLEMS

A few brief words are necessary on financial problems. Throughout its existence the modern Greek state has enjoyed a more or less regular budget deficit. If a vast reservoir of national credit is available as in America or Britain, the annual balancing of revenue and expenditure becomes academic. Lacking such a reservoir, Greece has had to depend on foreign loans and currency devaluation. Currency devaluation, or inflation as it is now more politely called, is a question of degree. In some measure it is necessary to our economic system. In Greece it has attained astronomic dimensions. The prewar drachmae, and consequently bonds, bank deposits, etc., simply ceased to exist. The postwar drachmae moved from 150 to 30,000 to the dollar (the last three zeros have now been removed by a change of name, so that a thousand-drachmae note has become a one-drachma note). As a result no Greek keeps his liquid funds in cash or bank deposits. He carries gold in the form of the old minted British sovereign (pound). This is now worth around ten dollars. No one knows how much of this monetary gold is held. Any adult who is not absolutely destitute holds some. The first step of any one receiving payment in paper drachmae in excess of immediate needs is to convert it into gold pounds.

Psychologically, it is virtually impossible to do anything about this position. A man who has lost his savings two or three times through inflation cannot be blamed for taking precautions. In the frontier districts and the districts affected by the civil war fear of trouble is a further cause. Gold will buy escape and food at any time. The effect is to sterilize a substantial amount of internal credit, which, if expressed in bank deposits, would materially assist industry and agriculture. The monetary gold, if deposited with the Bank of Greece, would provide a reserve for procurement abroad.

The banking system is virtually hamstrung by the absence of deposits, and the treasury has no source of short-term loans. Loan credit to industry, agriculture, and state operations is on a hand-to-mouth basis.* The author has personally known cases of ordinary workmen on American aid projects with four or five months' salary unpaid. Printing more money is the alternative, but this only sets the inflationary spiral going again. The need is for a period of currency stability to restore confidence in the monetary system.

---

* At the end of 1954 figures of note circulation, bank deposits, and short-term bank loans were, in millions of new drachmae at thirty to the dollar respectively, 3843, 4054, and 8035. Assuming a working population of two million, this gives average figures of note circulation and bank deposits of about sixty dollars per head.

PROSPECTS OF DEVELOPMENT

Excluding the special postwar problems, which have in fact been solved between 1948 and 1956, the special need of Greece was and is capital development. It is completely typical of a large group of countries that lack special resources such as oil, etc., which would attract private investment capital.

The average diet is a bare 90 per cent of the FAO standards of caloric intake necessary to sustain life and health in the climatic conditions of Greece. The substandard average necessarily implies that a substantial proportion of the population is existing well below this level. This in turn implies for the bulk of the population a life of austerity, devoid of any amenities and with no possible margin of saving. The wealth of a nation rests on the individual wealth of its people. As everyone knows, there are individual Greeks of very considerable wealth, but their wealth springs from their shipping businesses and other enterprises operated from London and New York. It is there, if anywhere, that their taxes are paid. Occasionally they visit their homeland, sometimes for a few months at a time. Some even invest at home in large apartment blocks and similar properties. In fact this "profit capital" provides Greece with some fifteen million dollars a year in foreign exchange (dollars and sterling), which is a very important help to the country.

Apart from this, gifts from emigrants, revenue from tourists, and the sale of tobacco, dried fruits, and some fresh fruit, Greece has no other income with which to pay for the vital wheat, sugar, and petroleum. The Greek economy has little margin to buy such essentials to increased production as fertilizer, pesticides, and chemicals. There is no margin whatever for capital goods such as farm machinery, heavy plant equipment, etc. Internally there is no regular budget surplus to support a program of state capital investment, and little saving margin to undertake private development works. In

1952, for example, internal saving was entirely absorbed by increased inventories and dwelling houses, which in total amounted to no more than 5 per cent of the gross national income.

Labor is not short, and potentially it is generally agreed to be of a better-than-average standard. Given natural resources to develop and the capital to develop them, the exports and consequently the imports would rise. It is generally accepted that agricultural production could be greatly expanded with improved techniques and investment. The development of industry depends on a solution to the fuel and power position.

CHAPTER 4.

The Plan of American Aid

GENERAL REVIEW

The brief synopses in the preceding chapter have indicated the problems faced by the American mission in 1948. The mission had available the reports prepared by the preceding UNRRA mission, information supplied by the British Economic Mission, and reports prepared by the Food and Agricultural Organization of the United Nations on agricultural problems. Various development plans had also been prepared before World War II by foreign specialists and by some of the Greek government departments.

It was obvious that the first need was economic aid to support the military effort to crush the Communist forces. Immediate measures were also necessary to alleviate the plight of the war refugees, and ultimately to resettle them in their devastated homes. It was clear, too, that, until political and economic stability were attained, it would be necessary to provide credits for basic imports and to cover the budget deficit internally. These activities were clearly within the mandate of congressional legislation.

Something beyond these steps was needed. It was essential for strategic considerations that the position of Greece as part of the Western alliance be stabilized.

The map shows at once the special strategic position of Greece. Its surrender to Communist influence would bring

Russia to good Mediterranean ports, completely turn the flanks of Italy and Turkey, and directly threaten the Near East and Africa. The widespread dissemination of Greek peoples through the Mediterranean area and indeed throughout the world would constitute an additional embarrassment if the homeland was lost. The loss of China was serious. The loss of Greece in 1948 would have been a totally irreparable disaster. Its security was beyond price. The United States and Britain have already spent billions of dollars in military and economic aid, and must go on spending indefinitely.

Greece is vital to the West. Every Greek knows it. Greece is fundamentally loyal to her NATO allies. Of that there can be no question. Western culture and beliefs were mainly transmitted through Greece to the younger members of the European family. Democracy, politics, economics, are Greek, not English, words, like most of our philosophical and scientific terminology. To the Greek, therefore, Western civilization and culture are peculiarly and particularly his own creation. To betray them would be to betray nearly two hundred generations. The Greek, however, is traditionally a merchant, and he sees no reason why he should not get a good price for his loyalty, especially when he considers that he has a just and fair claim to economic aid to lift him to a prosperity approaching that of his allies. Recent political pressures must be viewed in this light.

How far this position was appreciated in the early planning is not clear. That something beyond rehabilitation was intended is quite evident. The objective was at least to initiate substantial capital development to offset Communist propaganda. The American mission to Greece appears to have intended to make the maximum possible development and to obtain from congressional credits the largest possible share for development in Greece.

Following the AMAG allocation of $105,000,000 in 1947–1948 for economic aid, the amounts provided in the calendar years 1948 to 1951 to finance imports were respectively 111, 254, 263, and 259 millions of dollars. In 1951–1952 the program was considerably cut, following the Korean War and the congressional limitation of MSA objectives to economic support of the military program. Levels therefore fell to 99 and 59 millions of dollars in 1952 and 1953 respectively. The above figures differ considerably from the actual aid voted, since there is necessarily a long time lag between allocation of funds and their final absorption when the goods procured are actually delivered. This may run to several years.

The original plans were necessarily made on a year-to-year basis, dependent on congressional vote. A change in policy cutting back funds was always considered possible, but the actual cut in 1951–1952 did result in major program reductions. This was particularly felt in the counterpart support. In earlier years considerable quantities of heavy machinery for productive development were imported. The cutback in counterpart from 1952 onward resulted in very real difficulties in mobilizing this equipment for utilization.

A further radical change in policy in 1952 has to be noticed. Until this time the American Mission had directly participated in the program, with experts working with all Greek government departments. From June, 1952, the Mission carried out a progressive withdrawal from program participation, so that now virtually no contact with Greek government operating departments exists. Mission personnel strength is now about 10 per cent of the 1951 figure.

The following sections summarize the Mission planning in the period 1948–1952.

ECONOMIC AID TO MILITARY OPERATIONS

Apart from essential military supplies and the common-use items necessary to maintain an army in the field, such as food, petroleum products, and clothing, the first necessity to re-establish security was adequate and assured communications.

Under the initial AMAG program, continued under ECA, groups of American contractors moved into Greece to rebuild the port of Piraeus, open the Corinth Canal, repair the damaged railways, and build or repair principal strategic roads. This work was conducted under the supervision of the U. S. Army Corps of Engineers by two principal groups: Atkinson-Drake-Park and Steers-Grove.

Piraeus was put into full use, the Corinth canal was reopened, and the principal bridges and tunnels on the main railway from Athens and Salonika to the north were repaired. The main north-south road from Salonika to Athens (375 miles) and the Peloponnese roads, Athens-Corinth-Patras and Athens Corinth-Tripolis, were repaired and resurfaced. The Army Corps of Engineers and the contractors withdrew in May, 1949, after eighteen months of operations. At this date the Communist armies had been finally forced out of Greece, and the stage of pacification was completed.

RELIEF TO REFUGEES OF THE COMMUNIST WAR

Before the Communist war had reached its climax the bulk of the inhabitants of the affected areas had fled or been moved to safety zones. The care and maintenance of destitute masses constituted a heavy burden which was borne in large part by American aid funds. Their re-establishment in their devastated homes constituted a continuing problem and expense in the years that followed.

From 1949 onward American aid in foreign exchange and drachmae was provided for this purpose. Draft animals and livestock, tools and farm equipment, seeds and housing materials and repair were essential to this program of resettlement.

THE BALANCE OF TRADE

Between 1948 and 1952 United States aid met the bulk of Greek import needs. The following table indicates the degree of United States support:

BALANCE OF PAYMENTS (in millions of dollars)

	1948	1949	1950	1951	1952	Total
Imports	395	373	411	443	285	1,907
Exports	89	83	85	102	115	474
Shipping receipts	18	15	23	31	36	123
Foreign remittances and donations	11	9	14	17	18	69
Private capital	11	18	27	14	14	84
Total visible and invisible exports	129	125	149	164	183	750
U.S. Aid:						
Direct	222	120	130	145	58	675
EPU	6	136	133	115	42	432
Total U.S. Aid	228	256	263	260	100	1,107

During this period imports were also supported by one hundred million dollars from reparations (largely made possible by United States economic aid to Italy) and fifteen million from international agencies.

Some two-thirds of the imports were therefore carried by United States aid, and the nature, kind, and quantities were subject to United States Economic Mission approval. A peculiar position applied to exports. The exporter was obliged to surrender 50 per cent of his foreign exchange to the central bank. The use of these funds was also rigidly controlled. However, as an inducement, he was authorized to sell one-half of his foreign exchange for the best price he could get. The buyer might use it to procure luxury or semiluxury items such as motor cars, refrigerators, radios, which normally could not be imported through United States aid or other controlled funds. These controls applied until 1953, when trade was liberated on the devaluation of the drachma.

Analyses are available of the commodities procured from direct aid, but as nearly half the aid was expended in other European countries, a review of total imports gives a clearer picture of the position.

Quantitatively, the largest imports have been wheat and petroleum products. In value these account for more than 25 per cent of imports. Grain has amounted to some 400,000 tons per annum, mainly from the United States. In 1953 and 1954, due to exceptional harvest and reduction of aid allocations, this figure was halved. Currently the greater part of the reduced aid is provided in wheat from United States surpluses. In present circumstances this assistance causes no additional cost to the American taxpayer since it is a transfer from the farm support vote to the aid vote.

Petroleum products (including fuel oils), averaging one to one and a quarter million tons per annum, have largely displaced prewar imports of coal from the European countries.* United States coal has also been supplied under aid, displacing that from German, British, and Polish sources. In this context, Greeks have made many recent complaints concerning the quality of aid wheat and coal.

Sugar, around 80,000 tons per year, is the most considerable food import after grain; it is followed by meat, dried fish,

* Coal, 1938: 896,600 tons; 1953: 268,700. Fuel oil, 1938: 243,000 tons; 1953: 900,000 tons.

dairy products, pulses, and coffee. In aggregate these basic food items account for more than 10 per cent of imports. Sugar was and still is a major procurement under the aid program. Meat imports originate mainly from Yugoslavia and arrive on the hoof. Currently substantial imports of dairy products are drawn from the United States agricultural surplus program, but ordinarily the principal sources of processed milk are the Netherlands, Switzerland, and Scandinavia.

Raw materials, predominantly wool and timber, account for around 15 per cent of imports. Paper pulp and hides are other significant items in this category. Lumber for reconstruction has been and still is mainly financed by aid and is drawn from Finland, Sweden, and Austria. During the period imports have ranged between ten and twenty million dollars per year.

Manufactured goods account for another 20 per cent of current imports, of which nearly half consists of iron and steel products: sheets, tubes, pipes, etc. Wood, paper products, tires, and textile yarns are the other significant items.

Machinery, motor vehicles, and road and rail transport are the principal capital items imported, covering some 20 per cent of current imports and perhaps the same proportion of United States aid.

The only other major imports are chemical goods, consisting mainly of pharmaceutical products and fertilizers.

It will be seen that during the controlled period imports were confined to necessity items. The liberation of trade in 1953 obviously released demand for certain items. Meat imports doubled in quantity and value, and importation of motor vehicles nearly doubled. Other significant increases were in manufactured textiles, watches, photographic supplies, and similar items. However, the Greek economy, as we have already indicated, has a comparatively small rich group, and the ordinary farmer or worker is too concerned with basic subsistence

to consider luxury items. To him a new suit and a pair of boots
are luxuries.

RATIONING AND IMPORT CONTROL

In a state of emergency, when there are acute scarcities
of basic necessities, state intervention and the enforcement of
controls on consumption are inevitable. On the arrival of the
American Mission in Greece, such controls had already been in
force for some years as a result of enemy and allied occupation
and UNRRA assistance.

In a highly industrialized and well-organized country
like England, rationing, import controls, and foreign exchange
restrictions can be and have been imposed with almost 100
per cent effectiveness. In an agricultural country with less developed administration such as Greece, rigid application was
impossible. The control systems therefore aimed to secure distribution of adequate basic supplies, while tolerating the existence of a "free" market fed from the uncontrolled proportion
of foreign exchange earnings. Many Greeks and foreigners
were extremely critical of this "free" market, which allowed
the sale of additional necessities and certain luxuries to a
privileged few. However, there were advantages. A safety valve
was provided. Moreover, the peculiar position of the wealthy
Greek shipping hierarchy had to be considered. There were
obvious advantages to Greece as a whole in encouraging them
to stay in or at least visit the homeland, and thereby to re-
patriate part of their international profits. There is strictly
no reason other than sentiment why so many of this group live
in Greece and operate in London, or maintain homes in both
Athens and New York.*

---

* There are taxation considerations, but these can also be met by living in,
say, Monte Carlo, or on a yacht.

Excluding this deliberate loophole, then, the Greek government and the United States Mission endeavored to secure a fair and equitable distribution of such basic imports as wheat, coal, fuel oil, sugar, and other essentials. The bulk of these items were procured and distributed to regular trade channels through the Ministry of Supply. Other major imports such as fertilizers, pesticides and agricultural equipment, seeds, animals, etc. were handled by the government-controlled Agricultural Bank. Control was also exercised over certain home-produced items, especially wheat and olive oil. Exports of olive oil were forbidden. Collection and distribution was made through government channels. Part of the wheat crop was procured by the Ministry, and the milling industries were supervised.

Progressively as the state of emergency passed, government intervention was relaxed until the last steps were taken in 1953. For reasons of credit and price support the government still undertakes procurement of part of the local wheat and exercises control over grain imports and the price of bread. Regulatory measures also apply to certain other commodities. For similar reasons the Agricultural Bank still maintains a trading inventory in fertilizers and other agricultural supplies.

Apart from basic items, the Greek state during the aid period was the principal importer of machinery, lumber, and other items for the program of reconstruction and capital development. These imports during the period amounted to some 250 million dollars. They covered literally almost everything from experimental seeds to entire power stations. They are treated more fully in a later section of the chapter.

CURRENCY, CREDIT, AND BANKING

Something has already been said about the problems of credit in Greece. During the German occupation inflation entirely destroyed the prewar currency. The occupation currency had also ceased to exist. The "liberation" drachmae moved from 160 to 10,000 to the dollar in three years, and over the aid period further deteriorated to 30,000. It is difficult to understand the impact of rapid inflation without actually experiencing it. The effect is to destroy at a blow the entire working capital represented by cash and bank balances, book debts, government bonds, mortgage deeds, fixed interest stocks and charges, etc. Liabilities are simultaneously destroyed. The trader is left with his inventories, which he must realize to continue production or distribution. Obviously he will sell only for immediate cash of the new issue, to utilize immediately, or for some commodity, such as gold, that is of stable value. As we have seen, the Greek economy holds a limited amount of gold, mainly drawn from Allied distribution during the war to support underground activities, and from old supplies of British minted sovereigns (pounds) which have long been current in the Middle East.

The effect of acute inflation on the banks is to eliminate the entire assets and liabilities of their balance sheets, except buildings and office furniture. Strictly all banking ceases. Loan accounts and deposits no longer exist. Trading can be restarted only by the central bank issuing to them, as a loan, paper currency printed by the government. Obviously they are going to lend these new funds to only the most creditworthy borrowers. Equally obviously their former depositors are not likely to open accounts with them for a long time to come. The trading banks in Greece therefore became in effect branches of the government-controlled Bank of Greece and were entirely dependent on it for funds and directions.

The policy of the government and the Bank of Greece in turn was completely subordinated to the actions taken by the American Mission in making essential imports available to the economy. The actual control of bankers' credit rested in a body known as the Currency Committee, consisting of

Greek government nominees and bankers, and an American and British nominee. However, apart from the policy control, the American Mission, through the counterpart account, was by far the largest depositor with the Bank of Greece, and consequently was able to influence the credit situation by manipulation of this account.

In general, within the limits of availabilities, the Mission policy was generous during the emergency period, with the objective of re-establishing the smooth workings of the economy.

Until late 1951 the guiding principle seems to have been to expend counterpart balances as quickly as was possible within the limits imposed by the necessity to check inflationary tendencies. The practical policy observed was to "block" a portion of the counterpart fund equivalent to the Greek state budget deficit currently incurred, and to release the balance for active projects of constructive capital investment.

The major items on the balance sheet of the Bank of Greece therefore were:

On the liabilities side, the counterpart funds, the compulsory deposits of entities of public law (social insurance, municipal, port, and similar funds), and the note circulation.

On the assets side, the advances to the Greek state to cover budget deficits and current operations, and the advances to the private bankers.

The following table indicates the progress of re-establishment of the banking and credit system. This does not include directly controlled medium-term loans made to industry under the CLC program (see Chapter 8), which ultimately aggregated some eighty million dollars.

The sharp drop of about twelve hundred million drachmae in expansion of all items at the end of 1952 reflects the application of a new deflationary policy. The upward trend in the following years reflects the favorable harvests and the rise in prices following devaluation of the drachma.

TABLE OF SALIENT BANKING STATISTICS

AT YEAR END (DECEMBER 31ST)

(Expressed in millions of new drachmae)

	1949	1950	1951	1952	1953	1954
Note circulation	1,859	1,887	2,198	2,475	3,503	3,843
Sight deposits (Private)	402	484	766	888	1,422	1,891
Other deposits (Private)	196	226	251	269	476	924
Deposits (Public entities)	555	828	1,101	1,039	1,306	1,239
Short term loans	3,118	4,258	5,219	4,962	5,467	7,431
Agricultural	(845)	(1,077)	(1,293)	(1,597)	(1,730)	(2,243)
Other	(2,273)	(3,181)	(3,926)	(3,365)	(3,737)	(5,188)
Long term loans	270	302	392	465	510	604
Agricultural	(190)	(203)	(224)	(249)	(260)	(262)
Other	(80)	(99)	(168)	(216)	(250)	(342)

The loans described as "agricultural" relate to the agricultural credit section only; that is, they are primarily production loans. The item "other loans," however, includes advances to state organizations for procurement of agricultural commodities under price stabilization and rationing programs.

Greek banking is divided between the commercial banks catering to trade and industry and the Agricultural Bank. The latter makes almost half the loans but has virtually no deposits. Over the period it has been financed entirely by the Bank of Greece, largely from Mission counterpart, and it recently requested that it be permanently endowed with a substantial proportion of these loans as working capital. It is theoretically a cooperative bank controlled by and controlling the agricultural cooperative movement under government supervision.

The commercial banks have built up deposit accounts to some degree, but all suffer from the fact that many of their loans are in practice frozen, with little hope of liquidation in the present state of Greek industry. The chronic shortage of working capital has already been mentioned and is referred to again in Chapter 8.

This question of "frozen loans" was raised somewhat heatedly in the deflationary period in 1952 in connection with industrial expansion, since these were mainly given to the larger establishments. By contrast agricultural loans were mainly advances to the farmers, individually and as cooperatives, for financing production through procurement of fertilizers, seeds, and similar basic supplies.

There is also some financing of "crop carry-over." Something like a million farmers are financed directly or through cooperative groups. In actual practice a large proportion of the loans are not given in cash but in supplies, the farmer receiving an authority to draw such-and-such a quantity of fertilizer, seed, or other supplies from the warehouses of the Bank or Kydep (the farmers cooperative supply organization).

In effect these loans, too, are frozen, since immediately on repayment from harvest proceeds the Bank must replenish its inventories to prepare for the next year's advances. As will be seen in later chapters, virtually no funds are available for medium-term credit, which is so vital to farm improvement. The Bank executives contend that some medium-term credit is essential to extricate themselves from a vicious circle which condemns them to continuous financing of farmers who without improvement credits can never operate on more than bare subsistence level. This position is usually blamed on the deflationary policy pursued by the American Mission since the end of 1951.

DEFLATION AND DEVALUATION

Until the end of 1951, the economy was controlled and partially hedged against external price changes.

Officially the drachma was pegged at five thousand to the dollar, but as we have seen the exporter had the right to sell part of his foreign exchange on the free market at a premium. An average rate of ten thousand to the dollar was thereby determined, and in actual fact deposits in counterpart funds against aid imports were made at this rate. Following general devaluation of European currencies in 1949, this average rate also changed. Finally the official rate was consolidated in June, 1951, at fifteen thousand to the dollar. The exporter now became entitled to a premium subsidy on certain commodities, while the importer of certain nonbasic categories of items, assuming that he could get a licence, had to pay perhaps thirty thousand drachmae to the dollar. The fifteen thousand parity was admittedly an overvaluation of the drachma, established temporarily to prevent price increases in the basic items. Consequently exports had to be subsidized to enter world markets, and nonbasic imports had to be valued at something around true exchange rates. This condition prevailed until April, 1953, when the drachma was devalued to thirty thousand to the dollar, and the premiums and subsidies were abolished. This valuation is currently in line with purchasing power parity.

The peculiar insulation from devaluation was made possible only by United States aid in the supply of basic commodities, which were arbitrarily undervalued for purposes of deposit in counterpart fund. The price of basic imports was therefore directly subsidized to the extent of 50 per cent.

During the period a steady upward trend of internal prices was maintained, as the following indices show:

TABLE OF PRICE INDICES, 1950–1954.
(Athens/Piraeus)
(1952=100)

Wholesale price indices	1950	1951	1952	1953	1954
General	83	101	100	117	131
Food	86	103	100	114	127
Raw Materials	77	101	100	128	145
Finished Goods	79	98	100	111	127
Fuel	72	91	100	129	143
Beverages and Tobacco	88	96	100	111	124
Cost of living indices					
General	85	95	100	109	125
Clothing	76	95	100	102	126
Food	90	96	100	108	121

In connection with this table it should be remarked that there are certain peculiarities that tend to cause a difference between wholesale and retail prices. The wholesale price of wheat has risen over the period from 2.46 to 4.14 drachmae per oke (2.8 pounds) while the price of bread has only risen from 3.20 to 3.70. This is the result of deliberate pegging (and the initial establishment of a price inducement for home-grown wheat in excess of world levels). Sugar, rising in the wholesale table, has fallen in the retail due to derationing. The general upward trend of prices, however, continued and has given rise to talk of further devaluation.

The general barometer, however, is not the price indices but the unique position of the daily market prices of the gold pound, the established medium of exchange in Greece. If you want to borrow money from a friend or a moneylender, the loan is, illegally, expressed not in drachmae or dollars but in gold pounds; and it was this unique position that the United

States Mission, in theory, sought to solve by a stabilization of the drachma. The justification usually quoted for the deflationary policy was the success in Germany as a result of the stabilization of the mark in 1948. (There was, however, a big difference between the German economy of 1948, which had considerable productive capacity, already held substantial inventories, and was shortly to receive substantial United States aid, and the Greek economy of 1951, which lacked productive capacity and inventories and had a falling level of aid.)

The new policy was preceded by the sharp drop in economic aid that represented a congressional reaction to the Korean War. This necessarily resulted in an immediate curtailment of the importation of capital goods projected for the development program. Strictly speaking, due to the time lag between approval and actual delivery of heavy machinery, this cutoff may be felt only two or three years later. There were, however, cases where spares, ancillary equipment, and even essential parts of major projects were cut off from the program, with the result that utilization of imports already made was wholly or partially paralyzed.

Apart from the availability of foreign exchange funds, a new condition was imposed on the importation of capital goods for state account. As explained in Chapter 2, in Greece a procedure had been established that was equivalent to waiver of counterpart. As from July 1, 1952, if, for example, the Greek State Railways wished to purchase a locomotive, the drachma equivalent of the dollar cost had to be deposited in the counterpart fund. This drachma equivalent could only be found from the national budget. The Mission now insisted on budgetary stability, so that this capital requirement had to be found by taxation. The objective was to impose a check on reckless procurement. In fact, it virtually stopped all procurement for a time.

In late 1951 the Mission imposed a cutback on all major investment projects in progress by imposing a restriction on the release of counterpart funds.

From July 1, 1952, the Greek government was required to finance its own program of capital development from budget surplus over ordinary revenue. The Mission, contingent on budgetary stabilization and an adequate provision from the Greek state for capital development, was prepared to make a limited contribution toward capital investment: in the fiscal years 1953, 1954, and 1955, respectively 525, 705, and 300 million drachmae. As these figures were less than the actual dollar aid, the effect was deflationary. This was further emphasized in a restricted credit policy pursued by the Currency Committee, and the requirement of a balanced budget.

FINANCES OF THE GREEK STATE

The Greek state budget, like those of so many other underdeveloped countries, is ordinarily in a chronic state of deficit. The table of recent state budgets indicates the typical problems.

Average annual income per head in 1953 (an exceptionally favorable year because of good agricultural weather) was 5,000 drachmae ($160). Average family income was therefore around $650, of which $150 was paid in taxes etc. As in most underdeveloped areas, the bulk of the revenue is raised by indirect taxes. Luxury imports are heavily taxed, but in fact the bulk of the revenue is drawn from a heavy taxation on sugar, gasoline, and fuel oils, with tobacco and salt as further substantial yielders.

Income tax is difficult to apply where the majority of people are on or near subsistence levels, and is lightly laid on the few industrialists to encourage further development.

GREEK STATE BUDGETS
(Expressed in millions of new drachmae)

Revenue (Excluding Aid Contributions)	1950–51	1951–52	1952–53	1953–54
Annual Direct Taxes	645	1,000	964	1,321
Extraordinary Direct Taxes	220	295	586	521
Indirect Taxes	3,220	3,792	4,072	5,354
Other Annual Revenue	307	394	406	513
Other Extraordinary Revenue	316	242	239	357
Total Revenue	4,708	5,723	6,267	8,065
Expenditure				
Civil Ministries	3,412	4,056	3,992	5,387
Public Security	407	515	575	704
Defense	2,220	2,000	2,020	2,873
Dodecanese	34	41	45	52
Earthquake Expenditure				183
Total Expenditure	6,073	6,612	6,632	9,200
Total National Income	24,840	29,361	30,571	41,279

It should be added that Greek state salaries are low: a clerk earns $30 to $50 per month, a general director $150, a nomarch (in administrative control of a county) $150, a graduate engineer $130. The economies in 1952–1953 were largely obtained by heavy staff cutting. The increase in civil expenditure in 1953–1954 was accounted for by increases in staff salaries and pensions (three hundred million) following devaluation, and by the absorption of the capital investment program previously borne by the Mission.

The impossibility of establishing budgetary equilibrium without cutting the military expenditure is obvious. Consequently the Greek government and press stated that unless the United States supported the budget by a definite grant, the army establishment would be cut. As a result a specific grant (described as for military aid) was provided to meet the 1953–1954 deficit of 750 million drachmae, increased to 1050 million in 1954–1955 estimates.

In the preparation of the 1955–1956 budgets, prior to the general election, it is no secret that the government requested and obtained additional aid in view of the prevailing discontent in the country following the slowdown of development and the restrictive policy.

In 1952, therefore, the United States withdrew from supporting the budget and the investment program, and pressed on the Greek government a policy of budget stability, cutback in development plans, and a progressive withdrawal of aid.

This policy is now abandoned for a practice of budget support and expanding aid, without effective control of investment program expenditure.

THE PROGRAM OF INVESTMENT AND CAPITAL DEVELOPMENT

In the period from 1948 to 1952, by contrast, all expenditure on capital development was directly controlled by the American Mission. Each major field of aid was the subject of a formal agreement of economic cooperation. Specific project agreements were made covering each major item or class of smaller items within the cooperative agreement for the particular field of activity. These agreements specified objects, intentions, conditions, procedure of administration, and funds required in drachmae or in foreign exchange, for the entire project and for the particular fiscal year. Periodical amendments were made in material particulars as required. The project agreements were signed by the United States Mission, by the interested Greek ministry or entity, and by the Ministers of Finance and Coordination (Economic Policy). The last-named ministry, newly established by transfer of personnel from other ministries, from the central bank, and from academic and scientific bodies, was specially charged with the supervision of the investment program, and worked in day-to-day contact with the Mission on all phases of the program. Fund releases to support projects were approved by the Mission on request of Coordination.

In coordinating planning, short- and long-term objectives had to be considered. Restoration of war damage to capital assets not already covered by the UNNRA, army, and AMAG programs clearly called for first attention. This particularly affected communications by road and rail, the ports, and the devastated mountain villages.

However, the extremely adverse trade balance required immediate steps if Greece were not to become a pensioner for an indefinite time. Quite obviously a considerable expansion of agricultural production, not only up to, but well beyond, prewar levels, was essential. For forty centuries Greece has imported grain in exchange for more specialized commodities, but the trade depression from 1929 on forced an intensified home production. It is highly possible that from the long-term point of view the traditional policy is correct, but in conditions of 1948, the immediate expansion of exports of the semiluxury products (tobacco, dried and fresh fruits, wines, olives) was hardly feasible. Consequently an intensification of the immediate prewar policy of increased self-sufficiency in basic food products, especially grain, would show results in a substantial reduction of imports. At the same time, and parallel with this, the longer-term policy of development and expansion of meat and dairy products, olives, fruits, and vegetables was to be initiated. This combined agricultural policy found its expression in two sections: technical development, and land improvement works involving construction. These two sections can be separated only on broad lines, since they constantly interact on one another.

The technical development projects are considered in more detail in Chapter 5. Primarily, these were concerned with educational activities in improved techniques, use of fertilizers and pesticides, new crops and better varieties; and with research and experiment designed to improve production or quality of existing products or to introduce new ones. For these purposes counterpart funds and technical assistance were made available for the educational program and for financing various special development projects in seed improvement, cattle breeding, veterinary medicine, and horticulture. Equipment and selected seeds and livestock were imported.

Land improvement works covered a multiplicity of activities, large and small, which are surveyed in more detail in Chapters 6, 7, and 9. The investment program provided counterpart funds to finance these works and foreign exchange to import heavy earth-moving equipment, well-drilling rigs, pumps, pipes, and similar items.

Inevitably, increased agricultural productivity stimulates an increased demand for industrial goods. As the limited Greek industrial production was well below prewar levels, it was imperative to step up that production to cope with current needs, restore war devastation, and at least reduce some of the demand for imports. Capital re-equipment, financing of expansion by long-term loans, and provision of working capital were obvious steps. An urgent need, however, was to provide additional and cheaper power to avoid burdening the imports program with an expanding demand for coal and fuel oil. A program of hydroelectric power was developed, and a new thermal generating plant utilizing local lignite was constructed.

The industry and power program was financed from counterpart for local currency advances to industry and for labor and materials in the power program. Foreign exchange allocations were made to import machinery, generating plants, and equipment. Steps were also taken on similar lines to revive and extend existing Greek mining enterprises. The whole field is covered in Chapter 8.

The health of the workers and farmers and their families is now recognized as a significant factor in productivity. Sanitation, particularly through improved domestic water supplies, and public health, through construction of hospitals and sanatoria and the introduction of modern equipment, covered a large group of Mission projects considered in Chapter 10. A combination of local currency from counterpart to cover construction costs, technical assistance, and imported equipment and water pipes formed the financial basis for the program.

As in all underdeveloped countries, communicatons in Greece are indifferent. Costs of road, rail, and port facilities and airports are among the heaviest charges to be met by all countries outside Western Europe and North America. High transportation costs and the limitations thus imposed on marketing constitute one of the greatest difficulties to the developing economies. In Greece a great deal of the effort in this direction was absorbed by restoration of war damage alone, and even at the present time this is not complete in some sections. In other areas the program has gone much further by improving trunk roads and developing a vast network of village roads, where previously only mule tracks existed.

The program of rebuilding the devastated villages and rehousing the refugees required a substantial financing of the production of brick, tiles, cement, and similar local products and the importation of large quantities of lumber, fittings, and other materials, as indicated in Chapter 12.

In addition to these major programs a complex of minor programs was involved. In forestry to reduce lumber imports, in fisheries to increase indigenous supplies, in education and vocational training, in hotel improvement and museum devel-

TABLE OF AID INVESTMENTS

	Counterpart (Millions of new drachmae)	Foreign Exchange (Millions of $)
Agricultural Improvement	383.6	9.0
Land Reclamation	675.9	31.0
Forestry	40.0	0.6
Fisheries	18.1	1.3
Power (including Lignite)	883.2	66.7
Mining	12.7	1.3
Industry	328.1	23.3
Tourism	60.0	1.2
Highways	494.4	10.8
Railways	190.7	43.6
Ports	141.6	4.6
Shipping	—	19.7
Civil Aviation	84.4	3.0
Telecommunications	26.5	6.5
Housing	797.0	15.8
Public Health	122.2	7.3
Water Supply	64.3	5.3
Education, etc.	80.2	3.2
Special Relief Programs		
Care of Refugees	1,300.0	—
Replacement of Farm equipment, etc.		15.0
Rehabilitation of war-destroyed industry, etc.	18.7	2.6
Earthquake Relief	150.0	—
Advances to State Budget	2,026.6	—
Miscellaneous	112.9	1.4
Technical Assistance	171.4	0.5
Total	8,182.5	273.7

opment to stimulate tourism—projects were progressively developed with three types of assistance: technical guidance, local currency funds, and imported supplies and equipment.

However in another field, as we shall see in Chapter 14, aid was provided primarily in the form of technical assistance. This is the multiple field of administration, which covers many highly developed specializations that only the most advanced economies of the United States and Britain, and perhaps Germany and France, can supply. Sometimes even these countries lack adequate competence and experience, and any one of them may be totally lacking in particular fields.

The evalution of program success is made in the individual chapters. The reader may however be interested in the summary of program financing contained in the adjoining table. As will be seen, some 4,680 million drachmae have been drawn from counterpart to finance reconstruction and development. This was accumulated at various rates, but may be averaged at fifteen to the dollar, that is 312 million dollars. To this should be added imported supplies, including certain items from Italian reparations, of 273 million dollars. The bulk of this program was carried out from 1948 to 1952, when, as we have noted, a change in policy took place.

GREEK STATE INVESTMENT PROGRAM

In fact, the bulk of expenditure under the investment program was compressed into the three calendar years 1949, 1950, and 1951, representing an average of 150 million dollars per year spent on constructive investment, apart from relief and budget support. This program of direct United States investment was severely cut back in the second half of the fiscal year 1951–1952 as a result of the new deflationary policy.

In the following fiscal year this program was to be continued by the Greek state. The only American contribution was some 525 million drachmae (equivalent to about 30 million dollars in counterpart) to which the Greek state contrived to add about 80 million drachmae. The net result was wholesale cancellation of programs, or at best a slowing down. Greece was literally spattered with works at all stages of completion, liberally plastered with such signs as "Marshall Aid," "Gift of American People," etc. until the Mission decided that diplomacy required that they should be removed. All social service construction, all work on roads, rails, ports, houses, hotels, museums, schools, stopped dead. The power program was continued at full scale, but the bulk of the agricultural improvement schemes were cancelled, as were the well-drilling and most of the medium-size land improvements. Work on larger schemes progressed at very reduced pressure. It was strongly argued within the American Mission that, however justifiable a cut in nonproductive activities might be, the abandonment or limitation of the productive schemes, mainly at a time when they were near completion, was not deflationary. There is considerable validity in this claim. I recollect one drainage scheme that had absorbed a million dollars and was complete up to installation of pumps. It required only three thousand dollars to complete the installation. Like a considerable number of other projects in the same stage, it was cut out of the program and remained incomplete for four years. A large part of the mechanical equipment for road construction and land improvement became immobilized for lack of credits.

The Greek government sought additional credits from America and elsewhere but was not immediately successful. A further United States counterpart contribution of twenty-five million dollars in 1953–1954 again had little budget support. In 1954–1955 an increased budget support of twenty million dollars was counterbalanced by a fall in counterpart of eight million. A large part of expenditure in this year was not true investment, since it involved reconditioning of roads, previously constructed but now deteriorated, and of other structures left unfinished by the earlier cut. In 1955–1956 the crisis was so acute that the annual budget (due in July) could not be submitted until December, after pressure for additional aid, with the imminence of an election, had brought extra United States contributions.

It is not necessary to emphasize that the four years have been a period of unrelieved depression to interested American Mission personnel and to Greek government officials. Fortunately, partly as a result of the earlier investments, largely through favorable weather conditions for agriculture, and partly through increase of tourism and other invisible revenues, the period has been favorable to the balance of payments. Revived German and British buying of standard prewar exports has been of major help.

Recently German credits have made possible the initiation of construction of a refinery which will ultimately substantially reduce the cost of petroleum imports, and a scheme to develop another thermal electric plant with German capital has been initiated.

Unfortunately these plans do not touch the country's most vital needs, as the succeeding chapters show.

CHAPTER 5.

Agricultural Productivity

AGRICULTURAL DEVELOPMENT

Most underdeveloped countries compare unfavorably in levels and in varieties of agricultural production with the nations of Western Europe and North America. This is due in part to lack of advanced techniques and in part to the inability to meet the capital costs of drainage, irrigation, and other land improvement works. Any program to develop agriculture must cover both these aspects, which are largely interdependent. However, it is necessary to explain the two parts of the program separately, without overlooking their close association. Succeeding chapters deal with capital works of land improvement. This chapter is concerned with technical improvements.

Agriculture covers a wide range of products and activities—field crops (grain and legume), garden crops, industrial crops, arboriculture, viticulture, animal husbandry, etc. Man's developments of improved techniques of cultivation go back to earliest times, and all ages have contributed.

The present century, however, despite its primary emphasis on industrial expansion, has perhaps contributed more to the advancement of agriculture than of any other industry.

The enormous developments of fertilizers, weed killers, and pesticides have made possible substantial increases in yields. Improved tools and equipment may increase productivity as well as reduce costs. The development of new varieties of seeds and trees has provided greater disease resistance, made cultivation possible in areas not previously considered suitable, and provided improved qualities and larger yields. Research in animal husbandry has bred many specialized producers and provided greater knowledge of feeding techniques, new standards of products, and the entirely novel process of artificial insemination. New manufacturing processes have introduced canning, preserving, concentration, and extraction of agricultural products, and new uses and techniques are regularly found. Scientific research by the Western nations continually provides returns in these fields and in many others.

We must remember, however, that introduction of new practices has not been immediate, even in the West. The new knowledge has to be disseminated and the improved methods progressively introduced. In America, Britain, and elsewhere, apart from the numerous technical publications and the publicity of interested commercial corporations, it has been necessary to introduce county organizations to intensify the dissemination of new knowledge.

The peasant of Greece, Iran, or India does not receive the *Farmer and Stock Breeder* weekly, nor does he have access to highly organized agricultural schools, colleges, and research institutions. His knowledge has been derived from his father. In the majority of underdeveloped countries the farmer is a very small landowner. In Greece there are approximately 1,330,000 landholdings of an average size of six acres. More than half the country's 9,000,000 million acres are in units of twelve acres or less.

Small farmers must be conservative. They cannot afford to take any risk that would jeopardize a fraction of the subsistence, and an unsuccessful experiment with a new variety or crop means tightened belts for all the family in the coming winter. Similarly, expenditure on fertilizer, pesticides or other new methods will reduce family income unless it brings about a clear and definite increase. Most rapid agricultural development has been made by large landowners and corporations that can afford to take long-term risks. The peasant farmer cannot.

In America, Britain, and other Western countries agricultural education has largely consisted in proving to the smaller farmer by practical demonstration that he can safely change his methods. The small farmer of Greece or Asia is by no means stupid. He can understand the evidence of his own eyes, and he can understand possibilities, but he must be convinced that he is going to benefit from a change.

Radio, publications, visual aids, films, photographs may all help this. In the last analysis, however, personal contact with experienced and trained agriculturalists, and practical demonstrations such as special plots, are the deciding factors. The dissemination of knowledge and consequent increase in production of underdeveloped countries depend on the establishment of agricultural education through schools, short courses, and a service of agricultural extension agents in close contact with the farmers.

There is a corollary. To create the extension agents there must be agricultural colleges. There must also be properly staffed research institutes. The research of Britain and America cannot be transferred automatically to Greece or Pakistan. Climatic and soil conditions differ. The interchange of scientific knowledge and the results of research must take place between Oklahoma and Tehran, but the application of Oklahoma results to Tehran must be checked locally, and any necessary modifications must be made before the new information is generally released.

There are, therefore, three definite steps required to increase agricultural productivity: higher technical institutes to train local research staff and extension agents, development of research institutes, and popular dissemination through primary agricultural schools, publicity, and a county extension service. In these connections the wide diversity of agriculture must be considered. Animal husbandry is almost a subject on its own and requires the specialized backing of a veterinary college, animal clinics, stock-breeding research, and institutes concerned with fodder crops.

The farmer's wife and daughter also have unique contributions to make. Apart from the obvious feminine interest in improving amenities, sanitation, babycraft, and child care, there are possibilities of improving living standards by training in home crafts, by introducing modern methods of preserving fruit and vegetables, and through improvement of dairy products.

To back the educational activities there must be organization and credit to distribute fertilizers and pesticides, to provide new tools, to distribute new varieties of seed, and to introduce new animals. These amenities are laid on in the advanced countries. They were built up over a long period, and cannot spring up overnight without assistance.

To these needs we must add improved marketing, and often processing plants to absorb new or increased production. We must also develop quality controls such as meat inspection, examination of herds, and measures to control plant and animal disease. In a simple subsistence economy these regulations are not so essential, but export crops require sanitary controls.

These paragraphs can only indicate the problems involved and the steps necessary to solve them. It must be remembered that the entire program must be balanced and it must be integrated with capital works. There is no gain in introducing an irrigation system which is dependent for success on the conversion of a wheat-growing economy into one producing cotton, fodder crops for dairy herds, and tomatoes, unless the farmers are educated in the new techniques, cotton gins and a pasteurization plant are ready for the new products, and marketing facilities for tomatoes exist. It is, of course, self-evident that the seeds for the new crops should be available, and that loans should be available for the farmers to buy good-quality disease-free cows. However, more than once it has happened that, though the need might be self-evident, project planners have omitted to make the necessary arrangements. I recollect visiting one American aid project of this type. A vociferous group of farmers explained that engineers and contractors had appeared and obligingly dug a concrete canal some three miles long to the village fields. It was now filled with water. As the farmers tersely explained, only wheat had been grown on this land for a mere four thousand years or so. They knew that with the water they could probably grow tomatoes, cotton, watermelons, hybrid corn, vegetables, alfalfa, clover. They added that they were quite prepared to do so but they just did not have a clue as to how to do it, nor did any one else for at least fifty miles around. They recognized that they needed cattle and processing plants. These, they added truculently, they were quite prepared to buy, cash down. The village had always been frugal, and the land yielded excellent wheat crops. They had written everywhere for some specialists to give advice, but no replies had been received. (The explanation incidentally rested in the Mission economy and deflation policy, as a result of which the Mission specialists had been "axed" and the Greek government department reduced by about 90 per cent.)

AGRICULTURAL PRODUCTIVITY IN GREECE

Prior to 1929 productivity levels in Greece were exceptionally low, in wheat, for example, little more than half those of neighboring Italy, which has fairly similar soil and climatic conditions. Principal concentration was in the three main cash crops—tobacco, currants, and olives. In these fields Greek ability and ingenuity had been concentrated. As a result, in the first two the country held a virtually unchallenged position, and in the last did not fall too far behind Italian standards, but this was too narrow a basis for the economy. The post–1929 policy had concentrated on wheat as a matter of necessity, but Greece has never, except in a few regions, been an efficient grain producer. Rice cultivation was unknown. Some cotton was grown, poor in yield and quality. The acreage under potatoes was small, and the production was poor. Tomatoes and some other vegetables were being developed.

Despite favorable climatic condition, citrus production was comparable neither in quantity nor quality with that of other Mediterranean lands. Other fruits were limited and poor. Even in 1952 most Greek apples gave the impression of leather bags stuffed with wood pulp. Dairy products were of low standard, and the half-starved cattle gave about one-fifth of Western European yields.

Sheep were the main source of meat, and even of dairy products. For the latter reason the lambs were killed while still milk-fed. Centuries of devastation and grinding poverty had turned the average Greek farmer into a vegetarian subsisting on bread and olives eked out by occasional salads of dandelions and similar weeds. His meat and dairy products generally moved to the towns. (This is not in the least exaggerated. Visiting a mountain town famous for its sheep's-milk yoghurt, I was assured that it was quite unobtainable locally, as the whole production was shipped to Athens). The sheep's milk cheese was almost the sole source of animal protein, supplemented in some areas by goat's flesh. Beef has not contributed substantially toward Greek diet for centuries. It is mostly killed very young, and its quality is not comparable with imported beef.

This depressing picture is a result of unfortunate circumstances rather than unfavorable natural conditions. Ignorance and poverty were major causes. In ancient times Greece was "rich in flocks and herds," as Homer so frequently states. The heroes of antiquity appear to have been good healthy meat-eaters, with a taste for variety in their diet. Cattle and horses are the easiest plunder of an invader, and it is almost certainly this fact that caused the initial decline of Greek productivity. Without good cattle and good draft animals, the downward path was inevitable. Agricultural prosperity attracted the plunderer and the tax collector in the disturbed centuries. The Greek farmer had come to believe that it was better to be destitute but to live in comparative security, rather than to be enterprising and rich but insecure.

Gradually the habits of a low level of productivity had become so established that the condition was accepted as normal.

Twenty-eight hundred years ago Hesiod, a small Greek farmer, in his poem *Work and Days* gave the world its first known agricultural treatise, full of wisdom and experience of the land. Now the problem was to educate, or rather re-educate, the small Greek farmer in sound modern agricultural practices, to show him how to make the best use of his land. This task was rendered fundamentally more difficult by the democratic approach. Well over one million had to be taught, and the teaching had to be accepted willingly. Obviously it had also to be done in a friendly manner.

The initial concern was to step up the low average wheat yield. The traditional policy of importing wheat is probably, as we have said, the wisest over a period, but in the short run a cut in the enormous (proportionately) foreign exchange requirement for wheat was necessary. Improved crop rotation, fertilizers, new seed varieties were the obvious answers. From the long-term point of view increased production of animal protein was essential to improve living standards. Development of forage crops, improved knowledge of feeding requirements, new standards of animal health, and new varieties of cattle were needed.

At present the Greek is, without exception, the world's biggest bread-eater. His average wheat grain consumption is nearly five times bigger than that of an Englishman. Improved economic circumstances and the development of local meat and milk production should materially reduce the need for wheat imports. Development of rice and potatoes would provide alternatives more suitable to local soil and conditions.

Other cash crops were needed to supplement olives, vines, and tobacco, and especially to give products suitable for export. Cotton and rice were "possible," but the greatest hope lay in fruit (oranges, lemons, apples) to supply Western Europe and Middle East markets. The grades of Greek fruit available were only suitable for the lowest market. Systematic cultivation, new stocks, pest control, and organized marketing were obviously needed.

In agriculture, however, developments must be spread over long periods. As a short-term policy plans were concentrated on wheat, to relieve the impossible pressure on foreign exchange until production in other areas could be expanded or improved. Education and organization, backed by fertilizers, pesticides, etc., were the first need, initially to be concentrated on wheat production, but to be spread to arboriculture and animal husbandry.

AGRICULTURAL EDUCATION IN GREECE

The first step to reform old habits was taken over fifty years ago in Macedonia by the late Dr. House, an American missionary in the Balkans. Convinced that Christianity could be applied in a practical manner, he founded the American Farm School in Salonika in 1902 with a capital of five hundred dollars. He bought a small barren site and built an adobe house. This house is now the center of a farm and school that cover four hundred acres and provide a four-year training to one hundred boys. The course covers the full field of Greek agriculture but is not limited to purely agricultural subjects. Training is given in masonry, carpentry, plumbing, and other village crafts, so that a Farm School graduate is a jack-of-all-trades.

The school's objective is to train practical farm boys who will return to their villages to cultivate the family fields. In the village they will apply the lessons learned in the school. Their example will be followed by their neighbors, when practical evidence of the benefits of new methods is seen. The boys are encouraged in community leadership, and the teaching aims to build good Christian citizens even more than practical farmers.

In 1955 was celebrated the jubilee of the school's charter, at which the King and Queen of Greece and all the notabilities of Macedonian and Greek agriculture were present to testify to the debt Greece owes the pioneer work of the school. To the sorrow of all, Charlie House, son of the founder, who had run the school for thirty-eight years, announced his retirement.

Charlie is a true New Englander, and though he has devoted his life to Greece, his judgment of practicalities is never clouded by any sentimentality. Greece has no firmer friend, but equally no more unbiased critic. The school enjoys no government aid or support and has been maintained and expanded by its friends in America and the British Empire. The American aid program did, however, contribute towards its postwar rehabilitation, and the Point 4 program supported a number of scholarships over two years.

Recently part of the Farm School grounds has been placed at the disposal of the British Society of Friends, who have founded and are operating a school for village girls to teach housecraft and home economy. Between the wars several institutes of a nature similar to the Farm School were established by private benefactors or by state action.

All this activity was stopped by war conditions. After the war and during the aid period substantial repair programs were necessary, and much of the work had to be restarted from scratch. American aid was provided for this purpose, but except in the case of the American Farm School, no material gain has resulted.

Equipment for cheese-making costing around fifty thousand dollars, provided for dairy schools at Larissa and Yanina, remained for years in the original crates, and it is extremely doubtful whether it is in full use even now. Other schools are used solely to provide accommodation for extension short courses. The fundamental problem seems to be that no one has got around to deciding what is to be done in the way of agricultural education in Greece. The schools are under the authority of the Direction of Extension, which has been too busy with adult programs and youth clubs to formulate a school policy. So, apart from the Farm School and one other, all agricultural schools in Greece are more or less suspended.

EXTENSION TRAINING IN GREECE

Prior to World War II, the American Near East Foundation and the Ministry of Agriculture had taken initial steps in the development of extension. The American aid program converted these beginnings into full-scale operations, with four hundred extension officers, in three years. Greece was not by any means lacking in trained agriculturists with graduate degrees of the Athens School of Agriculture or the University of Salonika. But the country lacked any organization or technique for transferring this scientific knowledge to the ordinary farmer.

The American county agents had the task of training in this technique and assisting to build the organization. The American Farm School and the School of Agriculture in Athens provided the facilities for short courses and training programs to reorientate the staff of the new service. One American extension officer summarized the new outlook by saying, "The state agriculturist has to convince the farmer that he is his friend and not his enemy."

It is difficult to judge the effects of a service of this type. When my staff tried to evaluate it in 1953, we visited over a hundred villages and invited public comment on the service. The general consensus of farmers' opinion was that they had learned much from the new service, but they also stated that they had not by any means fully applied what they had learned, since caution was necessary in applying new ideas.

A later survey in 1955 was less satisfactory. The stringent fiscal policy to check inflation enforced by the United States Mission had been applied, as far as the extension service was concerned, by the withdrawals of jeeps and other transport provided from aid funds, and by rigid limitations of travel. The consequence had been a discouragement of the staff and a rigid limitation of their field of activity. It may be remarked that American Mission agricultural officials had vigorously protested, to the Greek government, against the application of these restrictive policies, without any result.

On one occasion the responsible minister remarked that the Mission could not have it both ways. Either the budget could be balanced or the country could be developed. So long as the Mission department holding the purse strings insisted on budget stability, the extension would be sacrificed. (This view was largely due to the fact that the extension service had been established at a working level, and the ministerial level of the Greek government was not informed on its policies, activities, or potential achievements.)

In practical achievements the wheat yield per acre had risen 50 per cent above prewar level by 1953. This was mainly attributable to improved varieties and the use of fertilizer. Indubitably, too, benefits have been felt in fruit growing. In the livestock field the extension service developed some fifteen thousand demonstration plots for forage crops, introducing many new varieties to the Greek farmer in 1954 and 1955.

However, there remains a wide field still to tackle, including the very important practical problems of grading and marketing, which are as yet untouched.

The extension service has been organized and trained. It has returned practical results, but it has much to do and has lost its original impetus. The American extension agents, with one exception, have moved on, mostly to other countries. They and Messrs. Christodoulou and Veriopoulos of the Greek Ministry of Agriculture are to be congratulated on progress made so swiftly, but one regrets that even more has not been accomplished.

RESEARCH

This regret becomes even more intensified in reviewing research developments. Nearly a million dollars were invested to modernize the Greek research institutes. The results achieved have been almost negative, because the operation is disorganized and is starved for current funds to staff and maintain itself. Good work that may be achieved is thereby sterilized. One exception has to be made for the institute engaged in research into wheat and other grain. There can be no question that the improved strains developed by this institute have been a major factor in doubling wheat production in Greece.

This institute in its operations, however, had the benefit of the support of the Seed Production service. This operation, supported by one and a half million dollars of United States aid, was able to multiply the institute's new varieties with great rapidity and distribute them on an organized basis to the farmers whom they would benefit. Publicity was supplied by the extension service. The author's strongest criticism of this useful and efficient organization is that the same result could have been achieved at half the cost. The balance has been absorbed by bad debts from farmers and similar losses due to failure in efficiency of the responsible state services. As no one, either of the American Mission or the Greek government, ever bothered to call for a balance sheet, this fact passed unobserved for years.

CATTLE BREEDING

In early 1948 the American Mission and the Greek Ministry of Agriculture initiated a program of livestock development. This program involved construction, repair, or extension of some sixteen livestock stations and stallion barns. A mission proceeded to France in 1949 to buy horses for some of these stables.

For some unknown reason a letter of credit for some $280,000 was established by conversion of dollars to French francs through the clearing agreement. As this event shortly preceded the European currency devaluation in September, 1949, an immediate loss of aid of nearly $80,000 was suffered before one cent was spent.

The Mission duly returned in 1950, having bought some eighty horses. The objective of these purchases was to procure stallions to service the horses and donkeys of the Greek farmers and thereby produce a stronger breed of draft animal in Greece. Further local purchases of horses were made from aid funds. Through foreign exchange the stations were also stocked with bulls, goats, sheep, pigs, and miscellaneous varieties of poultry. Total project cost exceeded one million dollars.

A survey was undertaken by the Controller's Office in 1954 to evaluate the project. During a visit to one of these stations, one of our staff remarked on the mettlesome nature of one of the animals at exercise. A closer scrutiny revealed that it was an Anglo-Arab race horse. Examination of the records then disclosed that half the horses imported from France were in fact Anglo-Arabs. Moreover, the horses procured in Greece appeared to be almost entirely purebred Arabs or Anglo-Arabs from Phaleron (Athens) race track.

One remarkable horse had been bought some two months before at the mature age of fourteen. I inquired whether he was up to his work. The stableman then volunteered the information that a week ago his first introduction to a mare had raised no interest in the old gentleman, who apparently lacked either experience or capacity. At another stable a beautiful Arab was introduced to us as a retired "flier." A special record was maintained of his progeny, and an eye was kept open for promising colts, so that the word could be passed to interested parties.

After this we made a rather exhaustive scrutiny of these stations. Our report described them in simple terms as a sinecure for their staff and a home for aged horses, which had cost the United States taxpayer $1,000,000 to establish and was costing the Greek taxpayer $250,000 a year to maintain, without a shred of benefit to the Greek people. We recommended immediate abolition, sale (or shooting) of the animals, and utilization of the land and buildings for practical purposes. Our opinion has not been contested, but no further action has been taken by the United States Mission and Greek government, although an additional recommendation to fetch in a livestock expert to review the future program had been implemented.

We exempted from this wholesale condemnation the importation of a number of Brown Swiss bulls, which had been utilized to develop a program of artificial insemination in Greece, which is proving highly popular and successful. It has, however, met with some opposition in the Turkish villages, where persons have felt religious scruples that the animals were not given a square deal. It was recently reported that some Orthodox clergy had expressed similar doubts. Another cause of dissatisfaction was that, for unknown reasons, the scheme had been confined to Brown Swiss, thereby limiting the possibilities for Jerseys and Guernseys in which the American Farm School had pioneered.

As a postscript to this story it is well to add that all experts recognize that a fully developed livestock industry is essential, both for the diversification of Greek agriculture and to improve the basic diet. The cattle-breeding program was only one aspect of a major scheme to develop this. Simultaneously the extension program and the seed service were pressing the expansion of forage crops, and schemes of land reclamation and irrigation were based on the assumption that there would be a major livestock industry.

VETERINARY SERVICES

The basic problem on the veterinary side has been shortage of veterinarians, who had to follow studies abroad. The major contribution of American aid was therefore the establishment of a veterinary college as part of the University of Salonika. The new college does not possess any palatial building but is currently housed in Nissen huts. Its first students graduated in 1956.

The shortage of veterinarians has of course been a severe

handicap. As Mr. Christodoulou, the General Director of Agriculture, expressed it on one occasion, "The veterinarians in private practice prefer to attend the dogs of Athens rather than the cattle of the provinces."

Nevertheless, the Mission and government embarked on a scheme of building veterinary clinics in provincial centers. Some have been successful; some have never been opened because no staff could be found; some, when opened, have generated public interest so small that the veterinarian was able to establish his bed in his office.

The same program arranged the procurement of nearly one million dollars in equipment and supplies and built a warehouse to contain these as well as surplus stocks from UNRRA and the Allied armies. Refrigerators were procured for the supervising veterinary officers in the provinces. Unfortunately this last purchase did not take account of voltage. Consequently, on a visit to one office, the veterinarian informed us regretfully that as the town's supply was DC and the refrigerator was AC, he could use a three-hundred-dollar refrigerator only for his lunchtime sandwiches. This affected almost all the other refrigerators.

The warehouse, on inspection, revealed a jackdaw's hoard. We calculated that certain stocks would last 170 years at present consumption rates. Antibiotics were time-expired, and certain cases of volatile liquids were found to be empty when opened. The government accepted our recommendation to dispose of the contents and close the warehouse.

To the credit side of the program must be set vaccination campaigns, at least partly successful, against various animal diseases. In general, however, the program must be counted a failure, due in large part to the shortage of trained veterinarians. When this is remedied, more constructive steps can be taken to safeguard public and animal health.

SCHOOLS OF TRADE SKILLS

A few words must be said here for the schools of farm skills developed by Mr. Pope, the American extension adviser, Mr. Melias of the Mechanical Cultivation Services, and Mr. Sinis of the Farm Machinery Station. We shall meet these gentlemen later. Melias especially has a capacity for introducing himself into any field.

The arrival of UNRRA tractors in Thessaly some years earlier had precipitated a crisis. Melias had hastily mobilized his own drivers to run impromptu instruction classes for farmers in driving and maintenance. The importation of more tractors under American aid was therefore met by the organization of "tractor short courses" at the American Farm School, the Farm Machinery Station, and the Mechanical Cultivation depots.

A field trip through devastated villages prompted Melias to suggest that short courses might be organized in masonry, carpentry, and blacksmith's work for young farmers and refugees. Thus were born the schools of farm trades. The graduation diploma was a bag of tools provided by the Mission. The teachers were a scratch collection of M.C.S. staff and outside technicians. Melias, believing that practice was the best teacher, let his students build office blocks and sheds at M.C.S. depots. The Volos office block, incidentally, withstood the recent earthquake unscathed despite the fact that a critical inspection reveals slight discrepancies in original alignment.

As a result the graduates were able to make a very substantial contribution to rebuilding their home villages, and imposed a salutary check on the inclination of the limited number of craftsmen to profiteer in the emergency following the Communist war. The schools still exist, though on a much reduced scale, under the direction of the extension service.

THE RESULT OF THE PRODUCTIVITY DRIVE

The agricultural productivity program has had successes. Total and average production are 50 per cent above prewar levels. A glance at a few statistics of production may be of interest.

	Total Production (in thousands of metric tons)		Product (in kilos per hectare)	
	1935–38	1953	1935–38	1953
Wheat	768	1400	903	1340
Barley	197	258	960	1204
Corn (Maize)	255	309	876	1162
Rice	4	66	2020	3764
Cotton	44	95	715	1110
Tobacco	61	61	658	693
Potatoes	148	445	6930	11420
Melons	203	393	8060	12900
Tomatoes	109	344	9491	16670
Other Vegetables	210	547	7241	11610
Livestock Meat	111	98		

The extension service claims the major credit, but not a little is due to increased availability of irrigation water for vegetable crops and to other land improvements. Equally significant have been the aid-supported imports of fertilizers, chemicals, etc.

Perhaps most deserving of credit is the simple Greek farmer who, working on his seven acre unit, with little or no capital and without scientific training, has been able to absorb and apply so many new ideas so quickly. It must be remembered too that this was achieved when many had lost all their possessions and lacked even a roof over their heads. I recollect one such farmer who in 1952 lived in a tree in which he had laid a rough platform of boards. This was the bedroom. Living room and kitchen were the ground under the tree.

Despite blunders and mistakes, which have hampered and obstructed well-intentioned plans, the Greek farmer has grasped the helping hand to lift himself up. Nevertheless he is not satisfied. His existence is often well below basic levels of subsistence. He sees and hears of better things. Far more are his wife and his daughters conscious of growing needs. He knows of mistakes and errors, and he lacks faith in his own government and officials, but he has also lost faith in America and Britain.

CHAPTER 6.

The Major Reclamation Works

WORKS IN MACEDONIA

Increased productivity from improved farm practices alone will not solve the deficiencies of Greek agriculture. In 1929 the Greek state initiated a program to drain the marshes of Macedonia and provide new lands for the Asia Minor refugees. Two major areas were involved: the plain of Salonika and the Philippi-Drama plain.

The Salonika plain is contained between sea and mountains; it runs in a great curve to north and east from the mass of ten-thousand-foot Olympus. Through this plain runs the Axios River, which breaks into it through a gap in the northern ranges. "Fairest of all earthly streams," Homer called it in the *Iliad*. Homer, as anyone who knows Greece can vouch, was ordinarily pedantically accurate in his background descriptions, but this statement is a "downright lie," as Mark Twain would say. Like the Mississippi, Axios carries half a continent with it. The silt from the drainage of the Balkans has created the plain of Salonika and is adding to it day by day. Within historic times the recorded shore line at points has moved out twenty miles. The lake of Gianitsa lay in the middle of this area. Under Turkish rule no management of this fertile plain had been provided, and it was waterlogged, marshy, and malarial.

The Philippi plain of eastern Macedonia was in even worse plight. Here had once stood a great city, where Julius

Caesar was avenged and where Saint Paul first preached in Europe. The broken arches of temples and public buildings, the prison of Saint Paul, and the remains of the great basilica that later Christianity erected to his honor, lie surrounded by malarial marsh.

In these two regions the American contractors, Monks Ulen and the Foundation Company, in prewar days had driven drainage canals to carry off the surplus waters, Gianitsa and Philippi had been completely dried, the rivers Axios and Strymon had been contained by flood levees, and the areas lay ripe for development. In fact new towns had sprung to life, and land had been distributed in the cleared marshes, although essential secondary and tertiary drainage systems had not been completed.

On the Strymon river, into which Philippi drained, the Bulgarian occupation forces appear to have enjoyed an orgy of destruction, to which later the Communist bands they supported were to add. The floodgates on the Strymon and many works, in addition to equipment and installations, were deliberately wrecked. The Salonika area under German occupation suffered primarily from neglect of the regular maintenance that must be given to works of this nature.

American aid was first concentrated on the salvage and repair of the completed works, and later on the addition of structures and secondary works to complete the original plan.

Two government agencies were charged with this responsibility. One, YSSYEM, was a civil engineering group of the Ministry of Public Works; the other, YPEM, was a composite group which, oddly enough, was controlled by the Direction of Extension of the Ministry of Agriculture. YSSYEM was responsible for the control of the rivers Axios and Strymon, and for the main canals and structures. YPEM was responsible for "valorization" of the land. This meant in effect that their work was to provide tertiary drainage and irrigation canals, and generally to get the area in a fit state to hand over to the farmer. This curious administrative arrangement has been the subject of a bitter feud for over seven years, within and without the Mission and the ministries concerned.

The project agreements under which United States aid in counterpart have been released in a sum of around twelve million dollars contain several important provisions. It is explicitly provided, for example, that the Greek government shall set up administrative organizations to take over the work of project maintenance. It is also provided that a scheme shall be devised under which farmers settled on the land shall pay the cost of reclamation or improvement to the counterpart fund. The objective of this last provision is to secure a revolving capital fund from American aid which will make possible a continuing program of reclamation.

To date these solemn undertakings have been ignored. Moreover, apart from a few slightly bellicose letters directed to the responsible ministers by the Controller's Office, and some more critical comments by Walter Packard, the former adviser on land and water resources development, the American government has over the last four years accepted this breach of agreement, which formed in effect an addendum to a treaty. The consequences are, of course, that the completed works suffer progressive deterioration through absence of any administrative body to give regular supervision, while further extension to the works is checked by a shortage of capital funds.

The staff under my supervision have visited the villages of the area and have talked over the problem with the farmers. The farmers have told us that they recognize the need for supervision and are willing to pay the necessary levy toward an organization established for that purpose. They are also prepared to pay a contribution toward the cost of completed works, with the proviso that they prefer that this repayment be made into a fund to extend the works in Macedonia to benefit their neighbors. The reason for this preference, they explain, is that any repayment to Athens would inevitably disappear without any benefit to Greece.

A few words of explanation of the Greek government's failure are necessary. First it should be said that, due to frequent changes of government and ministers, the top political level is in fact unaware of these provisions. As an example, when Mr. Apostolidis, Minister of Agriculture in 1953 was informed of this in a conference with Mission representatives, he immediately requested us to investigate and present clearly the practical steps necessary. Unfortunately he resigned because of ill health before our report was completed. Since then I have personally been in more or less constant touch with the responsible officials. They point out quite reasonably that this problem involves several ministers, is entirely new to Greece administratively, is outside the scope of authority of every one of them since it involves several departments, and consequently can be settled only at cabinet level. Four, perhaps five, ministries are involved, and a decision must be made handing over jurisdiction to one, or else carefully redefining each authority. As the problem ultimately involves all Greece, the consequence will inevitably be that delegation of responsibility to one minister will completely change cabinet precedence. It is therefore difficult for any single minister to present the issue. Furthermore, the permanent civil servants face the problem of fully briefing their ministers on the position, which involves many legal and technical pitfalls.

The civil servants have stressed time and again that this is an issue that must be raised by the Mission at cabinet level and fully explained by the neutral Mission experts. Just before my formal separation from the Mission I once more raised the question of following up the correspondence. Mr. Apostolidis, restored in health, had just assumed the post of Minister of Finance. I was told that in view of the present delicate situation it was not United States policy to "needle" the Greek government. Leaving Greece, therefore, as a private citizen, I wrote personally to Mr. Apostolidis reminding him of this issue. I quoted Packard's words of a year earlier that the reclamation works would soon become archaelogical monuments if this administrative difficulty was not faced.

THESSALY

It is not only in Macedonia that the problems of maintenance and repayment of capital cost arise. This clause was also included in agreements covering other Mission projects.

The next most important is Thessaly. This region is in peninsular Greece immediately south of Macedonia. Geologically it is an extraordinary area, a deep hollow surrounded by great mountain ranges. To the north Olympus lifts its snowcap; to the west the unbroken line of Pindus peaks towers almost as high; to the east Pelion and Ossa block access to the sea; and to the south, the solid mass of Othrys completes the circle. In a past age the area was a lake fed from the drainage of the surrounding mountains. The old legends say that Neptune the sea god with his trident smote the mountain ring between Olympus and Ossa to create the narrow gorge of Tempe. Through this single gap in the northeast the entire drainage must pass. The Penios River began to fail in its functions long ago. In 1937 British contractors commenced work to improve the main river channel and its tributaries, and to construct drains to handle floodwaters and clear the marshlands. They resumed work under American aid, which has invested around six million dollars in the project. The main works are virtually complete, as are also many of the supporting works.

Here, too, the Ministry of Public Works was responsible for the major engineering works, but the Direction of Hydraulic

Construction and Mechanical Cultivation Service handled the "valorization side."

Difficulties have arisen from time to time over this divided authority, since the Ministry of Public Works is inclined to be legalistic about the protocol involving formal transfer of works. This may delay the "valorization" by years. The agriculturists want to jump the gun and get results. This is especially the territory of Melias, the actionist who breaks regulations. In southern Thessaly the Selinon area had had primary drainage, so, regardless of technicalities, in moved the tractors of Mechanical Cultivation to install supplementary drainage and to level and prepare the land. No one has ever quite understood where they raised the money, or some of it at least, for this project. I personally think it came from an American Mission subsidy for brush clearing. Thirty thousand acres were ready for winter wheat, and the following spring brought a crop on this area six times the national average coverage per acre. Other drained areas of Thessaly did not show the same phenomenal results, but there was no doubt that the works had been beneficial, and the full fruit had not yet been gained. Shortly thereafter Melias was negotiating with a group of villages in southern Thessaly to introduce secondary drainage. It was planned to finance the project with a loan to the communities from the National Deposit Fund (the fund that holds trust accounts, legally disputed money, etc.) But some of the villages with left-wing councils held out for governmental assistance. They claimed that other areas had enjoyed this, and had not been asked to repay. This, of course, was one of the inevitable consequences of failure to enforce the repayment provision.

Again in Thessaly the major works are suffering for lack of an organization to supervise and maintain. In this case a law has been drafted to establish drainage authorities for part of the area that is within the jurisdiction of the Ministry of Agriculture, but it has not yet been passed.

ARTA

In Epirus, the northwest corner of Greece, the central mountains fan out to cover the entire area to the coast with subsidiary ranges. In the Arta area, immediately to the south of these ranges, the drainage rivers running into the Gulf of Ambracia have silted up the deltas to build an area of fertile land.

In 1937 drainage works were initiated in this area, too. Resumed under American aid, the scheme was expanded to include irrigation for some fifty thousand acres. The major works have been completed, and the irrigation system has been constructed by the Direction of Hydraulic Construction and Mechanical Cultivation Service.

Practical results have been phenomenal. In three years the value of local production has been quintupled. In recent talks with the agricultural specialists of the area we were told that a much greater deferred effect will be felt as changed crop patterns are established to make full use of summer water.

In this area Mission staff and staff of the Ministry of Agriculture pressed on with plans to organize the farmers. A strong cooperative irrigation authority, whose executive is elected by the farmers, has taken control and assumed responsibility for maintenance of the major part of the technical works. This cooperative levies on its members for the supply of water and utilizes these funds for maintenance and for some improvements in the works. However no steps have been taken to initiate repayment of project costs, but the farmers have been definitely informed that this will have to be done as soon as necessary legislation is passed.

PLANS FOR IRRIGATION WORKS

The American consulting engineers Knappen-Tibbetts-Abbett-McCarthy had contracted to undertake surveys and prepare plans for new hydraulic works. The Arta project is an example of the benefits that were envisaged from irrigation works.

The low summer rainfall limits the cultivation period in Greece and the type of crops that can be cultivated. In the Arta area, availability of irrigation water has made possible both double-cropping after winter wheat and the introduction of cash crops that previously could not be economically grown, such as rice, cotton, forage crops, and potatoes.

K-T-A-M were concerned to ascertain how far it was possible to provide similar opportunities elsewhere.

Originally, possibilities of major irrigation schemes had been foreseen at a later stage in the Macedonian schemes of Axios and Strymon, but in the then state of the land it was impossible to plan.

K-T-A-M presented major schemes for irrigation in the Salonika plain by means of storage dams on Axios and Aliakmon rivers. A similar plan was presented for the Nestos River, which separates Macedonia and Thrace. These schemes are, of course, of vastly greater dimensions than the Arta project, involving around one million acres.

Another major scheme is planned to reclaim 100,000 acres in Western Greece, south of Arta, now under shallow-water lagoons and lakes, and to irrigate this and the adjoining area of around the same size through a dam on the Achelous River. It is estimated that this scheme alone will increase the agricultural productions of Greece by around 400,000 tons.

Of course these four schemes involve a very considerable investment, well over 100 million dollars. Besides these schemes, seven other surveys of around the same size are planned.

With the present expansion of population, Mr. Walter Packard, the Mission's former Adviser on Development of Land and Water Resources, calculated that, in order to maintain present Greek living standards, all these projects should be completed during the next fifteen years.

In the present financial state of Greece the availability of investment for major works of land reclamation on this scale cannot be envisaged easily. Nevertheless, the Greek government under political pressure initiated work on the Axios, Aliakmon and Achelous dams in 1954. Work has progressed slowly, with intermittent stops because of cessation of funds. Following floods on the Evros in early 1955, the initial stages of this scheme have also been commenced.

The American Mission was generally opposed to this policy, feeling that priority should be given to fully "valorizing" existing projects and undertaking smaller works, rather than to committing long-term capital in the major schemes.

One is tempted to ask why such a large number of surveys, manifestly beyond practical realization with present available funds, were undertaken. The simple existence of plans, which in some cases are extremely detailed, necessarily presents a temptation to pressure groups. The consequent dissipation of available funds over several projects prevents the realization of any single one.

Furthermore a source of grievance is established, in that it is felt that Mission support was good up to the planning stage but then was deliberately withdrawn. Of course, more rapid progress could be made if steps were taken to recover the earlier investments from the beneficiaries, but this has never been clearly associated with aid limitations and reductions.

EVALUATION

The major schemes so far carried out have brought considerable benefit, but no provision has been made for administration and maintenance of the completed works. Provisions were included in the covering project agreements, but these were never enforced. The American Mission, which introduced technicians and advisers in most other fields of land reclamation, rather oddly never provided for an expert in administration and management of authorities for drainage and irrigation works.

The Greek government has failed to introduce any legislation to oblige landowners to pay for improvement costs, despite provisions in the formal agreement. The Mission has failed to protest this failure at a top level. The surveys and plans for later extensive works paid for by American aid funds look very nice on paper and have cost some $500,000. The likelihood of early application in the absence of unexpected windfalls is poor. Their effect, therefore, is tantalizing and acts as an irritant.

There are at the present time two possible sources from which accelerated construction could be financed: repayment of past costs of existing schemes and external aid. For three years the government has sought the latter from the United States, Germany, Britain, France, and Italy. The present stages can be described as "political demonstration only." Regular, sustained investment of ten to fifteen million dollars per year is a minimum essential for a period of ten years. Some contribution from private sources is possible, but the comments in Chapter 2, in which the difficulty of withdrawing capital from a developing country were pointed out, must be borne in mind. At one time I suggested that this field might be made the subject of a public loan for, say, forty years, floated with the guarantee of the United States government, on terms requiring the establishment of organized water authorities with properly trained staffs, the institution of regular loans for maintenance, and a systematic scheme for repayment through irrigation water charges and flood protection levies.

Unless some such constructive steps can be taken to initiate a serious program and to maintain the support through the entire period of construction, we must necessarily count any support from Greece as obtainable by temporary bribes. There is no other way of lifting the standard of living in those important border areas along the Bulgarian frontier.

Proffering some aid this year, perhaps some next year, but threatening all the time a definite cutoff, is the height of stupidity. Any intelligent Greek or American must recognize that this single group of projects is beyond the present capacity of the Greek state; and it is only one section of the problem and will meet the needs of only a limited portion of Greece or the Greeks.

Any well-wishing foreigner must recognize the dilemma of Greek politicians, anxious to meet the needs of their constituents, forced to spend a little here and a little there to hold public feeling in check, and constantly having to ask the United States Mission for more generous treatment. The alternative is to look across the northern borders and forget a war of six years ago.

It is therefore not incomprehensible that so many of the newspapers, and many politicians and civil servants, say that America is not interested in Greece, and that the only real prospect of meeting needs lies in withdrawing from NATO into neutrality.

CHAPTER 7.

Land Reclamation and Improvement:
Small Schemes: Mechanical Cultivation

INTRODUCTION

Major schemes of land improvement like those considered in the last chapter are applicable to only a small proportion of Greece. In a country where the land is largely level and traversed by major rivers, such as Iraq, Egypt, or certain provinces of India, this type of scheme may be of enormous value. In a broken and rugged terrain, like Greece, any attempt to improve the standard of living must be dispersed over a wide number of smaller schemes providing different types of land improvement for comparatively small areas.

Perhaps some mountain torrent in times of rain pours its flood and gravel over the fields of some narrow valley. Check dams and small levees may double the annual yield. In another valley a bubbling spring fed from the snows of Taygetus can be channeled a mile or two to water the orange groves and rice of Laconia. Or perhaps a short canal may divert the waters of rivers such as Alpheus, Eurotas, or Achelous to rice fields, potatoes, maize, or forage crops along their banks.

In fertile Elis the winter rains running down from the steep slopes of Chelmos and Erymanthus bog the land, so that winter planting becomes virtually impossible in many sections. Late crops are not possible in the dry summer. A few drainage canals can work miracles and bring thousands of acres into cultivation. In another area clearing of brush, terracing of hillsides, systematic ditching, leveling by mechanical techniques, and similar schemes of land improvement bring large areas into use. These are examples of a multiplicity of undertakings that can benefit areas ranging from a few acres to thirty or forty thousand.

The principal difficulty in undertaking these operations lies in the fact that the small farmer with five to twenty acres possesses neither knowledge nor funds to undertake these works. Prior to 1939, the Direction of Hydraulic Construction of the Ministry of Agriculture, the Refugee Resettlement Committee in North Greece, and the Mechanical Cultivation Service of the Greek state had initiated works of this type.

In the early stages of the aid period two main projects were initiated for "medium schemes." One ultimately provided some five million dollars for hydraulic construction in South Greece, the other about the same sum for YPEM in Macedonia. In addition the Mechanical Cultivation Service presented a plan for bank loans to be given for private schemes through agriculture banks. A further project provided a subsidy of 10 per cent to 30 per cent of the cost of private schemes. Later the extension service began to develop village self-help schemes toward which the Mission project provided over three million dollars for material and hire of equipment.

The governing agreements for the medium schemes provided that plans should be prepared for repayment of capital costs and for the organization of small irrigation and reclamation authorities. The "small schemes" were originally on a grant basis but from 1952 were established as loans. In this case, although unregulated, repayment has been started. In the medium schemes nothing has yet been done to organize repayment.

Obviously an essential to the improving of land was the provision of adequate equipment to undertake the various works. Under a special project agreement, some seventeen million dollars were expended on tractors, bulldozers, excavators, etc., and on the workshop tools necessary to maintain them. Some five million of this total related to wheeled tractors and other machinery, which was bought for demonstration purposes and was later resold on an installment basis to farmers. The balance was assigned to the Mechanical Cultivation Service of the Greek state, a long-established organization which customarily undertook land improvement works for state or private accounts, and which already held equipment imported by UNRRA and other agencies.

MECHANICAL CULTIVATION SERVICE

This formidable organization has been described as the spearhead of the Greek drive for increased productivity. Its interests are not solely in land reclamation but cover many other agricultural activities. It is perhaps the most intensive of all Greek state services, because its personnel are imbued with a sense of mission. Its activities are closely bound up with those of its former chief, John Palaeologos, director of Farm Crop Cultivation of the Greek Ministry of Agriculture, who still exercises a close supervision despite his more general responsibilities for Greek agriculture.

In 1925 J. P., a Smyrna Greek who had just completed his own schooling, was teaching at the Higher School of Agriculture in Athens. At this time the resettlement problem was at its height. J. P. visited the offices of the Resettlement Committee and was met by an old family friend, who demanded in fierce tones why he was lingering among the girls in Athens when every trained Asia Minor Greek should be helping his brothers in North Greece. J. P. wrote out his resignation and took the night train to Salonika.

Arriving there, he was promptly given charge of a group of threshing machines. After a few weeks he received a bald notification that he was now chief of the tractor group, about forty machines, which constituted the Mechanical Cultivation Service of the Resettlement Committee. Convinced that a mistake had been made, as he was only twenty-two and had no experience, he did not take up duties until a week later, when a deputation of tractor drivers arrived to ask for instructions.

The original objective of the service was to break up the land for the holdings of the Asia Minor refugees. Powered with heavier machinery, it took on land-clearing responsibilities. Later, with new equipment, it took over the valorization of the land reclaimed in the Giantsa and Philippi areas and in Macedonia generally. J. P. was moved back to Athens, and M.C.S. depots spread south from Macedonia and into Crete and the isles. Agricultural services such as heavy ploughing were its principal work.

In 1941 M.C.S. tractors mobilized to resist the Italians in Epirus, and the war left only a few survivors. Through UNRRA, the tractors and bulldozers from the British and American armies in Italy were transferred to M.C.S., and J. P. returned from a fruitful visit to Germany with 150 units as reparations.

The first postwar effort had been to concentrate on ploughing to secure the wheat harvest, which the shortage of draft animals had imperiled. With the arrival of UNRRA, followed by Marshall Plan farm tractors, M.C.S. progressively disengaged itself from common ploughing, sold its wheeled tractors, and concentrated on the heavy caterpillar track units. The provision of some ten million dollars in United States aid credits made possible additional heavy units, excavators and other specialized machinery. M.C.S. now had a disposable force of around nine hundred self-propelled units plus ancillary equipment.

In 1952 the Chief of Mission requested the Controller's Office to investigate this agency from a practical business viewpoint. First, we were to consider whether a state agency of this type was essential or whether it could be replaced by private initiative. Secondly, we were to present plans for correction of any faults discovered in practice.

Our earliest contacts with this agency presented us with a problem. There was no doubt that it had many critics, American and Greek. There was equally no doubt that it had faults. However, we were immediately impressed by the high morale and almost crusading fervor that characterized its activities. We were even more impressed by the reception we met at the thirty depots from which machinery operated. Every manager welcomed our inspections, placed his entire staff and organization at our disposal, and proceeded to give a full exposition of the situation, meticulously reporting failures, faults, and difficulties as he saw them. In the whole of my professional career I have rarely known any organization so prepared to accept an investigation and so ready to accept criticism.

Some time later we heard the explanation. Palaeologos had issued a directive somewhat in these terms: "The American people gave us most of our machines. Their representatives are visiting us to ask for an account of our stewardship. You are instructed to disclose complete information on all material facts, irrespective of whether you are asked or not. The objective of this investigation is to help us to perform our functions better. It is in our own interests as Greeks that the investigation be in a position to make a fair and unbiased report."

When the report was finished we were asked to provide a Greek text. The Service then proceeded to distribute this to all responsible members of its own staff, to all senior government officials in Athens and the provinces, and to the higher academic, technical, and commercial bodies of Greece. They explained that this was the first important management investigation in Greece, and they wished to set an example in giving it publicity.

A meeting was arranged with Minister Apostolidis, Mission representatives, and the Service chiefs. Palaeologos prefaced the meeting with a formal statement that he and his senior staff had carefully considered the report and had asked for clarifications and explanations where necessary. There were a few differences on minor matters, but they were prepared to accept the report in full and to follow its recommendations. The Minister then stated that as no difference existed between the American Mission and the Greek state, we would now proceed to take the necessary steps. So the reorganization started. Later the British Ministry of Agriculture extended an invitation to the United Kingdom, and this reorganization became a cooperative assistance scheme.

REPORT ON MECHANICAL CULTIVATION SERVICE

This report is significant because it represents, so far as I am aware, the first complete appraisal of a major American aid project in the manner in which a commercial organization would be investigated for investment purposes. An investment of nearly twenty million dollars in machinery, installations, and subsidies was involved. The investigation cost fifteen thousand dollars.

Our assessment of private initiative versus state enterprise may be of interest in its application to other countries. The Service had originally held a virtual monopoly position in the light-wheeled tractor and harvester fields. Over a period of thirty years it had introduced agricultural mechanization to Greece, but as soon as private initiative had developed in a particular activity it had progressively withdrawn, meanwhile exercising a market control to prevent exploitation.

In the summer of 1952 we were disturbed to find that on orders of Palaeologos a group of fifteen heavy modern combine harvesters was totally immobilized. His explanation was that these were imported in the aid program by the Service and had been operated on a limited scale in 1950 and 1951. Thus contractors owning old-fashioned threshing machines had been given the opportunity of seeing the most modern type in action. An undertaking had then been given to the contractors that their applications for importation under the aid program would be approved, and that the M.C.S. combines would not be operated in competition except in a national emergency or to prevent "price rings." The combines were held for several years on that basis and sold in 1955, when continuing imports had replaced the old threshing equipment throughout Greece.

Similar methods had been applied in the wheeled tractor field. M.C.S. had now sold to private farmers or contractors all wheeled tractors and their equipment imported by UNRRA and Marshall aid, and had abandoned regular ploughing and similar light operations except in a few backward areas.

In the caterpillar tractor field it retained equipment exceeding sixty horsepower. Our review of the situation disclosed that similar equipment was held by a number of private contractors operating mainly in road construction. However these were small-scale operators. They did compete with M.C.S. occasionally in agricultural works, particularly in reclamation. The M.C.S. organization included engineers, agriculturists, and ancillary personnel who could plan smaller works as well as carry them out. It was spread in thirty depots with supporting factory equipment over all Greece. Around 50 per cent of its operations were on state account or for municipalities and communes. This investment had a replacement value well in excess of twenty million dollars. It was quite obvious that with the chronic shortage of capital in Greece, no private agency could overtake this enterprise. Even if capital were available it would be drawn from other productive enterprises. Moreover the interest, risk and profit factors would enormously increase prices. Market investigations revealed that the bulk of the work could be undertaken only at marginal prices, due to the poverty of the people. Moreover the pool of funds was strictly limited. Greek state budget allocations for work were limited not by demands but by the budget ceiling. Communal activity was limited by local budgets, and private activity by the loans authorized for the purposes by the Currency Committee. The same total fund was therefore available irrespective of work quantity. Contractors' work on roads was substantially higher, as were excavation works for other ministries (as much as seven or eight times in certain cases).

The investigators considered that M.C.S. prices were below theoretical costs and that this made any private computation impossible.* This was actually due to an incorrect basis of competition. The investigators therefore defined the function of M.C.S. as to continue its activities in the present fields at a fair competitive price, which would give opportunity for a slow but steady development of private enterprise. However, our opinion was that the period of present operational activity would not be less than ten years and might easily be twenty-five. In the meantime it should be the objective of M.C.S. to operate on a basis in which revenue provided a sum sufficient to meet current expenses, provide for replacement of machinery, and show a small surplus.

At that time M.C.S. was falling short of meeting current

* This was pointed out to Palaeologos during the investigation, and a provisional increase of 3 per cent was computed. The investigators found that this had been implemented within three days, as it was not M.C.S. policy to conduct unfair competitions.

expenses. This position should be remedied by a reorganization spread over two to three years. The causes of deficit were outlined. Previously there were no prices for services below standard costs, together with an inelastic market which prevented full employment being given to all machinery. This was due to the credit restriction policy applied on Mission instructions by the Currency Committee, and to the limited funds available for state investment. The work was there to do, but the finance was not. At that time and later the Controller's Office criticized a rigid deflationary policy which did not take account of the type of activity to be financed. It is self-evident that the wages and standard charges of an organization such as M.C.S. are rigid. The effect of increased work is merely increased fuel consumption. The surplus revenue in our plan would pass into an account limited in purpose to expenditure in the United States for replacement machinery. The effect of the work would be deflationary in that, as considered later, its immediate effect would be to increase available goods. For some reason this argument, clearly comprehensible to any intelligent man, meets a solid psychological block in the mind of an economist. As a consequence millions of American aid dollars, in the form of valuable productive machinery owned by M.C.S., Well-drilling Services, and other agencies in Greece, rust in idleness.

In the author's opinion these comments could be expressed with considerably greater violence. The economist is taking the place of the lawyer in inhibiting productive activity by hidebound restrictions. Perhaps more clearly than anyone else, the public accountant, whose field is the practical financial problems of trade and industry and whose tools are statistics and financial data, realizes the harm that college-trained theorists, who possess very little of the practical knowledge essential to real assessment of his data, may do through following some theoretical formula.

THE FAULTS OF M.C.S.

M.C.S. had some major internal faults. Principally it lacked any proper system of accumulating accounting, costing, and financial data. Secondly, it was deficient in the fields of workshop administration and mechanical engineering. These deficiencies are characteristic of the Greek economy as a whole, due to its rapid growth, the lack of time available for training managerial staff in these fields, and the lack of contacts with more developed centers which would make these shortcomings evident. The combination of these defects tends to create major faults in fields of management and administration. Supply channels cannot be organized, and policy decisions are made without essential facts being available.

As a result of these deficiencies a large proportion of earth-moving machinery (nearly one-third) was consistently immobilized, and this proportion was continually growing. Not a few machines had been out of use for a year or more. Lack of essential spares was a partial cause, but even more significant were the breakdowns and inefficiencies due to faulty repairs. If a part broke, the enterprising Greek mechanic often decided that this was because the maker had just not made it strong enough. He therefore machined a substitute out of some really strong material. The consequence on intermeshing parts in a finely balanced machine can be guessed. I have often heard the engineering adviser moan in anguish and agony over the wreckage of some ten-thousand-dollar machine.

To remedy these defects we proposed that a group of foreign technical experts be employed to train the staff of the service and to introduce modern management practices.

We further suggested that a number of M.C.S. personnel pay a short visit to another state operating a similar service, so as to compare activity and administration.

The latter proposal crystallized into a visit to the United Kingdom, where a State Machinery Service is operated in certain areas. Palaeologos, accompanied by Dr. Frixos Letsas, a mechanical engineer employed by the American Mission, was given fullest facilities to see modern organization, repair shops, and mechanical accounting systems. Later the British government loaned to the Greek state the experts to assist in the reorganization. (Mission and Greek state, after consideration, had judged that experiences of United Kingdom conditions, with a restricted field of operations and similar terrain would be more helpful than those of the United States, where farm sizes were generally huge by comparison and marginal cultivation had not the same significance.)

Over the next two years the reorganization progressed. Modern systems of accounting, storekeeping, and costing were introduced. Then a management meeting completed the arrangements for statistical control of machinery utilization and spares procurement by punched card accounting. Almost all units are reported to be active, although the fleet has been reduced a little by scrapping overage UNRRA equipment. Workshops, stores, and supply lines are now well organized. It is pleasant to see the M.C.S. depots in early spring, with lines of machinery and equipment, freshly repainted and reconditioned during the slack winter season, ready for the new battle in the struggle to establish freedom from want in Greece.

M.C.S. has two complaints. First, they object to the limitations imposed by the credit policy. Secondly, in January, 1956, M.C.S. lost the British organizing team. This is a loss for which Greek state and Mission were equally blamed. Last year the Mission promised to pay their salaries from United States technical assistance funds; then, to the surprise of the Ministry of Agriculture, wrote three months later to say that the Greek state budget should bear the cost. As a consequence of the mix-up the team was unpaid for seven months.

In 1956 M.C.S. was unable to get any reaction from
the Mission, which was pursuing a noninterventionist policy,
or from a stopgap government, which was preparing for elections. Regretfully, therefore, they said good-bye to the team,
with the hope that later in the year they could be invited to
return, if certain plans described in Chapter 9 matured.

SMALLER WORKS OF LAND IMPROVEMENT AND RECLAMATION

The constructive work of M.C.S. is so closely associated
with the reclamation program that a joint account of them is
preferable to separate treatment. M.C.S. works closely with five
agencies: the Agricultural Bank, the Directions of Hydraulic
Construction and Extension of the Ministry of Agriculture,
the county officers of the Minister of Interior responsible for
community works, and YPEM in Macedonia.

The Agricultural Bank is a semigovernmental institution
formed in conjunction with the Cooperatives of Farmers to
provide short- and medium-term credit to agriculture. Since
the war it has practically no deposits, and its entire disposable
funds are obtained from the Bank of Greece or American
Mission counterpart. It is stretched to its utmost to provide
short-term credits for cultivation and marketing. Certain funds
provided from counterpart and state budget are earmarked for
medium terms. A substantial part of these credits is devoted
to land improvement works such as brush-clearing, terracing,
breaking up new land, replanting vineyards, very deep ploughing, and small drainage and irrigation works. These enterprises
are undertaken by individual farmers or cooperative groups,
usually performed by M.C.S., and financed by the Bank on
two- to five-year loans. Credits actually provided are only a
fraction of the potential demand. Nevertheless American aid
investment in this field, partly repaid, has probably averaged

$550,000 per year over the aid period. This, of course, is a revolving fund.

The community development program of Extension and the Ministry of Interior are now combined.* Construction under these programs is usually performed by the local authority using labor contributed by its members. External aid may be given from counterpart and state budget funds to procure materials or hire machinery from M.C.S.

A very substantial number of small land reclamation projects have been carried out by this means, involving drainage, irrigation, and similar operations on a community basis, as well as other community improvements. Agricultural schemes, originally provided for by grants, are now to be repaid over three to five years.

The most considerable part of this type of work was the construction of rural roads, either under the Extension or Interior schemes or from community funds if these were available. Before this investigation I had never realized the "productive" value of market roads. We consequently made a rather thorough investigation of this type of work. It is possible to illustrate the economic benefit by a wide range of factual accounts. Papaconstantinou, the M.C.S. epoptis in West Greece, had a vivid story of a "sales" visit to one mountain village. After a long discussion one gentleman of eighty stood up and said, "Boys, I now keep two mules. If this road project goes through I shall save at least the keep of one mule. I start the road fund by giving my second mule for sale."

The M.C.S. since 1948 has driven some six thousand miles of road. As the bulldozers of Thessaly and Macedonia cut their way to link the mountain villages of Olympus with the trunk roads, an expanding production of fruit, dairy products, and meat moves to the cities.

---

* This type of program has now been initiated by other underdeveloped countries, notably India.

Behind this lay a forceful sales campaign by M.C.S. staff and workers, who often trudged the mountains to tell the villages of the gains of a road. Perides, who pushed the road campaign in Boeotia and Euboea, liked to talk about the village that formerly fed its pigs on fine apples, but had now trebled village income through direct shipment to Athens' market.

There is an amusing but pathetic story of Perides' excursions into small works. The maximum expenditure claimable against the small works fund was fifty thousand drachmae for any project. Perides wanted to do a flood protection work which he estimated at three hundred thousand (ten thousand dollars). He therefore had to present it as if it were six different community schemes through different villages. An American Mission extension agent discovered this and insisted that it be taken up as a medium work. The Direction of Hydraulic Construction replanned and presented it for approval by the Reclamation Committee at three million drachmae. At this stage it was claimed by the Mission and Public Works engineers as a major work, and replanned by them at ten million drachmae. As such it was accepted, approved, and initiated as a Mission project. It was cut as part of the "credit squeeze" in 1952. In 1955 I heard that it had been reinitiated by M.C.S. as eight small works, and it has, I believe, been completed.

MEDIUM WORKS

This last story is sometimes said to illustrate the real basis of distinction between small, medium, and large works. It is not, of course, 100 per cent true, but there is sufficient truth about it to be disturbing. It is indubitable that a work initiated by M.C.S., Extension, or Interior would cost more if planned by Hydraulic Construction, and still more in the hands of Public Works. The fact is that the small works group plans a job with a "ceiling," and manual labor and local materials are provided by the farmers or the community generally. The finished job is, of course, often very rough-and-ready, but it serves its purpose of expanding production.

Hydraulic Construction has civil engineers who survey and then draw to engineering standards. The work is then performed by contractors. Hydraulic Construction engineers do not, however, possess the funds of Public Works, and they are much closer to the earth, in the sense that they must relate costs to profits assessed by agriculturist colleagues. Public Works live in a rarified atmosphere where their surveyors and engineers draft to standards unaffected by sordid considerations of profit. Medium works normally are on a scale demanding engineering specifications. Excluding the Macedonian program of YPEM, some six million dollars of United States aid have passed into such operations.

A few typical examples will illustrate. The villages surrounding the favorite tourist resort of Delphi are world-famous for their olives, which form an important dollar export, but the region suffers chronically from summer drought. Some of my readers may have traveled the Delphi road. Over the little town of Arachova (three thousand feet) rises one of the giant peaks of Parnassos. Into a shallow plateau above the town pour the melting snows of the peak in the spring. The Arachova project has made this plateau into a reservoir. A tunnel (of some fifteen hundred yards) has been bored through the lip of the plateau. Its exit can be seen high on the mountainside from the road just beyond Arachova. Down the slope the water travels along a concrete channel, from which branches pass on either side to water the olives of Arachova and Delphi. The surplus water then passes into the Pleistos River, which runs down the deep gorge below Delphi. Along the river it is syphoned off to irrigate the left-hand section of the great sea of one million olives that carpet the valley as one looks down from Delphi. The balance of the olives are irrigated from a second project drawing water from a source behind Amphissa. The two schemes together have cost the United States taxpayer around $400,000 and are not fully complete. It is difficult to measure benefits in terms of a variable crop like olives, but we were frequently assured by the communities concerned that the schemes have been and will be of enormous benefit, not only in increasing crops, but more particularly in assuring regular crops irrespective of rainfall.

The unquestionable benefits of the Konitsa project on the Albanian frontier cannot be disputed. Here the Aoos River falls steeply through a narrow gorge of the Pindus range to traverse a broad plain locked in by surrounding mountains. The town of Konitsa is notable for its gallant and successful defence against the Communists, who were anxious to seize a point so near the frontier, and the project had a morale factor.

It was planned to build a diversionary dam up the gorge to syphon the water along a tunnel parallel to, but above, river height. This section was undertaken by Public Works. From the mouth of the gorge the water was to be piped across the valley and along a series of irrigation canals, to provide summer water for the famous Konitsa melons. This section fell to Hydraulic Construction and M.C.S. With summer water, Konitsa could also grow forage crops, and the townspeople plan to increase their cattle and build a cheese factory.

No scheme has been so bedeviled with problems. An argument about the dam plans between Public Works, which drew them, and the Mission and other parties, was finally settled by the dam structure being swept away. Another argument about the tunnel was settled by rock falls wrecking the first works, so that the line had to be moved farther back, as Public Works were told it would have to be. These and other errors have probably doubled the cost of the works (originally estimated at around $300,000), and delayed completion by three years.

Another project which had its humorous if tragic aspect was launched in Epirus, in the village of Phiniki. Again Public Works built a small dam and led the water down a concrete channel for two miles to the village fields. Unfortunately the spirit level of surveyor or contractor does not appear to have functioned correctly. In the middle of this run, half the water spills over and back into the river. In the ultimate outcome this is as yet no loss. The Epirotes share the reputation of the Scots for canniness in financial matters. The surveyors and engineers came and left without one word on payment or formal agreements. The villagers cannot reconcile such incredible generosity. This is not a backward village although it lies a hundred miles off the beaten track. Its inhabitants are well known for their habit of migrating to America, England, Egypt, or Turkey to make a "pile" and return home. Being astute, they scent a trap. So for four years, as they told us, they have let a water supply that cost eighty thousand dollars in aid funds run past their fields unused. This is not the only incident of its kind, and it illustrates the important point that the Mission, Public Works, and Hydraulic Construction engineers functioning alone, without the cooperation of M.C.S. or Extension who know and understand the farmer, have great difficulty in "valorizing" their works.

ALKALI LAND SCHEME

This failing has not characterized the alkali land scheme. Something of this project is already known to televiewers in the United States, who saw and heard its principal architects, Packard, Letsas, and Palaeologos, on a program in June, 1955. *Time* has also featured the story.

To be fair and to award proper credits, the plan was apparently developed separately by Kalinsky and Michaelides (Hydraulic Construction), Palaeologos (Field Crops and M.C.S.) and Christides (YPEM). The cement, consolidation, and initiative were provided by Packard and Letsas.

The alkali land reclamation provided a double solution. Greece before and after the war was a substantial rice importer, while neighboring Italy was a high producer. Greece lacked irrigation water. The estuaries of most Greek rivers are characterized by mud flats built up from the silt, but due to high evaporation these flats are impregnated with salt, which limits herbage to a coarse and scanty grass. Some 300,000 acres of this potentially good land lie idle. Obviously cleaning by continuous flow of fresh water is necessary. The combination of this leeching process for three years with the cultivation of a profitable, salt-tolerant, crop of rice made reclamation economically feasible.

Hydraulic Construction and M.C.S. in cooperation developed experimental reclamation in the Antheli (Sperchios) region, in the Arta area, and on the Achelous at Missolonghi. M.C.S. and YPEM collaborated in the deltas of Axios and Nestos in Macedonia. The success of the initial scheme and the high price of rice attracted private speculators, for whom M.C.S. performed the necessary reclamation works and land preparation. Around four million dollars of aid funds have been invested, of which part has been returned from rice sales. Reclamation costs run around two hundred dollars an acre.

The general application of the scheme has received recent checks for several reasons. First, of course, is the "credit squeeze." Second is the large increase in Greek rice production from these and other irrigated lands which has made Greece in the last three years into a rice exporter. This has discouraged private capital. Palaeologos has been seriously considering banning rice cultivation except in the salt flats.

A third, technical problem has risen in certain areas. It appears that the leeching operation as originally carried out sets up chemical reactions, which over a period adversely affect the soil structure. Rinnan, the Mission soil specialist, has evolved a solution involving heavy dressing with gypsum. Until final results are known, and the effect ascertained in other areas, a check on expansion is inevitable.

An obvious and urgent need is a suitable and economic follow-up crop to rice, since the alkaline effect is not necessarily completely cleared after three years leeching. Sugar beets have been suggested, but at present there are no processing plants.

Greece of course is a cane sugar importer, while neighboring Turkey now produces beet sugar. Schemes of sugar beet production have been propounded several times, notably by Packard. They have, however, been checked by the American Mission. This has been a major irritant to Greeks, who rightly consider introduction of sugar beets imperative to their agricultural pattern. The Mission policy is considered to be dominated by the desire to maintain the Greek sugar market for United States surpluses. This issue affects the good will of the very important and constructive aid achievement in alkali land.

YPEM IN MACEDONIA

This chapter cannot be closed without a brief reference to the operations in North Greece. YPEM, as we saw in the last chapter, is the final executant in the large reclamation schemes in this region. Within that territory it also assumes the functions exercised elsewhere by Hydraulic Construction.

YPEM is an exceedingly efficient and well-integrated organization, headed by a very able and conscientious official in Orestes Christides. YPEM not only undertakes engineering works but maintains its own experimental fields and research services, and backs up reclamation by extension activities. It also has a very efficient and organized forestry service, which supplements the reclamation works in the plains by tree-planting and by anti-erosion and torrent control works in the northern hills. It has no machinery of its own, but operates a group of tractors and excavators loaned by M.C.S.

It has unfortunately neither the equipment nor technical services to maintain these machines, and continuous difficulties have arisen. Unfortunately, frequent Mission recommendations to return the equipment to M.C.S. control, though accepted in principle by the ministry, have been delayed in application. Consequently much of it is now immobilized or wrecked.

The alkali land scheme was developed with outstanding success in a model estate in the Axios delta. Experimental rice crops in the Serres region led to major developments by the farmers, which produced some phenomenal yields. One man reported over four tons of paddy rice to the acre.

YPEM operations since 1948 have been financed almost entirely by United States counterpart funds to an amount of nearly six million dollars. There can be no question that, all in all, the results have shown more than a fair return. As in other cases a great deal depends on personal leadership, in particular that of Christides and of Loucopoulos, the forestry section director.

AN EVALUATION

This group of activities represents a United States aid investment of nearly forty million dollars. Perhaps its most important benefit has been the establishment of a new major crop in Greece—rice, of which around ninety thousand tons per annum* are now produced. Greece is now self-sufficient and

* Production figures (hectares and tons) are: 1947, 3,000 and 6,000; 1950, 10,000 and 32,000; 1952, 21,000 and 75,000. Imports, 1938, 28,000 tons. Exports, 1953, 20,860 tons.

is building up exports. Every credit must go to the vision and hard work of those primarily concerned. It has revolutionized existence in certain areas and increased the farmers' gross income by nine million dollars a year. If this were the only benefit it would be a reasonable return, but the benefit from the complex of other schemes is even greater. In total it is impossible to calculate, but the detailed studies of my staff disclosed scores of villages where large gains in income had resulted.

Nevertheless, no one of the primary movers in these projects is satisfied. The irresistible, effervescent Packard left Greece in June, 1954. The United States government refused further T.A. funds for his salary, as he was over the retirement age. Since that date the United States Mission, so the Greeks say, has taken no interest in reclamation.

Packard had planned a reorganization of Greek state services to develop and expand land improvement activities. Since that time these plans have been passed from hand to hand but never implemented. The deflationary policy pursued by the Mission has resulted in virtual sterilization of all schemes, and much of the machinery is idling.

The cuts in aid funds and the iron clamp on the Greek budget have caused severe reductions in technical staffs, so that no one is available to organize the farmers in irrigation or drainage districts. Meanwhile all over Greece completed works are deteriorating because the simple farmers do not understand the requirements for operation and maintenance. The Mission could solve these problems, but when the Controller's Office suggested strong representation at ministerial level, we were told not "to needle the government."

CHAPTER 8.

Power and Industry

PROBLEMS OF INDUSTRIAL DEVELOPMENT

The increase in agricultural productivity of underdeveloped countries is simple by contrast with the complexities of even limited industrialization. Unfortunately, the nineteenth-century concept of specialized agricultural producers supplying the intensely developed industrial economies has had to be abandoned. The growth of economic nationalism is a major cause of this change in viewpoint. The shortages resulting from the two world conflicts, which particularly involved the principal industrial countries, have encouraged the tendency.

However there are natural trends that would inevitably have forced a certain degree of industrialization in most countries. The most important consideration is the need to make the best economic use of the labor force that is surplus to agrarian needs, both quantitatively and qualitatively. This labor force can be fully exploited only in an urban society. Every society has always had some measure of industry. The current problem is presented by the demand voiced in so many countries for a virtually self-contained, highly developed industry. Industrial expansion and development became a panacea, which is strongly pressed by the groups of specialists, technicians, and clerks who feel that they lack opportunities in the simpler societies. Greece is no exception to this general rule, and throughout the aid period, loud pressure has been exercised for greater industrial development. Inevitably, as

131

elsewhere, the United States in this instance (Britain in others) has been accused of deliberately throttling this part of the program in the interests of its own industrialists. There are two intrinsic types of difficulties in industrial development. The expansion of Britain, Germany, and the United States has been a steady evolution to which literally millions of people have added a contribution. It has been by no means a painless process. It never was and never could have been blueprinted in advance. One step has led to another, one invention to another, one process to another, one industry to another. The whole economy constitutes a pattern of the most elaborate kind, which virtually defies definition and explanation. Unfortunately we who have been born into this complex system cannot explain this difficulty to others. If we try, we are simply accused of belittling the capacity of others. Nevertheless it would probably help us a great deal more in our relations with underdeveloped nations if we frankly admitted that we created London and New York by accident rather than by conscious planning, and that the achievement owed much to circumstances and accidental combinations.*

Another major difficulty rests in the underdeveloped countries themselves. There is an acute shortage of capital and of managerial ability to undertake modern industry. Our own capital and managerial skill were developed during a period of 100 to 150 years, in which the size and capital equipment of our industries expanded by degrees. Unfortunately we cannot apply the same procedure to other countries. They have to start off at our level, but must do so without the elaborate systems from which we benefit. A textile mill in Lancashire or New England is usually a public company to which many people have contributed capital in the form of preferred stock, equity

---

* We are, of course, handicapped by Soviet claims to have carried out a process of deliberate industrialization. This is partly false as industrialization goes back to Peter the Great, and the speed-up was undoubtedly very costly.

shares, and mortgage debentures. Ordinarily its bulk purchases of raw cotton will be covered by a bank loan or by the intermediary of the produce market. The directors and management have perhaps little or no investment. In Greece the entire capital and management must almost inevitably be contributed by the proprietor and his family. There is no wide market of potential investors on which to unload stock. (This is due to past inflation and to the lack of any substantial savings in a subsistence-level population.) Once the industry is established it is virtually impossible to realize the investment. The small private capital available tends to be invested in trade rather than industry, because the commitment in trade is to an inventory that can be adapted to circumstances and liquidated if desired. This is generally symptomatic of most countries in an underdeveloped condition. The position is vicious, in that labor remains unused and the rising group of "educated" become malcontents for lack of opportunity. The obvious solution is to induce European and American industry to develop branches, but this policy is often opposed by the pressure against "colonialism" and "exploitation."

GREEK INDUSTRY IN GENERAL

In the past Greeks with available capital have been drawn toward the long-established businesses of shipping and trading. Industrial development in Greece is extremely limited and employs no more than 300,000 people. Even with the best possible development of agriculture, the limitations of the country and the continued upward trend of population inevitably imply the necessity of industrial development. Psychologically this is also necessaary. The Greeks are undoubtedly one of the most brilliant and diverse peoples of the world. The younger generation demands the scope and opportunities given by modern technologies and administration.

The prime necessity for modern industry is cheap power. The only substantial generating plant in Greece in 1948 was owned by the British-financed Athens-Piraeus Electric Company (APECO) with an installed capacity of 130,000 kilowatts, driven by imported fuel. Outside Athens, power and light were provided by numerous independent small generating plants with a total capacity of no more than 80,000 kilowatts. Some were owned by municipalities and communes, some by a company enjoying the concession in several of the larger towns, and some by individuals. Clearly a first step was to increase capacity* and develop a unified "grid" system.

Industrial development presented a more complex problem. The first aim was to get existing industry moving again. The index of production for 1947 was computed at 65 (on the base of 1939=100). New plant was an obvious need, and working capital was certainly required. The possibilities of new enterprises depended on a review of existing enterprise.

The principal group was the textile mills, mainly cotton but with some wool, employing some 70,000 people in the cities of Athens, Piraeus, Salonika, Volos, Patras, Levadia, and Naoussa. It is the major labor employer in all these centers. Some 2,000 establishments were recorded in the industrial census of 1951, but many of these were small, specialized units. The trade is largely in the hands of a few major family groups. All plants were out of date and inefficient—some, especially on the woollen side, markedly so. At Naoussa, the mills had been burned by the Communists.

The other principal employers of labor were the clothing and footwear industries (50,000) and the food and beverage group (60,000). Both of these groups were almost

---

* Comparative figures for other small countries in millions of kilowatts: Switzerland 2.9, Norway 2.9, Netherlands 2.4, Finland 1.1, Denmark 1.0, Austria 1.9, Yugoslavia 0.7, Eire 0.2. All (except Yugoslavia and Netherlands) have substantially less population than Greece.

entirely very small-scale enterprises. Some 45,000 establishments report under these two heads. Except for a few of the
larger and more enterprising units, little could be done for
these groups as a whole. For these exceptions—the flour mills,
processing and canning plants, wineries, olive oil refineries—
there were possible opportunities for expansion, re-equipment,
and additional capital.

The next significant employer, metal products, with
around 25,000 employees in 10,000 establishments, was the
likeliest field of development. In this field lay the greatest
opportunity to displace or reduce imports. These possibilities
extended into machinery (7,000) and electrical goods (4,000).

The dominant establishment in the chemical group
(15,000 employees in all) was the enterprising Bodosakes Industries, the only Greek industry with wide international contacts.
It required almost unlimited assistance in a rapid expansion
program.

The industries particularly affected by the requirements
for the building program were wood (10,000) and the cement
group (12,000). The cement industry also had opportunities
for export if additional plant could be provided. Other minor
groups, including furniture (10,000), leather (5,000) and paper
(3,500) had more limited scope.

The opportunity for new industries was dependent on
many factors. Canning clearly had a priority in view of the
drive for increased agricultural productivity. Cold storage,
juice extraction, and milk processing were also advocated, as
well as other types of packaging and processing plants.

The agricultural demand also lent force to the Bodosakes plans for fertilizer development. This demand also indicated possibilities in various metal industries. Pumps and
motors might be assembled locally or manufactured under li-
cense. Welded pipe production presented no major technical
difficulties. The availability of considerable quantities of scrap

from war materials etc. suggested the possibilities of a small
foundry industry.

These plans were laudable and practical, but some suggestions went beyond this. Extruded pipe, however significant
the imports, was generally regarded as impracticable by reason
of the heavy capital outlay and the technique required. So too
were elaborate plans for the development of an aluminium
refinery based on the native bauxite ores, and for a large-scale
industry in this field. How far existing industry, re-equipped
and with the benefit of protective duties, could compete with
imported supplies might depend a great deal on the new power
program.

THE POWER PROGRAM IN GREECE: CONSTRUCTION

Existing power resources were entirely dependent on
imported fuel. The new program planned to double capacity
by using local resources.

On the island of Euboea, some fifty miles north of
Athens, substantial deposits of lignite had been located, which
technical experts considered suitable for use in a generating
plant. The island is separated from the mainland by a narrow
arm of the sea. It was in this protected anchorage that Agamemnon collected the Greek fleets preparatory to the attack
on Troy three thousand years ago. On this shore, at a small
village called Aliveri, overlooking the sound in which a thousand galleys once gathered for a never-forgotten war, now
stands the new power station provided by American aid. The
power cables traverse the strait to serve the new grid system
supplying southwestern Greece. The lignite mines are connected
with the power station by light railway. The lignite lies near
the surface and can be partly mined by open-cast methods.

The station has a capacity of eighty thousand kilowatts,
and since its opening in 1953 it has made a material contribu-

tion to the power supply of Athens. To absorb additional capacity, transmission lines not only connect with the APECO network in Athens-Piraeus but run north to supply the towns of Thebes, Lamia, Levadia, Volos, and Larissa in Boeotia and Thessaly. Power is also available to service certain of the larger villages.

South of Athens the transmission lines link with another scheme to supply the Peloponnese. In the narrow, winding gorge of the Ladhon River, not far from the historic site of Olympia, a large retaining dam has been built. A tunnel cut through the mountainside provides an outlet through which the waters flow to power a generating plant of 55,000 kilowatt capacity. This station is primarily designed to serve Patras, Tripolis, Corinth, Argos, and Kalamata. The connection with the Aliveri-Athens section permits equalization of load.

In Western Greece, in the gorge of the Louros River a little north of Arta, another hydroelectric station (capacity five thousand kilowatts) powers the cities of Yanina, Arta, and Preveza. The transmission lines do not link with the other systems.

Macedonia is supplied by a hydroelectric plant located at Edessa in the mountains that border the eastern edge of the Macedonian plain. Edessa was the ancient stronghold of Philip, father of Alexander the Great; there the Macedonian dreams of world conquest were born. The town crowns a steep ledge rising almost sheer from the plain. It is characterized by a series of most attractive waterfalls, whose sources are seepages from lakes lying back in the mountains. The Edessa power station is driven by a constant flow tunneled and piped from these lakes. This station with a capacity of 40,000 kilowatts has the obligation of supplying Macedonia and the western towns of Thrace through transmission lines as far as Kavalla.

The Macedonian system is not yet connected with the Athens-Aliveri-Ladhon grid. It was originally planned to make this connection through a further thermal electric system at Ptolemais, a small town in the eastern Macedonian mountains, some fifty miles from Edessa, and thereby hangs a curious story.

Here substantial deposits of lignite had been located. A Greek industrialist in association with Swiss interests projected a development of this field, with the establishment of a briquette-manufacturing plant and a power station. Loans from aid funds to provide part of the cost, amounting to more than ten million dollars were earmarked for this purpose. In fact letters of credit were established to cover part of the equipment. However negotiations were prolonged and finally broke down. The responsibility is often placed on the Mission, although it is, as so often, difficult to allocate the blame. Now Bodesakes has taken up the Greek interest in association with Krupps. An agreement was recently signed, under which, it is said, German credits will be made available to cover part of the costs of the Ptolemais scheme. The new plan links the briquette plant and power station with a factory for the production of nitrogenous fertilizer.

To the south, in Thessaly, the Greek state also negotiated an agreement to construct another hydroelectric station in the gorge of the Megdova River. This scheme was examined by Knappen-Tippetts-Abbett-McCarthy and is associated with a plan for irrigating southwestern Thessaly. Oddly, and rather inexplicably, the Mission refused to meet the costs of the original survey of K-T-A-M, which were paid by the Greek government from its own funds. Currently French credits have been negotiated to underwrite part of the costs of this scheme.

Finally, the remaining gap in the transmission lines between the northwest Greece system at Arta and the rest of the network is covered by two other plans. The K-T-A-M plan for reclamation and development of the Achelous River provides for two small plants on the river to supply this region.

A further plan, prepared some years ago, provides for a major hydroelectric station in the Chremasta gorge higher up the river. This would be the largest unit in Greece and would link up with the transmission lines of Arta, Peloponnese, and Athens-Aliveri in a complete grid. Recently attempts were made to negotiate part of the costs of this scheme from the unsettled balance of Italian reparations.

The writer is extremely doubtful of the early fruition of any of these supplementary schemes. The German, French, and Italian credits cover imported items only. Local costs have to be found by the Greek state, and the source is not evident. Generally the Mission has been antagonistic to any proposals to expand the power program beyond the initial plants. Limits of Greek state capacity to support investment have already been underlined, and any surplus generated from sale of power is likely to be committed for some time to the extension of the low tension network to service smaller towns and villages.

The total cost of the scheme to date has exceeded 50 million dollars in foreign exchange and approximately 1200 million drachmae, that is some 120 million dollars in all. Assuming that this expenditure represented economical performance, considerably greater expenditure would be required to undertake the further extensions to capacity. The work at the hydroelectric stations of Agra (Edessa) and Ladhon was performed by the Italian Edison Company. Materials supplied from Italy for this purpose and lira payments to contractors and staff formed part of the Italian reparations for war damage. The Louros dam and the low-tension network were supervised by French contractors, while the high-tension system was technically supervised by British contractors. The Aliveri project and mine were undertaken by American companies. The overall supervision of the scheme rested with Electric Bond and Share Company (EBASCO) on the power side and Pierce Management Inc. for the lignite development at Aliveri.

THE POWER PROGRAM: OPERATION

As indicated in the earlier paragraphs, the largest power producer and distributer in Greece, APECO, was a foreign private company, which was moreover in a position to expand its investment to improve and extend distribution within the capital area. The remaining capacity was also mainly in private hands. Many of the local networks, however, presented a complex pattern of varying voltage and capacity, both direct and alternating. Even within the fairly efficient capital area much of the system was becoming obsolete: in the provinces it was sometimes set up to no recognizable technical standards. M.C.S. in most areas found it necessary to set up its own generating equipment for small workshops, due to the impossibility of depending on the local systems. Tariffs were obviously high.

An early decision had to be made on the form of administration for the new facilities. The well-known conflict between private and public utility control showed signs of appearance. EBASCO* had been in previous negotiation with the Greek government and was interested in the ultimate decisions. Finally a compromise was reached. APECO and the efficient Greek concessionaires were to continue their interests, but they contracted to buy power from the national system in lieu of or additional to their generative capacity.

The new national network was controlled by an entity of public law, known as the Public Power Corporation (PPC). PPC was responsible for supervising construction and operating the new supplies. It had a board of management and executives appointed by the government. However, for the time being, by special contract and legislation the management authority was vested in EBASCO as regarded power, with more

* Ebasco had previously formed part of a public utility empire in the States but following American legislation, had sought investments and concessions abroad.

or less unrestricted rights to handle construction; and in Pierce Management for lignite. The companies were to organize and train the necessary Greek staff and develop procedures and systems of operation. This special arangement applied until June, 1955.* EBASCO provided American technical staff to supervise construction and to set up the systems and procedures of PPC. The American, British, French, and Italian contractors to develop lignite and undertake construction were introduced under direct contract with the Greek state and PPC or under subcontracts. The "power group" finally constituted a major foreign colony of several hundreds. At the expense of aid funds, they enjoyed salaries and allowances, travel and accommodation of dependents, and other privileges that compared extremely favorably with Mission salaries and conditions of employment, and with those usually accorded to other technical personnel. Comparative high pay rates and concessions were applicable to the Greek staff employed by PPC, EBASCO, and contractors, and employment in the group became the ambition of many Athenians. (This applied to junior levels and not to those of the senior executives, in which few Greeks were employed.)

It is extremely difficult to assess the values and benefits of the power scheme or the results achieved. There has been a little backbiting between the nationalities. This seems to be roughly a lineup of all the others in criticism of the Americans. Many troubles have appeared on the local distribution side. The local distribution networks are often crude and operate on varying voltages, direct or alternating, which have been determined for purely arbitrary reasons. The low standard of living necessarily affects the power consumption and consequently the economics of "breaking" the cable systems to meet rural needs.

* Pierce Management withdrew in 1954.

Of course, there are striking exceptions. Anthili village rose from absolute poverty to comparative wealth as a result of the alkali land scheme. The Power Corporation proposed to supply the irrigation pumps, but some difficulties arose about the domestic supply, some distance away, which might require separate transformers. The Anthili council, in its new-found pride, thumped the table to demand why any question should arise about providing a transformer to a community well able to buy two or three for cash down.

There are psychological problems, too, since it is sometimes difficult not to oversell. One village off the new power lines had a large number of shallow wells driven by diesel engines. Chancing to pass on other business, I was persuaded by the village elders sitting in café conference to take their part in a demand that power be supplied for their wells. I asked them whether they had checked power costs to see whether conversion was worthwhile. They answered in the negative. I advised a careful study of this angle before pressing too far. They then told me that they had heard that with electric power you just pushed a button; was this true? On this being confirmed they again insisted on help in securing a power line. As the subsequent conversation developed, it appeared that this button pressing had a hypnotic fascination for the village.

Perhaps the most indignant community in all Greece was Mycenae. The center of disaffection was the Belle Hélène, the little inn that with its proprietors was made famous by archaeologists. I have listened many times to Agamemnon's seething flurry of indignation at the refusal to supply a village of such vital significance. Over our heads loomed the vast bulk of Mount Zara, on which the beacon fires signaled the fall of Troy. Behind us lay the historic ruins of Golden Mycenae, in front the green vale of Argolis, whose history goes back to man's earliest days. And as we ate Orestes threatened to defeat the PPC by buying a generator to supply not only the inn but the entire village.

Arachova, high on its mountaintop, investigated the possibilities of utilizing its irrigation water (see Chapter 6) for power generation. When I last talked to the irrigation committee they had offered a deal to PPC to supply surplus power in winter, when the flow is adequate, against free supply from the grid in the summer, when it is not. Arachova is primarily a shepherd town, but the motor road to Delphi has brought contact with modernity. Once we met an old shepherd dressed in the traditional style familiar to all. In response to my wife's request to take a photograph, he languidly replied that he guessed from the public demand for his picture he must be very photogenic. This combination of tradition and wider knowledge is typical of the power program. It can bring a tremendous change to the rural areas of Greece, but its results have still to be seen. I am regretfully unable to add any comments on the actual capital costs of the program or of the economic future of PPC. The reason is that this vast expenditure of American aid has never been investigated. The Controller's Office planned it, and has even undertaken tentative probes, during which the need for further investigation was duly reported to Washington. However, we have never been given the authority to go ahead. In fact when we proposed to do so our staff was so drastically cut that any practical possibility of undertaking it had to be indefinitely deferred, which is to say abandoned.

LOANS TO INDUSTRY: ADMINISTRATIVE PROCEDURE

Power was intended to develop industry throughout Greece. Loans to industry were primarily directed to the sophisticated Athens area. A special machinery known as the Central Loans Committee whose administration operated within the American Mission, was originally established for this purpose. In 1955 this organization under another name passed under Greek government administration and is now an independent entity known as EDFO.

CLC theoretically worked through the banks, which submitted to it requests for long-term loans involving capital development or reconstruction. Such loans might involve expenditure in local currency or in aid dollars.

As in the United States, in Greece it is not legal to express a loan in terms of gold or equivalent. Special legislation was therefore passed under United States pressure to provide that all CLC loans, whether of drachmae or foreign exchange, be expressed in dollars and be repayable as to capital and interest at the exchange ruling at the time.

Let us consider the case of a man who secured drachma working capital, new machinery, or buildings in 1948, when the exchange rate was ten drachmae to the dollar. If he got it from an ordinary bank, a friend, or a private source, he now repays the exact number of drachmae loaned. If he got it from CLC, he repays at present at thirty drachmae to the dollar, or three times the local currency loaned. Of course, if the machinery was foreign-procured the value has risen. However the odd thing is that if he had bought an American aid tractor or deep-well pump in 1948 on deferred terms, or had received a medium-term agricultural loan, his debt was fixed in drachmae. So that we have entirely diverse treatment applied within the aid program.

This peculiar arrangement is said to be enforced by congressional requirements. I relate a story of a small-town blacksmith, a hard-working honest man, who was pressed by American Mission staff in the early days of American aid to set up a workshop to manufacture agricultural implements. He was loaned by CLC part of the funds to build his workshop and buy machine tools. His debt and interest rocketed to three times its currency value, but prices, sales, and profits did not rise accordingly, and at last he was sold out, lock, stock, and barrel.

I quote two Greek opinions. One man, a senior employee of the American Mission, a well-informed and intelligent man, described the dollar clause as a deliberate conspiracy to strangle Greek industry in order to maintain American importations. The other man, a senior government official associated with the program, described it as a criminal folly, opposed to every principle of sound business and economics, which had hamstrung a large part of Greek industry. I am also assured that the aforesaid legislation authorizing this clause is at best of doubtful constitutional validity and would have been contested long ago if it were not for the embarrassing consequences to United States relations. As a result almost every debtor affected is trying to delay or postpone his CLC payments in the hope of a later concession.

Of course the retort can be made that the borrower had no need to resort to CLC. Unfortunately this does not take account of the fact that the United States Mission absolutely controlled credit in Greece, and only limited medium- and long-term credit was available outside; i.e., the borrowers were forced to CLC by deliberate restriction of other sources.

An amusing story incidentally can be told of the attempt to enforce a similar position on agriculture in 1951. The Mission devised a project for establishment of oil storage tanks for olive-growing areas. As an afterthought, some unknown authority in the Mission included the dollar clause. The tanks to a value of $180,000 arrived, and erection commenced. The farmers' cooperatives, presented with dollar loan notes, refused to sign. In 1954 we started to check this project. We had by this time long developed our system. We would arrive in the village, sit down in the café, and ask for the village president. Normally he would arrive accompanied by some of his council.

He would start a low-voiced conversation. In a short time curiosity would replace politeness, and the entire village would be pressing around our table. The more diplomatic utterances of the leaders would be replaced by blunt-spoken opinions from the crowd.

Our first village opened with the polite statement that the olive tanks were not installed for various reasons, but the crowd soon had us informed of the true position. The tanks, unassembled, were in storage, and they could remain there forever before the people would sign this loan note in an unknown currency. Where were they going to get dollars to settle? The next village had completed its tank but refused to sign the note. For three years it had only held rain water.

The next visit to a larger town produced a businesslike committee of well-to-do farmers. The tanks were in full use. The loan note had been signed. I attacked directly. Why this action, when their neighbors had been so canny? A delighted roar of laughter rose from the group. They had hired the best lawyer in Athens. After mature deliberation they had been formally advised to sign, but to make payments only on the basis of a drachma loan. Application of the dollar clause was of doubtful constitutional validity in CLC loans, but it was certainly invalid in all other cases. This was not a CLC loan but was under another project, and therefore the loan note was completely unenforceable.

LOANS MADE

Loan applications could be referred for review to a firm of foreign public accountants employed by CLC. Some were so referred: some were not. It has never been clear on what basis this decision was made. It has never been clear on what basis loans were granted. As a public accountant I can see no point in a loan that provides a business with enough to buy some machinery, when the request was for machinery and working capital to operate the machinery.

This policy appears to have been especially applied to loans for textile industries. Unfortunately these industries, processing raw materials in an international market on a seasonal basis, are in special need of working capital to procure bulk supplies when available, in order to maintain steady production in succeeding months. This is not so essential in Britain and America, where the organized commodity markets provide the necessary carryover and credit. In Greece, however, these do not exist. Further, the Greek textile mills must sell to a primitive distributive chain, which is itself chronically short of credit. As a result of these and othe causes, aid to textiles, especially the destroyed Naousa plants, has been blunted and made ineffective.

Aid in other directions has often been completely ineffective. For example the port of Irakleion was provided with nearly a million dollars to buy and erect a complete cold-storage plant for the export of grapes and other fruit. For nearly six years this plant lay unused because funds were not available to complete the building. A complete fruit-packing plant and a canning plant stood idle for years. Equipment provided by a loan made to the wine growers of Euboea has been largely sterilized because phyloxera destroyed the vineyards. (The odd thing was that phyloxera were already in the island before the loan was made). A long list of these "wildcats" could be made. A review of their balance sheets is sheer tragedy.

On the other hand there are fields in which the loans have been of unquestioned value. The chemical and associated group of companies under Bodesakes has developed, expanded, and prospered. The cement industry has been greatly expanded. So too have the metalworking trades, thanks to new plants. Electrical appliances show the most considerable expansion due to establishment and growth on industries in such fields as refrigerators, cookers, and heating appliances. Oddly, however, the radio field does not show a similar expansion.

Another interesting field of CLC loans was the tourist industry. As a result of the construction of modern hotels such as the Athens Palace in the capital, and hotels in Rhodes and elsewhere, Greece was able to gain considerable benefit in foreign exchange with the development of tourism betweeen 1953 and 1956.

Help has also been given to a number of mining enterprises. The projected loan for Ptolemais lignite referred to earlier, although approved, was never utilized to any great degree, but other loans were made. Apart from CLC loans, advances to mining enterprises were made by other United States agencies, to be settled in the form of ore deliveries (bauxite, chromium, etc.).

Greek minerals are not as yet substantial, but they include a rather mixed group. According to mining engineers, it is probable that only the fringes of development have been touched to date.

The following figures of comparative mineral production may be of interest:

PRODUCTION OF MINERAL ORES (in metric tons)

	1929	1938	1950	1953
Iron	253,025	348,613	4,623	88,333
Lead	44,800	14,889	1,665	6,487
Zinc	29,011	10,338	6,428	11,198
Nickel	4,309	50,306	—	—
Antimony	137	—	2,500	5,003
Chrome	24,214	42,464	12,630	36,759
Bauxite	6,280	179,886	77,448	328,241
Iron Pyrite	133,399	244,000	87,678	237,323
Magnetite	84,023	168,243	26,256	106,938
Lignite	156,526	108,010	163,455	444,500

The nickel mines are in process of restoration with a recent loan. Lignite reflects the increased use for power production. Bauxite has been largely expanding for United States procurement programs, but is likely to maintain its position.

Other fields, though reflecting improvement over 1950, do not show the progress which might be expected on the prewar basis. The same trend is reflected in manufacturing statistics. General production was up around 50 per cent over 1950 levels.

This table shows comparative indices for industrial groups:

INDICES OF INDUSTRIAL PRODUCTION
(1939 = 100)

	1950	1954
Metallurgy	79	194
Metalworking	82	164
Building Materials	100	232
Textiles	107	149
Foodstuffs	107	152
Chemicals	90	160
Leather tanning	92	122
Paper	118	156
Wearing apparel	44	81
Woodworking	82	115
Cigarettes	168	174
Electric apparatus	152	302
All industries	100	155

The introduction of improved equipment implies that the number of employees will not rise in proportion to production. In fact in textiles it has markedly declined. Only in metalworking (30 per cent) and electrical apparatus (20 per cent) have substantial increases occurred. Between 1950 and 1954 the total number of persons employed in industry has remained static. With an expanding population it is obviously essential that both production and opportunities for employment should increase. It may, therefore, be assumed that capital financing of industry has not been adequate to meet the needs of the economy.

PRODUCTIVITY COMMITTEE

Despite the greater growth of industrial production in relation to the labor force engaged, Greek productivity per capita in many industries is low. This, as in textiles, necessarily reduces its competitive capacity and thereby checks development. In the absence of development adequate to absorb the labor force, it is not politically feasible to intensify productivity per man, as such proposals inevitably meet resistance from the workers.

The United States aid program set up a fund of one and a half million dollars from 10 per cent counterpart to expand production. This fund provided for loans to new types of enterprise and to schemes of productivity. To the end of 1955 none had been granted, and the only withdrawals from the fund have been administrative expenses. These loans are issued on extremely short term (five years) during which little benefit can be accomplished.

EVALUATION OF INDUSTRIAL LOANS PROGRAM

Loans to industry have borne some fruit, as witnessed by the table. However, in relation to the real problems of balancing the economy, absorbing surplus labor force, and increasing living standards, virtually nothing has been achieved. The full benefits of the power scheme have not yet been felt, and statistics of production and employment in Athens area to January, 1956 show a definite correlation. However any unbiased observer must recognize that for political and economic stability, it is an imperative necessity to absorb the surplus labor force. It must be remembered that, serious as this burden is in direct costs, it is felt far more in indirect costs, where transportation, handling, marketing, and distribution are heavily loaded with labor that should be engaged productively.

The problem of underemployment is acute in more industrialized Athens and Piraeus, but it is felt still more in the other larger cities. Athens has benefited primarily from new and expanded industries: Salonika, Patras, and Volos have not.

Some months ago I talked to the Catholic parish priests in Salonika and Patras. They described their flocks as the most distressed in Europe. They reckoned that few of their parishioners earned fifteen dollars per month. These semi-industrialized port towns are consequently completely depressed.

In all three of the major cities the predominant mass of labor is in the depressed textile and apparel industries. Salonika is rather more diversified, with food processing, furniture, metalworking, and machinery. Volos has a substantial cigarette factory; Patras, nearly 40 per cent textiles, has some food processing and papermaking.

Each of these cities is urgently and desperately in need of new industry, not only to absorb its own surplus labor but to take up the surplus labor of the surrounding agricultural area and to check the progressive drift toward Athens-Piraeus. This has long been recognized by the Mission, but nevertheless no results have ensued. The picture is even worse if extended to the smaller towns. CLC support has been concentrated on one area.

PROBLEMS OF PRIVATE INVESTMENT IN INDUSTRIALIZING GREECE

Much lip service has been given to the possibilities of foreign investment. So far this has been infinitesimal. Groups of Americans, particularly Greek-Americans, have talked in terms of multimillion-dollar enterprises, but little has happened.

It must be remembered that any rapid development of new industry must depend initially on foreign capital, techniques, and management. Almost necessarily it must be a branch of an existing organization.

So far, to private enterprise, Greece is a security risk because its continued political and economic stability are completely dependent on American and British foreign policy. The foreign industrialist consequently asks for the guarantee and support of his government. All he gets is a pious blessing.

Germany, the country's largest individual customer, is a little more generous, as the recent Krupp agreement over Ptolemais indicated. However, one plant will not solve the problems. Only a consistent and progressive policy based on constructive planning, backed by government guarantee but financed by private risk capital, can achieve any serious results.

It is probable that Britain can help more than America in actual establishment of new plants to supply Middle East markets, but only if a common policy front and mutual agreement can be established. Without this, British capital will not move into an area that at the moment is under American economic and political control, and therefore incapable of being influenced.

SOME SIDELIGHTS AND AFTERTHOUGHTS

One particular American aid credit goes to the canning industry, which is now making excellent strides in Greece. This is an industry with real significance although not a big employer of labor. To date, milk-processing plants established by UNICEF and Mission funds have not achieved a great measure of success. Cotton gins and seed crushing have also made progress, and so have olive oil pressing plants.

In food processing it is well known that the sugar-beet industry is the most important absorber of labor. American private risk capital toyed with this for some time but was ultimately driven out by Mission opposition. How far this results from pressure groups in the States, as Greeks allege, it is difficult to know. At the moment, Greeks regard this industry as vital, not only to the agricultural balance but for the mass employment it will give to labor gangs in lifting, transporting, and processing. The Greek government has had a full report and plan developed by industrial consultants and is trying to find the twenty million dollars necessary to set up the plants.

Other significant industries such as motor body and railway car building, bicycles, radio, furniture, and leather goods could comand a Middle East as well as a local market. The only present manufacturing exports (with values for 1953) are chemicals and fertilizers ($3,000,000) cotton fabrics ($1,750,000) and cement ($1,750,000). By contrast manufactured imports exceed $100,000,000 (excluding food items).

Quantitatively imports have increased, and there is no real improvement in the position from American aid.

CHAPTER 9.

Agricultural Development through Well Drilling

POSSIBILITIES OF IRRIGATION FROM UNDERGROUND WATER

The program for the development of underground water resources has been the cause of more harsh words and more bitter controversy than any other field of American economic aid to Greece. As the total loss of an investment of over ten million dollars may be involved, this is understandable.

What tends to exacerbate the issue is that there is no question of dishonesty or misuse of funds; and there are no grounds to believe that all concerned, American and Greek, did not act honestly, sincerely, and to the best of their abilities. It is a tragedy of good intentions.

The tragedy is even more heightened by a sense of deep frustration and a feeling that a great opportunity to really benefit the Greek people has somehow eluded our grasp.

In preceding chapters we have already seen the significance of water to the Greek economy. Water means life and prosperity to the Greek farmer. The total annual rainfall in Greece differs little in aggregate from that of north temperate zone countries such as Britain, but the greater part falls during the winter and practically none during the period from May to September. During that period the combination of hot sun and water can produce miracles of productivity, but less than 7 per cent of the total cultivated area of Greece is at present irrigated.

154

American readers who saw the TV show on the Anthili rice fields will recollect that in five years water has converted five thousand acres of barren salt flats into rich rice fields producing yields well above world averages. The bust of Walter Packard commissioned by the villagers to whom the scheme had brought a new life stands in the village square to record forever their gratitude. Once a broken-down collection of hovels, Anthili has now become a thriving community prepared to pay cash down for civic improvements, as we have seen in the last chapter.

Across the river from Anthili lies another village and a monument known to all the world. It was here that three hundred Spartans held the pass of Thermopylae against the innumerable Persian armies. A little mound covers the bodies of the heroic few, and a simple stone records: "Traveler, say to the Spartans that we remain here forever according to orders."

Between this mound and the river lies another wide expanse of salt marsh, with a total potential equal to the Anthili flats. Unfortunately the Sperchios River, fed from the melting snows of the great central mountains, carries a summer flow barely able to meet the needs of the reclaimed area. A storage dam higher up the river could provide the additional supply, but unfortunately the topography of the valley would make this extremely costly.

Geologists and soil specialists maintain that down the narrow valleys of Greece two rivers may run. The one, visible to the eye, dries up in the fierce heat of summer to leave a mere trickle or a bed of dry gravel; the other protected from evaporation, runs continuously perhaps five hundred feet below the surface.

Oddly enough, the possibility of utilization of underground water supplies by deep well drilling has never attracted serious attention.

The originator of a practical program of development was Charlie House, the principal of the American Farm School in Salonika. This wiry New Englander had followed his father in devoting a lifetime to the training of Greek farm youth. Elsewhere I have told the story of the school.

Charlie's interest in well drilling goes back to 1918, when the British Army in Salonika fetched out drills and geologists to meet the needs of army camps. The drills struck adequate supplies at around one thousand feet down. According to Charlie's story, the geologists believed that underground waters in vast quantities passed under Greece from the great drainage areas of central Europe. His efforts between the wars failed to develop any serious response in official circles. Drilling was carried out in Macedonia for village domestic supplies only, by two or three old rigs of the Refugee Resettlement Committee.

When Charlie, fresh from internment in Germany, sat at the Greek desk of UNRRA in Washington in 1945, he found no provision for well-drilling equipment in the Greek reconstruction program. Nevertheless he removed two surplus army rigs from the Yugoslav program and cautiously consigned them to the Greek government c/o American Farm School, Salonika. On his return he tried to interest Kalinsky, then Director of Hydraulic Construction, in the possibilities of deep well drilling.

Meantime, by accident rather than design, the Greek state had acquired around twenty-five more rigs from UNRRA, from war booty, and from British Army stores, but no crews were available to operate them. Kalinsky and Charlie, therefore, started a training program in the Farm School grounds.

At this stage the AMAG program commenced to operate, and the possibilities of tremendous developments were
envisaged.

The salt flats like Thermopylae represent a small percentage of Greek land. Their reclamation would mean local
prosperity, but it would not benefit Greek farmers generally.
Something was needed to lift the productivity of thousands of
villages scattered all over Greece. So long as well over half the
arable land was restricted to annual crops of grain and a substantial area lay fallow under crop rotation, progress would be
limited. Storage dams might meet the needs of Arta and the
Salonika plain, and with irrigation introduce a new and more
profitable crop pattern, but neither these nor smaller irrigation
schemes could fully satisfy the obvious needs of Greece.

Thoughts therefore turned to the possibilities of shallow
and deep wells. Almost all existing irrigation was drawn from
shallow wells. The Argos plain, market garden of Athens, maintained its lavish production of tomatoes, watermelons, and
fresh vegetables from this source. Shallow wells had already
been greatly helped through UNRRA importation of pumps
to substitute for the primitive water wheels and similar devices.
This importation was continued through the AMAG and ECA
periods. Purchase was financed through Agricultural Bank
loans mentioned in Chapter 7. Moreover a local industry manufacturing pumps and pipes was supported by credits from this
and other sources. However, shallow wells are limited in capacity and are restricted to small areas. The water table in Argolis
has already fallen substantially under the influence of pumping. I was reminded of this very forcibly.

Lunching in front of the little hotel at Mycenae, I noticed one of the earlier percussion rigs working in the next
field. Orestes, the landlord, told me that water was now becom-

ing so difficult and so expensive on the periphery of the plain
that deep well drilling was the only possibility.

It was this possibility, and the possible application of
deep wells throughout Greece, that was foreseen in the early
AMAG program.

THE AID PLAN FOR DEVELOPMENT

A rapid survey of the resources available indicated that
the two rigs at the Farm School could be reconditioned, and
so also could three British Ruston rigs. The later UNRRA
rigs were of limited serviceability.

Promptly another bunch of rigs was requisitioned—bigger and more expensive models than before. The mixed collection of rigs already in the hands of the Greek state were all
of percussion type.* A percussion rig breaks up the ground by
the constant lifting and dropping of a heavy weight. Penetra-
tion is necessarily slow; ten to twenty feet, dependent on soil
conditions, represents a fair achievement for a normal working
day, working to a hole of eight-inch diameter.

Rotary drilling rigs, introduced in the 1948 program,
are the type used in oil drilling. A bit with cutting or grinding
edges is violently rotated to achieve a rapid cutting action. The
results in terms of depth achieved vary exceedingly according
to soil and rock strata. Depths of 250 feet have been drilled in
alluvial soil in an eight-hour day in Greece. The technique of
operation differs in other respects. With a percussion rig the
steel pipe is hammered into the hole as the soil is broken up.
The rotary rig, however, seals the sides of the hole with a water-
proof compound as it proceeds. The pipe is dropped later,
when the water supply is established.

Apart from special soil conditions, the percussion rig

* Except the two Farm School rigs, which were rotary rigs of lighter capacity.

is more suitable for exploratory work, whereas the rotary can be better utilized on production drilling in an area of proved water strata.

The AMAG officials prepared a master plan for development of underground water. The production rigs were to be sold to syndicates of contractors, who would carry out drilling for farmers. Twelve light UNRRA rigs were to be sold to farmers' cooperatives for drilling smaller wells; the remaining thirteen percussion and two rotary rigs were to be operated by the state for exploratory drilling and for domestic water supplies under the sanitation program. A group of American drilling foremen was brought to Greece to train the local crews in handling both types of rig and to teach the practical techniques of drilling.

With the advent of Marshall Plan aid, the original AMAG plans were vastly expanded. A procurement program of more than seven million dollars was developed, covering the importation of fifty more rigs, percussion and rotary, as well as auxiliary equipment, pipes, pumps, engines, and other materials. An even larger expenditure was envisaged, but it was cut back as part of the general reduction in program expenditure in 1951 and 1952.

In 1948 and succeeding years local currency was provided from counterpart funds to the Greek state for the exploration and training program and for working capital to an equivalent of nearly three million dollars.

In 1951, after a long series of negotiations with various American and foreign corporations, the British ADSCO Ltd. contracted to undertake a series of geological and geophysical surveys, supported by test drills to determine water-bearing strata in certain defined areas of Greece.

Total expenditures of United States aid funds in these plans have exceeded ten million dollars.

PERFORMANCE OF THE PLAN: PRIVATE ENTERPRISE

The initial stages of training drilling crews were generally agreed to have been successful. My own impression of the foremen was one of lively intelligence and keen interest in their work. Several have gone to Ethiopia to train crews in similar programs.

The first snag developed in the private enterprise plan. A company was formed which with the help of a bank loan purchased two of the rotary drills for around $100,000. After drilling some thirty wells the company went "broke." The rigs were taken over by the Agricultural Bank as collateral security for loans, and have been in storage for six years.

Bank executives reported that they have been unable to find buyers for the rigs. No private contractor can face the speculative risks of drilling in the absence of geological surveys, since potential customers stipulate that payment will be made only if water supplies are located.

The twelve rigs made available to the cooperatives were equally unsuccessful and have also been in storage for years. Technicians state that these rigs are too light for Greek soil conditions.

Faced with these setbacks, the Mission decided to support a State Well-Drilling Service on the lines of the successful Mechanical Cultivation Service.

STATE WELL-DRILLING SERVICE (1949 TO 1951)

During the experimental period the American drilling foremen had been training crews on the percussion rigs and on three new rotary rigs. Aid funds had been made available for wages and expenses, and a number of exploratory drills had been undertaken as part of the training.

A new formal agreement was made between the Mission and the government, which provided that the State Well-drilling Service should work as a contractor. Wells were to be drilled for farmers, cooperatives, and communities, on terms of repayment of drilling costs, pipe, pumps, etc. The United States Mission would provide working capital and funds for a limited training and exploration program.

The Well-drilling Service was a section of the Direction of Hydraulic Construction of the Ministry of Agriculture. This direction, originally under Kalinsky and later under Michael-ides, was also responsible for the irrigation and reclamation schemes that form the subject matter of Chapter 7, and for the general administration of irrigation and reclamation authorities throughout Greece. It was indisputably overburdened.

The American drilling foremen were pressing continually for work to occupy crews and rigs. This pressure was progressively increased as the fifty Marshall Plan rigs were delivered. Ultimately the state had a massed force of seventy-four rigs* at its disposal, including twenty-two rotary units, representing a capital investment including trucks and auxiliary equipment of three million dollars. It has been calculated that this force was capable of drilling around three thousands wells a year, a target which would increase the irrigated area by 150,000 acres annually, or nearly 2 per cent of the arable land of Greece.

During the two years of intense activity, 1950 and 1951, around seven hundred wells were drilled. A careful examination made in 1953 failed to reveal a single payment of any sort made, nor the existence of any agreements between the Service and farmers, communities or other persons. My own staff visited many of the well sites, but we failed to find more than

---

* Excluding the twelve light UNNRA rigs reported as unsuitable for local soil.

three wells functioning. The sites were scattered all over Greece.

In the majority of cases the local villagers were unable to give any explanation for the well. Typical statements were: "The drilling crew came. They made a well. They went away. We know nothing else."

We found "dry holes" with pumps and engines fixed, and we found "wet holes" with no pumps.

It is difficult to compute the amount thus wasted, but we estimated that in wages, fuel, pipes, and pumps, around three million dollars might have been involved.

During this period the American Mission was not entirely unaware of the actual events. Finally the differences of opinion between the Mission and the Ministry of Agriculture ended in open breach over this issue, and funds for working capital were stopped as from December, 1951.

According to the terms of a new agreement the State Well-drilling Service was to be self-supporting, but was to be endowed with any amounts it could recover from the wells already drilled as working capital. The immediate result was the withdrawal of all rigs to storage.

During the succeeding years several fact-finding investigations were made by American and Greek officials, and various explanations were given of the events. The Well-drilling Service claimed that their agreed function was training and exploration, and that the American reversal of policy did not take into account the problems involved. Enactment of legislation and establishment of operating procedures were a prerequisite to conversion to a trading operation. A cut-off date, a closure of operations, and a reopening on the new basis were essential. American pressure to use the rigs to maximum capacity prevented the progressive build-up of a trading service. Consequently the service had no alternative but to continue the program of exploration and drilling in the expectation that the well sites could be sold later.

ADSCO EXPLORATION DRILLING

One important criticism of the state exploration program was that it was uncoordinated and chaotic. ADSCO Ltd., an experienced British company, commenced surveys of four defined areas in May, 1951, using rigs loaned by the Well-drilling Service.

These were the Trikkala region of western Thessaly, the Xanthe-Komotine plain of Thrace, the Messara Valley in Crete, and the plain of Elis in western Peloponnese. The surveys, based on geological inspection and geophysical probes and proved by test drills, revealed substantial subsurface water in all four regions. "Water maps" were prepared and plans were laid to commence mass production drilling. This production program was to utilize the state rigs and crews in a systematic and organized manner. At this time, early in 1952, the United States aid program to Greece was seriously cut back, and as part of this economy the ADSCO contract was terminated. The company prepared final reports with detailed scale maps and plans for the full development of the four regions.

Some $400,000 was expended on this part of the project; yet apart from Michaelides and myself, I do not know one Mission or government official who has thoroughly studied the reports. Their content is most interesting.

The Messara Valley of southern Crete is sheltered by surrounding mountains and lies open only to the winds off the Libyan desert, with consequent minimum rainfall.

According to the survey a subterranean river traverses the valley, drawing its waters from the drainage of the surrounding mountains. Deep well-drilling could convert the greater part of the valley into a veritable garden of Hesperides, with all-year-round cultivation. One ADSCO official defined a gold mine as "fifty acres in the Messara with a deep well."

In western Thessaly, artesian strata were found under most of the area. ADSCO proposed the establishment of a connected network of production wells and supply lines to carry the surplus to other areas. Visits by my staff three years later revealed that no local officials were aware of the results of the surveys. Villagers, of course, recalled the ADSCO test wells but did not know the outcome. One village where an ADSCO bore had registered very high flows had sought further information in vain. Our investigator recorded that if he had been a canvasser with an order book for drilling, he could have made contracts for fifty wells in five minutes. To appreciate this eagerness, it is necessary to know that Thessaly land is excellent, but the dry summer restricts cultivation almost entirely to winter wheat. Summer water would make possible a second crop: potatoes, tomatoes, vegetables, even rice. Labor, of course, is mainly a family contribution and due to the wheat economy is available in full from June to September. As one frugal farmer put it, "With summer water I can quadruple my income, but I shall also save money by working instead of sitting in the coffeehouse all day."

In the Xanthe-Komotine region prospects are equally good. In Elis, due to the soft soils, subsurface waters have already been partly developed by local "drive-tube" contractors. (This is a simple drilling technique in which a narrow pipe is forced into the ground. It has obvious limitations imposed by soil conditions and narrow diameter of pipe). Though substantial water supplies exist, "pepper sand" in water strata causes difficulties.

As of the time of writing no practical steps have been taken to develop these regions. The entire investment is therefore sterile.

STATE WELL-DRILLING OPERATIONS, 1952-1955

After the complete shutdown of operations in early 1952 some requests for drilling did develop. The bulk of the small demand had to do with continued state financing of exploratory drills, domestic water for communities, state services, and industrial consumers. At best it constituted token utilization for purposes different from those for which the equipment was primarily supplied.

The Controller's Office of the Mission had taken up the issue, and a series of reports and counter reports passed between Mission and Ministry, terminating in a threat, backed by Washington, that the Mission would request refund of the aid involved. It was then mutually agreed that my Audit and Surveys Office should thoroughly examine the position and propound a plan for utilization. I was asked to make a careful and independent study of the situation, to find whether the rig fleet could be used and under what conditions, and to recommend either transfer to other countries or some practical plan of operations.

Initially, we were invited by Mr. Christodoulou, General Director of the Ministry of Agriculture, to discuss the position with Michaelides and himself. They assured us, and in fact gave the fullest cooperation and assistance. Mr. Christodoulou emphasized that he regarded the whole issue with the utmost gravity, and he wanted an absolutely true statement of the position. Bryce Mace, for the Mission, equally insisted on a true analysis of causes and position. "Let's hear it, even if it hurts."

Our driver suffered bitterly in the search for truth. Operating rigs and wells were situated in the most inaccessible places, and we meticulously examined well over a hundred sites from Thrace to Sparta, and discussed the question with innumerable farmers, local officials, bankers, and others.

A visit to the village of Agios Thomas, in Boeotia, brought a typical reaction to our enquiries. Near this village the Athens Water Company had undertaken a number of bores. Some of the smaller producing wells had been leased to the local farmers.

Passing through one day, we discussed the local problems with some fifty farmers in the community office, a rough stone building with a stamped earth floor, a rough table and three or four chairs. Finally I asked whether they were prepared to contract for well-drillings at a cost of around $2500, repayable over three years. The unanimous, immediate, deep-throated *"Pos!"** took me by surprise. Then one farmer spoke simply and to the point, "Three acres of my land are irrigated. Before, my income was $30 an acre from wheat. I still grow the wheat, but after harvest I plant potatoes, from which I now gross another $250. I have another twenty acres. I have asked for a two-year loan but cannot get it. Every man in this village is prepared to contract for a well this second, if we can get any loan whatever. Water is gold, since we are only forty miles from Athens."

I asked the same question at the American Farm School and was simply led to a point from which we could see irrigated and nonirrigated land. The difference in net income, I was told, was five to one.

In the rugged hills of Thrace the mayor of a small town showed a different story. For three years the town had been trying to raise the funds for a deep well, a pump, and a small water tower. The only sources of domestic water were the river and a few shallow wells. The consequences are evident in the medical statistics in terms of typhoid and dysentery.

---

* This is a Greek affirmative of which the strength is not translatable into English. It expresses astonishment that such an obvious question should be asked.

Our banker contacts were even more conclusive. How many deep wells, we asked one regional manager, have you financed? None, was the reply, because we have practically no allowance for medium-term credits, and none earmarked for that purpose. We could use unlimited credits on this and other land improvements. He called the regional technical director of the bank and asked for his estimate of the number of wells that could be immediately financed if credit was available. It was difficult to give a figure, for the farmers had given up applying as the Bank could not help. Three hundred, however, would be a minimum initial demand, increasing to a thousand in the second year. Our next contact assured us of an initial thousand. Thereafter the story became monotonous.

We heard the same story from the rig crews on location, a tale of so many who wanted wells and the prosperity they would bring, but had neither cash nor any possibility of credit.

After making due allowance for generous overestimates, it was nevertheless evident that the original planners had been justified but that something had gone very wrong. However there seemed no point in trying to pinpoint the blame. In fact it was extremely doubtful how far it could be allocated. We asked Michaelides about credits, but it was quite clear that he had asked both government and Mission repeatedly. When we sought to ascertain why credits were not available, our informants were mutually contradictory. One, a banker, remarked that perhaps my reports might modify the American Mission's views on credit control. This was echoed by the Greek government officials with whom I discussed the matter. On the other hand, one of my colleagues remarked that perhaps now the Greek government would be convinced of the need to constrict other credit in favor of agricultural medium-term loans, as the Mission had so frequently recommended.

FINAL REPORT ON WELL DRILLING

Our report, issued in May, 1955, was circulated to the ministers, the senior permanent civil servants, and various interested bodies. We recommended that the State Well-drilling Service be dissolved, and its functions, equipment, and staff be absorbed by Mechanical Cultivation Service.

The objective of this plan was to secure economies in administration, and at the same time to provide the organized selling service that was necessary to handle farmer demand. The M.C.S. had a local organization with proved selling capacity, as evidenced by their own "private initiative" programs. It was clear that a dispersal of the rigs all over the country was uneconomic and unsatisfactory. We accordingly proposed concentrated initial development in a few selected areas.

It was evident that a public demand for irrigation water existed, but that the ordinary farmer could not provide the two to five thousand dollars, cash down. We proposed the establishment of a program of credits for that purpose, to be made available by the state through the Agricultural Bank.

We emphasized that the failure to date was partly due to lack of proper administration and technical management, and recommended that the M.C.S. organizing team (see Chapter 7) should remain active a further one to two years to organize procedures for the combined service. In addition, a foreign geologist experienced in production drilling should be added to the team.

Our examination of available data and consultation with the various technical experts aroused strong suspicions, which gradually crystallized into conviction, that there was and had been a strong conflict between the advocates of deep well-drilling and the storage dam enthusiasts. This is not to say that the well-drilling plan had been deliberately sidetracked. In fact the strongest supporter of the ADSCO surveys had been

Walter Packard, the leading figure in surface irrigation. The original well-drilling master-plan committed funds on the assumption that subsurface water would be regarded as an economically feasible alternative. The personalities and early successes of the "surface storage school," combined with the initial failures of the Well-drilling Service, resulted in the deep-well program being regarded as applicable only to restricted areas where surface irrigation was not possible. As a result, well drilling was ignored in any plans for investment program funds.

During our investigations we learned from the soil specialists that Greek land has a very high porosity. Consequently the proportion of rainfall passing to underground storage is unusually great. This fact, combined with high evaporation of surface water, weighs in favor of deep wells as a more dependable source.

It is probable, though not proven, that the capital cost per acre of irrigation by deep well is greater than for storage of surface water.* Against this must be set the fact that a well is ready in a few days and will repay its capital cost in five to seven years, whereas a surface irrigation system may take ten years to complete. Benefit to national food supplies is immediate from wells. It therefore seemed that in a country short of capital, but urgently requiring increased production, the priority should be given to deep-well irrigation.

We therefore recommended that the first year of the new well-drilling plan should be concentrated in the proved production areas of western Thessaly, Messara, and Xanthe-Komotine. We added to this the sharp sting that six hundred multistorage deep-well pumps, worth at least a thousand dollars each, ideally suited for the development of Messara, had lain unutilized in the warehouse for five years. We suggested that

---

* This depends on individual circumstances. An artesian well obviously is far cheaper.

a responsible independent committee should decide on relative priority after the first year's program.

GREEK REACTIONS TO THE REPORT

A little to our surprise, our final report on well-drilling was received with complete approval by the permanent officials of the Greek ministries. We had taken some pains to solicit their views and to reconcile them as far as possible with our own, as we felt that cooperation and mutual understanding were essential to any attempt to salvage a ten-million-dollar investment.

On November 1, 1955, the controller and myself were invited to discuss this and other matters with the Ministry of Agriculture and Mr. Christodoulou, General Director of Agriculture. We were assured of complete concurrence with our conclusions, and that the plan would be put into effect subject to the Minister of Finance providing the necessary credits. In December, I was informed that necessary provision had been made in the budget for additional credits to the Agricultural Bank.

PROSPECTS FOR THE FUTURE

Despite these assurances I have no sense of certainty. Mr. Christodoulou, on whom administrative changes depended, had undergone a serious operation, and by March, 1956 no constructive steps had been taken. The American Mission is dominated by a conciliatory policy which requires that no harsh word of criticism shall be voiced against the Greek government. Moreover, all the Mission personnel who understood the problem and realized that ten million dollars had been thrown away have left Greece. On the Greek side, only Kalinsky, Christodoulou, and Palaeologos have any inkling of the practical possibilities. All are busy, overburdened, and tired.

To add to the uncertainty of the position, the Mechanical Cultivation Service managerial team left Greece without discussion of contract renewal.

This is a tragedy of good intentions. The virtually complete sterility of this investment is serious, but the human tragedy of the farmers of western Thessaly, Thrace, and the Messara is far more serious. This summer these regions should be blooming with new crops. This year family incomes should have risen from two hundred dollars a year to one thousand dollars. Operated efficiently as they were intended, the well-drilling rigs could bring this new life to thirty thousand additional Greek families every year. That they have failed to do so is due to bad administration on the part of the American Mission and the Greek government.

SOME AFTERTHOUGHTS

One small aside will indicate that not everyone in this story is devoid of initiative. Among the capital equipment acquired by the Well-drilling Service was a machine for digging shallow wells. Apparently this machine, after some years of neglect, had been "acquired" by the M.C.S. depot; that service appropriates any neglected machinery. I mentioned this machine in casual conversation to Palaeologos, under whom M.C.S. falls.

Some two months later Melias, M.C.S. chief in Thessaly, informed me with a cheerful grin that he and Palaeologos were not waiting for Michaelides' rigs any longer; they had started their own program. The shallow-well digger had gone into action and had already completed eighteen wells.

Melias is the most unbureaucratic of civil servants. After the Volos earthquakes he solved the problem of rehousing his staff in forty-eight hours. Flat trailers were immediately requisitioned from M.C.S. depots all over Greece and two-room wooden huts were erected on top. These were then towed to the sites of the houses and anchored in the garden or on the pavement.

His plans for well-drilling in western Thessaly, as soon as rigs are in his custody, are simple. Five rotary rigs are to start drilling simultaneously in a selected village and to work on full twenty-four-hour shifts until artesian water is struck. This should happen on the second afternoon. When the "gushers" come in, he calculates that he can fill his order book for a year or two ahead. In this dynamic little man rests the best hope that some day the American investment in rigs, equipment, training, and exploration will bear some fruit. His example will certainly be followed by M.C.S. chiefs in Crete and Komotine.

CHAPTER 10.

The Health Services

THE STATE OF HEALTH AND SOCIAL SERVICES

"When we came to Greece in 1923," a Smyrna doctor told me, "we came to barbarism. In Smyrna every workman ate meat every day. The Greek workman, we found, lived on bread and olives; he cooked so rarely that he could, and did, use the street as his kitchen. . . ."

Greece has changed since then; yet she is still a country of startling contrasts. Athens today, though she inevitably retains many of her eastern Mediterranean characteristics, may fairly be called a sophisticated modern city. So too may Patras, a main seaport and railway center in the Peloponnese; also northern Salonika, rebuilt on English lines. Shattered Volos, a clean and very pleasant modern town before the seismic disturbance, is now gallantly rebuilding according to the original design.

Today not only the Athenian plutocrat but also the ordinary Athenian has available a more than adequate supply of doctors and dentists with good degrees—degrees taken in schools as widely separated as Paris, London, Vienna, and Chicago, for the Greek traditionally travels far in his search for professional and technical qualifications.

Athens and Salonika have medical schools of international repute, yet public health and sanitation are comparatively novel throughout Greece. This is partly because the majority of Greek people live in small towns and villages, often situated in high, mountainous regions, not very easy of access and remote from the few main centers. However, although Greece's formidable natural features have tended to slow down the spread of technical, scientific, and medical knowledge, the suspicious conservatism of the Greek peasant and small-town dweller is also not without its effect, as any worker in the field can testify.

The villager draws his water from wells. Even modern "preseismic" Volos used house wells; also water tankers of various types, from the very primitive to the more sanitary, which dragged supplies along the road from distant Larissa. Volos hopes eventually to borrow enough money to pipe water to the town. Argos, not regarded as particularly backward, until recently drew domestic water supplies from faucets in the streets, the water being drawn from springs outside the town and piped along open channels past barns and cowsheds. Village sanitation is most frequently based on a "hole in the ground" (the so-called "Turkish toilet"), with probable seepage into the neighboring well.

Disease statistics for the pre-1939 period are unreliable; there was at that time no proper organization for the collection and preparation of such data. Indeed, general disease statistics for the postwar period are not altogether reliable; there is as yet no medical and social service adequate to deal efficiently with this particular branch of public health.

The death-rate figures are more dependable: a death rate of 17 per 1000 in 1923 declined to 13 in 1940, and the postwar death rate of 13 has declined to 7. The infant mortality rate has dropped from 133 per 1000 live births in 1931 to 43 at the present time.

It must be remembered, however, that the death rate of a country does not give the whole picture. One must consider what is the dominant disease in a nation. In Greece, until comparatively recently, this was endemic malaria. Some historians claim that the decline and fall of the Roman and Greek empires was due in part to the debilitating and disabling effects of endemic malaria on the able-bodied populations in key areas.

Nevertheless, the declining death rate in present-day Greece does indicate considerable improvement in the standard of national health, once so tragically undermined not only by the diseases due to malnutrition, bad sanitation, lack of elementary hygiene, and inadequate medical care, but also by endemic malaria and the diseases associated with and consequent upon it. The gradual improvement in political and economic conditions between the two world wars and the development of public works made their impression on the health problem. Fundamental to its solution were the sewage and drainage schemes, the improved sanitation, increasing numbers of medical men, and the founding of hospitals—although none of these, before 1939, was adequate.

In public health the most dramatic results to date are in connection with the control of malaria. In 1918 the Allied forces in Salonika regularly had one-third of their strength out of action owing to malarial infection. In 1930 about two million Greeks were suffering from the same disease. At the present time barely a hundred or so cases are reported annually. Extensive drainage systems and the wide and persistent use of DDT are responsible for this decline.

This battle was largely won before the arrival of the American Mission in 1948. The great drainage schemes in the Salonika area, the work of the British Army, the malaria control program of UNRRA and the World Health Organization, not only attacked and controlled but almost wiped out the dreaded scourge. The American Mission Health Service splendidly consolidated and extended the work of those earlier in the field. But it is unremitting work. At one time it was feared that the newly created rice fields would provide new breeding grounds for the mosquito, but these areas are keenly watched by the Health Service and are regularly patrolled by small aircraft carrying DDT spraying equipment.

Domestic water supplies and sanitation will be discussed later in this chapter.

THE GREEK WAR RELIEF ADMINISTRATION OF AMERICA

The Greek War Relief Administration of America, known as G.W.R.A., was initiated and organized during the first stages of Germany's occupation of Greece by communities of American citizens of Greek ethnic origin. During the war years G.W.R.A., using Red Cross channels, poured into Greece vital supplies of food and medicines for the sick and starving population.

In the immediate postwar period G.W.R.A., acting as a voluntary relief organization, moved into Greece and worked in cooperation with the Greek government, with UNRRA, and with UNRRA's successors.

During the fratricidal Communist war and the period of the creation and maintenance of refugee camps, G.W.R.A. provided for the refugees an excellent medical service of doctors and nurses, backed by a flow of medical and surgical supplies.

At the same time G.W.R.A. developed a plan for the permanent improvement of the medical services throughout Greece. Employing highly competent Greek and American staff, the organization devised and put into operation a widespread rural medical service.

The plan was in three parts: one, an improvement in major city hospitals was designed; two, "health centers" were to be constructed in key towns in the provinces; and three, the health centers were to be staffed and maintained by G.W.R.A. for a period of two years.

The local currency needed for wages and any local materials used in the construction works were to be provided out of counterpart funds. Equipment and installation materials procured abroad were to be paid for out of G.W.R.A. funds (the private donations of United States citizens). The funds needed for the maintenance of the health centers were also to be provided from G.W.R.A. sources. G.W.R.A. undertook the responsibility for the construction and completion of all necessary building.

The first part of the plan provided for some improvements at the Evanghelismos Hospital, the main Athens hospital. A new hospital was planned for Salonika, to be under the control of the university medical faculty. Improvements were planned for the hospital at Pyrgos, in the Peloponnese. A large modern general hospital was eventually constructed at Tripolis, also in the Peloponnese, to serve an area in which no such hospital had previously existed. Later, a smaller hospital was built at Rethymnon, in Crete, and a fine modern sanatorium at Knossos, also in Crete, to serve the island's tubercular patients.

The second part of the plan, the health center scheme, was even more important. The health centers were designed to meet rural needs; they were fitted up with X-ray and other necessary equipment for diagnosis and treatment, enough beds to deal with emergencies, and a permanent staff. The staff consisted of one or more doctors and enough nurses to serve the center and to provide a district nursing service. Some jeeps and an ambulance were provided as ancillary support.

THE MISSION-GOVERNMENT PLAN

G.W.R.A. had led the way. The Greek Ministry of Social Welfare and the American Mission Health Service were now concerned to fill in the details of a scheme that would provide basic efficient hospital services for the whole of Greece.

Sanatoria: Endemic malaria is often the forerunner of tuberculosis. Privation and neglect during the war years had weakened physical resistance, increased the risks of infection, and aggravated existing disease. It was felt that sanatoria for tubercular patients were immediately and urgently needed.

There had existed for years, at Asvestochori in the mountains above Salonika, the nucleus of a sanatorium for Northern Greece. Originally a former British Army camp of the 1914–1918 war, it had been enlarged by the use of Nissen and similar army huts. Here, cooking facilities had been installed and some six hundred patients established in what were intended to be their temporary quarters. Unfortunately, the second World War had interrupted the building of the sanatorium proper, and Asvestochori, except for the patients in the onetime army camp, appeared abandoned. Now, it was decided, the work was to be resumed and extended: Asvestochori was to have a thousand-bed sanatorium.

The town of Lamia, in eastern Greece, was also to have a new sanatorium; and at Yanina in Epirus, northwestern Greece, the existing temporary hospital for tubercular patients, an old Turkish barracks, was to be replaced by a new building supplemented by Nissen huts. In the Peloponnese, a sanatorium started before the war but never finished was to be completed and equipped.

Hospitals and Health Centers: Yanina's existing general hospital, also started but never finished, was now to be completed and given an extension that would double its capacity as originally planned. The Lamia General Hospital, in more or less the same state as the Yanina Hospital, was also to be completed and enlarged. The hospital in the port of Piraeus was to be enlarged by the addition of a new wing and was to have better and increased treatment facilities. The Hippocrates and Laikon Hospitals in Athens were to be modernized, and nurses' quarters were to be built. An extended health center program was to be undertaken.

Other Facilities: In addition, nurses' training schools and homes were to be built, also new modern warehouses for the storage of medical equipment; and the Athens Mental Hospital was to be remodeled. Generally, all pre-existing hospitals were to be improved by the provision of new and up-to-date equipment, especially X-ray diagnostic equipment.

THE HEALTH PROGRAM IN EXECUTION

The cost of the health program to the American taxpayer, in contruction and imported materials, amounts to fourteen million dollars. To this must be added a G.W.R.A. contribution running into millions of dollars.

In June, 1955, the United States Public Health Service (USPHS) officers operating the Mission's medical division were withdrawn, and effective Mission support for the health program came to an end. At the time of withdrawal, apart from the G.W.R.A. health centers, practically none of the facilities planned or constructed was in operation; this was attributable chiefly to delays in completion owing to increased construction costs and to the cutback in program funds referred to elsewhere in this survey.

Training schemes for the operators of the new equipment and various "control" programs had been instituted by the Ministry of Health and the American Mission, with some cooperation from the World Health Organization. (One odd feature: Greek industrial and commercial employees in the cities are insured with the Social Insurance Agency, I.K.A. I.K.A. pays members' hospital and medical bills and has its own hospital construction program; it does not, however, come within the province of the Ministry of Health, but is under the jurisdiction of the Ministry of Labor. During the "aid" period and subsequently, there appears to have been no cooperation between I.K.A., the Ministry of Health, and the Mission service).

REALIZATION OF THE PROGRAM

Asvestochori Sanatorium cost approximately one million dollars and was the biggest medical institution constructed under the health program; it was ambitiously and lavishly equipped with the most up-to-date service, laboratory, diagnostic, and treatment equipment. The director said that in the kitchen cooks were no longer needed, but a staff of highly skilled electrical engineers was essential. This epitomized the difficulties. Substantially finished in 1951, although some installations were not complete until 1953, for four years the great white empty building towered over the huddle of huts and patients below.

Work was carried on, patients and staff hoping that at any hour the rotted wooden huts and charcoal braziers might be exchanged for the clean stone and plaster building with its modern heating system.

Asvestochori during the long winters can be two feet deep in snow, with the Vadaris, the piercing north wind that tears through the mountain gap from the frozen heart of Europe, blowing so fiercely that even with chains a car will be unable to grip the icy and narrow serpentine road. The difficulties of administering a colony of tuberculous patients under such conditions, with no protection from the bitter winter nor from the blazing summer, are tremendous.

Money was the problem. Asvestochori is a foundation: patients contribute according to their means, but many are too poor to pay a drachma. The major portion of the moneys for running costs and maintenance comes from the national budget. It was clear from the start that the new sanatorium needed a much bigger and more highly skilled staff, including technical specialists, to handle the new equipment. The Foundation Committee and the Ministry of Social Welfare indulged in a long controversy about Asvestochori's establishment and financing; and the Ministry of Finance refused to make any substantial increase in the welfare appropriation.

In June, 1955, the Controller's Office of the American Mission determined on action. Strong letters, in which the language of diplomacy was abandoned, were sent to the Ministry of Coordination and to the Ministry of Social Welfare. The letters said that so shocking a situation was a grave embarrassment to the American Mission; and if some solution were not quickly found, we should be compelled to ask for the refund of the aid moneys involved.

The response was prompt: two weeks later, on a return visit to Asvestochori, we found that the removal of patients and staff from the hutment below, accomplished in three days, had been completed one hour before. Present in full force were the Foundation Committtee and Ministry of Social Welfare officials; the Minister was expected at any moment. The new sanatorium was in operation.

The story does not end on that note of triumph, however. Another visit, two months later, showed that the staff establishment was still far from complete, and that consequently much of the valuable equipment could not be put into operation.

The story of the Tripolis General Hospital is even less happy. G.W.R.A. had intended to endow the hospital but the sudden death, intestate, of a wealthy Greek-American who had verbally undertaken to contribute a large sum of money toward the endowment made this impossible.

The Tripolis hospital, designed according to the highest United States standards by G.W.R.A. engineers, was much more elaborately equipped than Asvestochori, and its complicated steam heating system was serviced by a water-softening plant to secure efficient working, indispensable in Arcadian territory, where the water has a very high alkaline content.

Tripolis has a pleasant cathedral and three reasonably good hotels, but the majority of its houses are one-storied, rough stone erections; it has no industry but is a main market center for Arcadia. The market and the incoming and outgoing produce block the too-narrow streets. A central market hall would be a great help to Tripolis.

Arcadia, austerely beautiful, is a mountain mass in the center of the Peloponnese. For nearly three thousand years poets have praised its primitive simplicity. Arcadia is today as it has always been: a land of shepherds grazing their sheep and goats on the mountain sides.

Arcadia's birth and death rates are higher than those of any other province in the whole peninsula we call the Peloponnese. Composed of 1,680 square miles, Arcadia carries a population of approximately 160,000; all except 30,000 live in small villages. Only 325 square miles are cultivated, and the cultivated land is divided between 44,783 landowners: an average of about four and a half acres to each family.

Fifty acres and a well mean riches in Argolis; and a man may live comfortably with only five acres on the narrow Tripolis plateau, given water, and if he is growing potatoes or garlic. But most of the Arcadian land is hacked from the stony hillsides. Langada, typical Arcadian territory, is a steep "bowl," on one side of which the village clings. Around the slopes are dotted the fields, of only very poor barley and corn. Long, hard winters are the rule in these mountains, and in the summers, which are hot and dry, the naked rocks and shale beat back the heat and dry the atmosphere to desert clarity. In Arcadia man is always striving for bare survival. When the whole of Greece was wealthy, we are told, Arcadia alone was poor. This was the province the beautiful Tripolis General Hospital was designed to serve.

"It was a bad joke," a Tripolis prefect said sadly, as we stood looking at the gleaming building. "It was a bad joke, to give us something so beautiful that we cannot use. . . . We told them that we could not support something so grand, but they said that the Arcadians in the States would look after it for us. . . . It was a gift to the homeland."

The army finally took over this white elephant; they have about thirty convalescent men there, and a small ward is used by civilian patients. The water-softening plant broke down, and as no one knew how to repair it the entire heating system became "furred" with the alkaline deposits that characterize Arcadia's water supply; it is now said to be almost unusable, and the damage irreparable.

South of Tripolis the river Eurotas cuts a deep valley to the sea. To the west the great Taygetus mountain rears its snow-capped peak, to the east the ranges of Painon, and to the south lies the sea: this is "hollow Lacedaemon," home of the race that has left a name synonymous with discipline. Sparta is a prosperous land, with a good climate; as it is enclosed by the mountains on all except the southern side, citrus fruits and the olive grow well there. Sparta is one of the best oil-producing regions in Greece.

There is a sanatorium here, situated on a small hill immediately facing the ramparts and walls of ancient Sparta. This is not a lavish enterprise; it was Greek-designed, on cruder and simpler lines, yet it stood unoccupied for years. Recently it has been reported as being put into operation, but this is not confirmed at the time of writing. The establishment of a sanatorium here was greeted with some hostility; the Spartans felt that a general hospital would have been of more immediate value.

The next unoccupied sanatorium stands on a site of even greater historic interest. To the west side of the ruins of Knossos stands a magnificent modern building: the great sanatorium built by G.W.R.A. and American aid funds, still quite empty three years after completion.

To the monotonous catalogue of empty monuments one can add the list of health centers unoccupied or only partly used, and of valuable and expensive equipment idle and rusting for lack of skilled operators.

Some of the buildings and equipment, it must be said, have been put to good use. The Evanghelismos Hospital in Athens is efficient and up to date. The hospital and the sanatorium in Lamia are both making satisfactory progress. So too is the university hospital in Salonika, although this is as yet a little unbalanced, since its facilities and equipment are based on the assumption that new wings will ultimately be added.

In many towns the work of the G.W.R.A. Health Centers has been excellent. In July, 1952, this operation was taken over by the Ministry of Social Welfare. The Chrysopolis center has since been closed, and within the Greek state budget it has not been possible to maintain the more extensive district service. Government economy measures in 1953 resulted in the withdrawal and sale of certain of the vehicles originally allotted to the health centers. In one district, an ambulance was purchased as "surplus" by a municipality and converted into a water carrier and street cleaner.

A BRIEF EXPLANATION OF HOSPITAL MANAGEMENT IN GREECE

A few words of explanation of the medical services in Greece are necessary. The greatest concentration of doctors is in the Athens area. This is not entirely due to such attractions as the greater sophistication and wealth of the capital; it is also because the civil government, private industry, banks, and similar organizations with mutual benefit schemes have a heavy proportion of employees in the region of the capital city. Another influential factor is that the social insurance scheme, I.K.A., applies only to workers in the urban areas, and more especially to Athens and the port of Piraeus.

There is no social insurance scheme in the rural areas. This lack raised an acute problem on one occasion, when a Mechanical Cultivation Service depot was moved from within the city to new premises just outside the city limits, which automatically excluded the staff from their former membership in I.K.A. Medical attention and hospital treatment in rural areas must be paid for by the patient; in cases of hardship it is provided free, but only on production of Ministry of Welfare certificates. In the rural areas almost all persons of moderate means apply for a "poverty" certificate before seeking medical treatment.

Some hospitals, sanatoria, and clinics were originally private foundations, although established by a municipality or by the state; but the repeated devaluation of the drachma has diminished, and in many instances destroyed, endowed funds, with only a few exceptions. Where this has happened the national budget must bear the burden of salaries and maintenance, or at least the difference between the running costs and the received fees. Due to the very recent economic and industrial development in Greece, workers in the medical field—doctors, nurses, skilled technicians, and trained workers in the various branches of medical therapy—are in very short supply, taken over the country as a whole.

State salaries are exteremely low—initially, fifty dollars per month for a well-qualified medical man; consequently, state recruitment of highly trained and well-qualified staff is handicapped and difficult. State-employed doctors inevitably supplement their salaries by private practice. Under economic pressure doctors may ultimately tend to detach themselves from the few big cities and to establish themselves in the rural areas and small towns where they are most needed, but at the present time there is little if any evidence of such a move.

I.K.A. is quite separate from the main public health scheme, and even provides competitive facilities. The latest Ministry of Social Welfare plan includes provision for a new rural health service, but the lines on which it will be established have not yet been laid down.

EVALUATION OF THE HOSPITAL PROGRAM

The principal failing in the health program is best expressed in the words of a member of the American Mission Health Division. "The Mission program," he said, "was a splendid ideal, but the scheme was prematurely put into operation. . . . Facilities were planned to our own first-rate and highly efficient United States standards, without full realization of the need to ensure that the trained people and the funds would be available to carry through the program. . . ."

Exactly how much of the imported, expensive equipment is in effective use it is hard to say; but certainly a considerable proportion has not been put into such use. Nevertheless, something has been achieved: an ideal has been put before the people and an inspiration given. On the purely practical level, many improved facilities have been established and some are being used. Perhaps it will be only a mattter of time before the administration reaches the standard of efficiency that the services laid down in the plan and that the donated equipment was designed to achieve. The American Mission, although it has done so much, unfortunately has contributed nothing toward an improved administration.

In 1953 we re-examined the position in an effort to find a solution. On the existing medical and public health facilities outside Athens, investigators' reports were clear and decisive: almost every public health institution was completely dependent on state aid; prewar private endowments had been dissipated by repeated devaluation; administration was uncoordinated.

I.K.A. was carrying out its program independently of the state. State officials told us of the virtual impossibility of obtaining state grants for needy institutions. Welfare workers complained of the low standards of efficiency of most nursing staffs. The theory of personal payment for medical services had become farcical, since "poverty" certificates could so easily be obtained.

Clearly, Greece needed, and still does need, a coordinated state health program. Whatever one's views on the idea of the Welfare State are, it must be recognized that a modified form of it may be the only solution to the urgent and pressing problems some countries are having to face. Certainly, no one with knowledge of the situation can deny that some form of national contributory health scheme is an absolute necessity to cover the large rural areas of Greece. In 1953, during visits to several of the provinces, made to discover whether such a scheme were feasible and acceptable, my investigators and I found that the small towns and rural areas generally were in favor of the principle of a health tax or some other form of national insurance.

In the latter part of 1955, the Greek government, as mentioned earlier, took independent steps toward the initiation of a rural health program; but how far forward it will go, or what will be its ultimate effects, it is as yet too early to say.

SANITATION

Clearly the health program has not been an unqualified success; but the operations of the sanitation program present a much more cheerful and encouraging picture, credit for which must be given to the American Mission Health Division. The vision, vigilance, and unremitting work of the Health Division's officers have brought great benefit to the whole of Greece, and especially to the rural areas, where the health and the working efficiency of the communities have been immeasurably improved.

Unfailing and ungrudging supplies of DDT and other pesticides for large-scale spraying operations, and support for the Greek state and World Health Organization programs, have conquered endemic malaria. The provision of large quantities of good-quality water piping has made plentiful supplies of clean water available to nearly every village. Soon the women carrying jerry-cans of water, filled at the spring a mile or even two miles from their homes, and the lines of donkeys with water drums strapped on their backs, will have vanished from rural Greece; for now clean and safe steel piping carries the mountain spring or well water straight into the village square.

The village of Anthili today has a faucet in every house, serviced by a five-mile conduit from Oiti, the mountain on which, we are told, Heracles burned like a beacon.

The modern village of Mycenae has tapped the Perseid spring which once supplied the ancient fortress of "Golden Mycenae"; and the brothers Orestes and Agamemnon have been enabled to put water closets and showers in their little inn, La Belle Hélène. Hundreds of villages throughout Greece are receiving the same benefits. The graceful girl carrying a pot of water on her head, picturesque but out of tune with modern needs, will soon be a mere romantic memory. Two million dollars' worth of steel piping represents unbelievably much health and happiness to an underdeveloped country such as Greece. Other very important parts of the Health Division's work has been the improvement of city water supplies and the overhauling of the sewerage system of Athens, both of which were urgently needed.

Plentiful supplies of clean water frequently make the difference between a diseased and a healthy nation, a poor and a prosperous one. The campaign for clean water is continuing; each little community is now educated to the need and so far as it can is facing the task of working for and paying for the water it needs. Well drillings, at present, are mainly for domestic water supplies. Water piping is now being manufactured in Greece, and funds are available on loan for community installations.

CHAPTER 11.

Road and Rail

COMMUNICATIONS IN GREECE

Roads, as discussed in this chapter, are not the rural farm-to-market roads of earlier chapters, but the main highways that provide the links of the country.

In my school days I could never understand why Saint Paul took ship from Verria to Athens. Having now traveled the road many times, I am no longer puzzled.

The spinal column of Pindus effectively cuts peninsular Greece in two. The projecting ribs compartmentalize the country so that access between the principal regions is best achieved by sea if the traveler has to depend on his legs to carry him up and down mountain ranges.

North Greece by contrast is level, and consequently the great Roman roads passed through it to form the corridor between Europe and Asia. Freight and passengers moving by land must still follow this route, although with modern steamers and airplanes the Macedonian corridor is considerably less important than it was.

In the following general comments road and rail have been treated together, as for practical purposes the topography gives little possibility for division.

A traveler entering Greece from Western Europe by road or rail moves through the Vardar gap from Yugoslavia. Salonika is the first significant town to be reached.

There is an alternative but much less important route farther west, through the Monastir Gap into western Macedonia. Lateral road and rail link the two routes near Salonika.

From Salonika we may turn east through Macedonia and Thrace to Turkey. By road there are two possibilities. One may proceed up the Langada Valley to reach and follow the coast to Kavalla, or one may take the longer route north through the important towns of Serrai and Drama to rejoin the first road at Philippi just outside Kavalla. The rail follows approximately the second route, with a detour north before reaching Serrai and a further detour in the Philippi plain due to the technical difficulties of piercing the mountain that overlooks Kavalla.

Beyond Kavalla road and rail run parallel through Xanthe and Komotine to Alexandroupolis, the frontier port on the Evros. Here, due to difficulty in crossing the delta, they turn due north up the Evros valley to Adrianoupolis in Turkey, and ultimately to Constantinople. This route is both the communication system of northern Greece and an essential part of trans-European connections.

The link between Salonika and Southern Greece faces far greater difficulties in terrain almost immediately, for the southern gate is blocked by a great ring of peaks rising almost sheer from the plain: Olympus, Pieria, Vermion. The road runs southwest to Verria and then starts the climb of Vermion.

No other spot in my travels has given me more anxieties than Vermion (the Kastana Pass) with the cold, barren peaks to left and right. With snow and ice, one-way traffic only is permitted; but it is in the mist, which may come any time with low-lying cloud, that one's sunlight memories of a twenty-foot road and five thousand feet of sheer drop become sharpest.

Beyond Vermion lies Kozani, chief city of western Macedonia, on a plateau at two thousand feet. In Kozani in the high winter the wolves visit the city square of an evening. Kozani has also a direct route north by road and rail to the Monastir Gap referred to above. Rail proceeds no farther south, but the road continues through a series of passes into Thessaly. From Salonika the rail parts company with the road to follow the coast and tunnel along the eastern slopes of Olympus. Following this much shorter route, rail rejoins the road in the Thessaly basin at Larissa.

Proceeding south in company, the road and rail traverse the Othrys range to Lamia, and then the Kalidromon range into Boeotia to Thebes. Here the rail again turns east to circle Kithairon and Parnes into Attica and Athens, while the road runs south over Kithairon and enters Attica and Athens from the west.

Before reaching Athens a main branch turns southwest to cross the Isthmus of Corinth into the Peloponnese. This route also is paralleled by rail. Both transport systems divide at Corinth. Northern branches follow the north coast to Patras and then south to Pyrgos and Olympia. The southern branches pass the plain of Argos and then climb into mountainous Arcadia. From Tripolis they run south to the port of Kalamata. The circuit of the Peloponnese is completed by road and rail connecting with the northern branch at Pyrgos, but different routes are followed.

In western Greece there is a main north-south road from the Albanian frontier through Yanina, Arta, Agrinion, and Missolonghi to a ferry across to the Peloponnese. The last section from Agrinion is paralleled by rail.

There are now three transverse roads linking eastern and western Greece over the spinal chain: a southerly route through Delphi from Boeotia to Missolonghi, a northerly route from Volos, port of Thessaly, through Larissa to Yanina in

Epirus, and a central route from Lamia through Karpenesion to Agrinion. A rail route from Volos traverses Thessaly but does not cross the outer mountains.

This rather extensive explanation has been necessary to prelude the description of the program of works under American aid. It will be appreciated that the North Greece connection line from the Monastir or Vardar gaps through Salonika and Northern Greece to Turkey has special significance as the only connecting land route between Europe and Asia not cut by the Iron Curtain. The Athens-Salonika road-rail link is the principal internal link and directly connects most of Greece with Central and Western Europe and Turkey.

Some indication will have been given by the comments, but it is almost impossible to picture these roads without actually traversing them. The main Athens-Salonika road continually rises and falls with the lines of the main ranges described above. In Greece these hill climbs excite little comment by comparison with the major passes. In Great Britain they would pass for major climbs.

The road distance along this route is 375 miles, but there are six passes over 2,500 feet, with almost vertical ascents and descents.

ROAD PROGRAM

The Greek problem of land connection has always existed, so the sea has normally been the chosen route. Main road development was initiated prior to World War II, but its extreme vulnerability resulted in enormous damage by the resistance, by the enemy, and by the Communists to all bridges over rivers and ravines and to many sectors in the mountains.

The initial United States program, aimed to support the Army against guerilla activities, was to restore the principal road sectors. This work was initiated by American contractors in 1947–1949 and resulted in the restoration and resurfacing of the main Athens-Salonika road, the northern section of the Peloponnese road to Patras, and the southern section to Tripolis.

Thereafter a service known as the Public Roads Administration, operating with the Ministry of Public Works, completed the Macedonian section from Salonika to Alexandroupolis in the east. In Peloponnese the AMAG restoration was carried from Patras to Pyrgos on the northern branch, and from Tripolis to Kalamata and Tripolis to Sparta on the southern branch. In western Macedonia the Kozani-Florina-Monastir road was restored, as was a parallel road to the west from Kastoria to Kozani.

This program was supported by considerable work on subsidiary roads linking larger towns and villages. This program was mainly carried out by Greek contractors working under the supervision of the nomos (county) engineers of the Ministry of Public Works.

Something should be said about these contractors. Due partly to war, and partly perhaps to the fact that prior to the war Greek contracts were limited in numbers, there was no organization or machinery to initiate the program. When the American consortium withdrew, their entire road-making plant was vested in an organization known as E.D.M.E. This organization was responsible for leasing this plant to the Greek contractors who obtained the work, or selling it on terms.

It was a frequent aim of the Mission construction division to set up these contractors in business. In the initial stages, they say, their entire business assets were represented by a briefcase. The P.R.A. and the road program backed by E.D.M.E. machinery sales gave the contractors assets with which to work.

To this can be added a factual statement that these contractors made considerable profits and in many cases have not yet paid for the machinery purchased. The Mission road program was heavily cut back in 1951, and many road works in process at that date are not yet finished. The quality of the initial United States roads was very good. So too was the work of some of the Greek contractors, but some of the contract work was terrible, which can only be attributed to very poor supervision by certain nomos engineers (or to even less creditable activities).

EMERGENCY WORKS PROGRAM

From 1951 construction was handled by a new group, and was concerned primarily with strategic works. Certain of the projects cut back were taken over, and other schemes were initiated. The new construction was now taken out of the hands of the nomos engineers and placed in the hands of a specialized organization known as Emergency Works National Defense Service (E.W.N.D.S.).* Most of the senior employees of this organization were engineers outside the regular state service, who were employed at much higher salary levels and operated from a limited number of regional offices.

E.D.M.E. was dissolved and the "rump" of the machinery taken over by a new Mechanical Equipment Service (M.E.S.). The first task was to get this machinery working again, since the intervening operations had more or less completely wrecked the whole outfit due to poor administration, gross carelessness, and mechanical incompetence. To the credit of M.E.S. it must be said that this was done thoroughly and effectively. The machinery was leased out to contractors on fixed terms and was very well controlled.

In fact this statement applies to most of E.W.N.D.S. operations. An orderly bidding system, clear contracts, and a

---

* The service was also responsible for port, airport, and similar construction works of a strategic character.

tidy accounting system were marked characteristics. Although it was a temporary organization, its efficiency was in marked contrast to the earlier performance of P.R.A. and the regular Ministry of Public Works. This credit must be shared by the Mission staff and the outside specialist who directed E.W.N.D.S.

Its program was limited. On the roads, work was mainly concerned with the repair, restoration, and completion of the central and northerly transverse roads between eastern and western Greece. It also constructed a secondary link on the north-south road, which avoided the difficult Vermion and Sarandaporo passes and followed a shorter line over Olympus to Katerini. In this area the program initiated other linking roads, mainly of strategic importance.

In the earlier programs much expenditure was incurred in macadamizing trunk roads. In the E.W.N.D.S. program the emphasis was on traffic compression of gravel surfaces for a period of years before macadamizing.

In Greece, E.W.N.D.S. was the victim of a consistent campaign of newspaper attack fomented, it is said, by the regular service of Public Works. It is said that prices were extremely high, that peculiar manipulation had taken place, that graft and corruption existed. The Controller's Office performed a fairly thorough audit, and we could find no major discrepancy or serious foundation for these stories. Nevertheless the Service was abolished in June, 1953, and road construction returned to the regular services of the Ministry.

COMMENTS ON THE PERFORMANCE OF THE EARLIER PROGRAM

The same audit comment, by the way, could not be made concerning the program that E.W.N.D.S. had superseded. A more entirely messy story it would be difficult to imagine. Due allowance must be made for the pressure on the regular service, and for the absence of the freedom enjoyd by E.W.N.D.S. to employ accounting and similar staff without restriction. It is obvious that there is a vast difference between the type of clerk you can get for thirty dollars a month and the type obtainable for one hundred dollars. Nevertheless there are good grounds for believing that confusion covered a multitude of sins.

The E.W.N.D.S. period was, of course, one of far greater monetary and price stability, and escalator clauses could be effectively applied. The prior period was characterized by price changes that involved constant strains on the escalator clauses, but it was clear that these clauses were often applied in what can only be described as a most generous manner.

LATER PROGRAM

The period subsequent to E.W.N.D.S. was mainly characterized by the appearance at the Ministry of Public Works of the dynamic figure of Mr. Karamanlis, now the prime minister. A new program was inaugurated to complete the works left unfinished by the earlier programs and to initiate a series of new works. The most important new work in progress is an alternative route between Athens and Salonika, following the shorter rail route round Olympus from Larissa to Katerini-Salonika.

A drive along completed sectors confirmed stories that this road will be the finest in Greece. Scenic attractions are considerable, since it passes through the famous Vale of Tempe between Ossa and Olympus. Tourism is of course now a major consideration in road location; and other recent road constructions have been of the route from Thebes and Levadia to Delphi, of the road through central Arcadia from Tripolis to Pyrgos via Olympia, of a new entrance road to Athens from the west, and of an elaborate coastal road along the bathing beaches east of Athens. In theory at least, these major projects have not been provided from American aid but from Greek state budget.

ROAD MAINTENANCE

The Karamanlis program has entailed a good deal of repair to and expenditure on the roads constructed by the earlier programs, and the state of repairs still leaves much to be desired. A word of explanation of the Greek system is perhaps necessary. The main "national" roads are, of course, a state responsibility. In every nomos (county) city there is an office of the Ministry of Public Works, with at least one qualified engineer, and possibly more, charged with the supervision of all state construction within that area. In theory, this county engineer is provided by the national budget with an allocation for maintenance and repairs. In practice, this is apparently so inadequate that maintenance and repairs never seems to be done.

I write this section with certain knowledge. In three and a half years my personal assistant and I drove over 150,000 miles in Greece. Houlis, my driver, and I often amused ourselves by speculating how many months or years a certain pothole or patch would have to wait for repair. The results of course varied markedly between districts. The general practice, however, was to allow a certain section to deteriorate to such an extent that a major work of repair was necessary. Then a contractor would have to rip up sections and replace them.

Much of this expenditure, however, could have been avoided by regular maintenance. Another marked cause of road deterioration was the failure to keep open the ditches and clean the edges and culverts. The heavy, almost tropical rains that fall from time to time very quickly undermine the road if they are not drained away.

I have a perhaps ungenerous theory that Greek civil engineers are taught only the higher techniques of their science, such as road construction, and do not demean themselves with the cruder question of maintenance.

Another contributing factor to road depreciation is absence of any police control of traffic. Heavy lorries are hopelessly overloaded, and I have seen private caterpillar tractors running happily along the asphalted highway on a hot summer day, leaving the marks of their passage behind them.

EVALUATION OF THE PROGRAM

The over-all cost of the highway program referred to above has amounted to around fifty million dollars, of which the latter part of the program, costing around six million dollars, has been drawn from Greek state resources. The balance, including ten million in foreign exchange, has been provided from United States aid.

The Greek system of road connections is so immeasurably better today that no comparisons can be made. The improvement, including, of course, the rural roads referred to in an earlier chapter, is summarized below in practical terms.

ROADS IN GREECE: LENGTH IN KILOMETERS

By Class

	1938	1951	1954
Trunk roads	9,965	11,622	14,033
Provincial roads	3,955	3,850	6,863
Community roads	1,840	4,437	7,582

By Type

	1938	1951	1954
Asphalt	3,730	2,827	5,043
Gravel	10,360	13,562	12,156
Unpaved	1,670	3,520	11,279
Total (All roads)	15,760	19,909	28,478

That vast and enormous waste occurred in the program is unquestionable, and there is strong presumptive evidence that there was some graft and corruption and not a little looseness in interpretation of contracts.

There has been a complete failure to apply any program of regular maintenance, and as a result considerable deterioration has occurred and will continue.

The actual construction work is, of course, of the highest importance, as it will improve internal communications and help develop Greece.

However, its impact on the alternative form of a transportation by rail has been less favorable. The improvement of communications was, of course, accompanied by an increase in the number of motor vehicles. The British Army and UNRRA provided Greece in the immediate postwar years with initial replacements for the prewar fleet of transport vehicles. During the aid period considerable imports of transport vehicles were authorized.

A less pleasant form of American aid helped restore taxis and private cars. Employers of the Embassy and of the Economic and Military Missions were authorized to sell their cars for drachmae. I recall one case, by no means isolated, of a colleague who bought a car for twenty-five hundred dollars and sold it a month later for around fifteen thousand drachmae (five thousand dollars). Isolated cases on the Army side are said to have imported two, three, and four cars for resale. The reason for these high prices, prior to 1953, was restrictions on imports of luxury articles, which made it difficult to procure private vehicles.

The sale of cars would not, however, have become big business if the American Mission had not been willing to change the drachmae for United States Treasury checks.

The cumulative effect of various sources of supply can be seen from the following data on transport vehicles:

MOTOR TRANSPORT IN USE

	1939	1954
Taxis	3,500	5,259
Private cars	2,700	7,633
Urban buses	1,043	2,133
Interurban buses	1,635	3,313
Trucks (private use)	1,845	7,081
Trucks (for hire)	4,155	12,090

The impact of this road development could be expected to affect the alternative form of transportation by rail. In actual fact the government has tried to limit this effect by restricting the number of transport licenses to its present level.

The American aid investment in the railways is around 55 million dollars more than the road investment of 50 million dollars, but consists to a much larger degree in overseas procurement. To this investment must be added a substantial sum in UNRRA equipment and in United States Army surpluses in Europe.

Prior to 1939 the Greek railway system was operated by six different organizations. The main line from Athens to Salonika and the lines in North Greece, with one exception, were owned by the Greek state (S.E.K.) and totaled 1,325 kilometers. This dated from the period 1900-1910 and was European standard gauge. The exception was some 176 kilometers of track up the Evros valley linking Alexandroupolis with Turkey and Bulgaria, which was in the hands of foreign concessionaires from Turkish occupation time. Until just before the war the section on the Turkish side was operated by an associated company.

The line from Athens to the Peloponnese (S.P.A.P.) was a meter-gauge system constructed in the 1880's by private risk capital and extended to 226 kilometers. In Thessaly another meter-gauge system of 231 kilometers linked the port of Volos with the rich grain-producing areas. In northwest Greece 64 kilometers of meter-gauge track and a ferry linking to the S.P.A.P. system was owned by another private group (S.B.D.E.).

The sixth railway of the group, as its name of Athens-Piraeus Electric tells, was a city line linking the capital and its port (12 kilometers). This alone now remains in private hands.

The Thracian Franco-Hellenic Railway for obvious reasons is part of the S.E.K. network, and after many years of negotiations was finally bought by the Greek state in 1953.

S.P.A.P. between 1930 and 1939 incurred severe losses through the depression, which affected the semiluxury exports of the area, and through mild bus and road competition. In 1940 the state took over as a receiver for creditors and public, with obligation to sell as a going concern. No prospective purchasers have yet been found.

Thessaly and S.B.D.E. earned steady profits before the war but could not face postwar conditions and were finally taken over by the state as receivers for unpaid C.L.C. loans.

The railways suffered more than any other section of the Greek economy. Prior to the new road program they formed the only orderly channel for distribution of supplies. Their vulnerability in a terrain like Greece is obvious. A well-placed explosive charge on a small bridge in the mountains may entail considerable time and expenditure in repairs.

Full advantage was taken of this by the resistance when S.E.K. was Rommel's supply line, by the Germans during their retreat, and later by the Communist guerillas. Thessaly does not have the strategic significance of the other lines, as it serves only Thessaly, and its meter-gauge equipment cannot run on S.E.K. lines. Nevertheless in retreat the Germans thoroughly and completely sabotaged every piece of rolling stock. In the later disturbances the guerrillas made a pleasant occupation of regular mining of its track. They (I quote a statement of

Thessaly officials) were not so efficiently destructive as the Germans, but caused extreme annoyance, and adversely affected the annual profit-and-loss account.

Resistance, Germans, and Communists enjoyed a field day with S.P.A.P. Main activity on the guerrilla side seems to have been a steady burning of country railway stations, accompanied of course by bridge blowing and rolling-stock wreckage.

S.B.D.E., oddly enough, very nearly profited from the war. The Italian occupation forces decided to extend it north through Epirus to Albania. When Italy abandoned the Axis this work was almost finished over the first forty-two miles, at the cost of destroying a small branch line.

This highly beneficial activity apparently was not appreciated by the farmers through whose fields the Italian Army had driven the track. Prompt and effective countermeasures were accordingly taken. One farmer rebuilt his house with the railway embankment running through his living room. Some meticulously and methodically removed the sections crossing their ground; others treated the embankment, culverts and all, as merely another of the obstacles that encumbered their fields, and regularly ploughed and cropped it each year. One ingenious gentleman had utilized a culvert as the base for an ornamental front gate, and another had used a cutting for his irrigation pipe lines. The section of track actually laid by the Italians has, of course, disappeared, and with time the scars will be covered. It is still possible for the interested traveler to follow the line as he moves up the road from Agrinion to Amfilokia.

S.E.K. actually did gain in one field from the German occupation, since the latter provided additional lines and sidings for their own convenience in the Athens and Salonika areas and at the port of Piraeus. However this benefit is no compensation for the enormous sabotage suffered from Germans, Bulgarians, and Communists to rolling stock, way and rails, stations, and telecommunications. In 1948 no more than two-thirds of the track system was operating with some 20 per cent of prewar rolling stock.

Apart from wanton destruction, all railways had suffered heavily from lack of maintenance during the period 1940–1948.

PROGRAM OF RAIL RECONSTRUCTION

Serious as were the losses to Greek railways, it must not be thought that they were always so disastrous as appeared. S.P.A.P. track was nearly seventy years old, and large sections were long overdue for replacement. I remember an early trip in the Peloponnese when to my astonishment we passed a locomotive laboring up an incline with the characteristic tall funnel that in childhood I associated with Stephenson's Rocket.

This museum piece had, of course, been relegated to branch-line activities, but it was surpassed by the S.B.D.E., which proudly operated locomotives bearing such dates as 1882.

Thessaly Railway operates a little branch line (sixty centimeter-gauge) which runs through the streets of Volos and circles between the bulk of mighty Pelion and the Gulf of Pagasae. Beside Volos station is an artificial mound, still crowned with Turkish houses, which the archaeologists say hides the palace of Iolcus by the sea from which, around 1500 B.C., Jason set sail on the voyage of exploration to develop the local textile industry which mythology and the nursery have forever enshrined as the Search for the Golden Fleece. Volos-Iolcus is still a textile town; and Pelion mountain, says the legend, was the location of Jason's old school.

Appropriately, therefore, the miniature traction unit of indeterminate age and ancestry that daily hauls the Pelion villagers to and from their market bears proudly the gilded name "Jason."

I confess that one of my simpler enjoyments is a stroll along the waterfront or in the streets of Volos. Nowhere in the world is there such an incredible huddle of epochs and times as in this, the world's oldest port and harbor.

The great landlocked gulf still shelters a modern port. A tanker is discharging into the new oil tanks the fuel to supply the roaring F—81's that wheel and dive overhead. On the south headland, past the brand-new white ice and cold-storage plant (erected through a C.L.C. loan) and the adjoining tractor lines of M.C.S., stand the ruins of the classical city, contemporary with the Athenian Acropolis and the once-flourishing Christian Byzantine city that succeeded it. Ancient Iolcus has remained unexcavated since Turkish Volos returned to the ancient site. "Jason" puffs his way toward Pelion, and a few minutes later the American-aid diesel unit rushes past toward Larissa. Textile and tobacco workers, and the shrewd commercial men and industrialists, pass and repass. An occasional mountaineer in traditional costume invades the scene. A sophisticated Paris fashion—short skirts, permanent waves, and all modern improvements—is etched sharply against a wrinkled old peasant woman with rough black homespun to the ankles, neck, and wrists, sacklike in shape and texture. The gnarled hands and stooping shoulders tell the story of work in the land of which it is said that the mule feeds before wife and child because it is the essential of life.

There is a malicious story of this primitive life which expresses a grain of truth. In the villages the position of women has changed since 1939. Then it was customary for the man and the mule to be followed by the wife. Now the order is reversed. The wife precedes. Antipersonnel mines sown by the armies and the guerilla forces have caused this improvement in women's status.

Pelion of a summer evening does not wear the badge of harsh nature but of a gentler, more pleasant world. Dark masses of foliage dot its vast bulk. The lights of the quaint and attractive villages so aptly called "the diamonds of Pelion" rope it with sparkling necklaces from the base almost to its seven-thousand-foot summit. Along the lower slopes cluster the olives that give life if not wealth to its inhabitants, and on the plateaus are the trees that bear its characteristic barrel-shaped apples.

That vast bulk sloping to the water's edge and dipping steeply below the surface provides the pressure to set off the subterranean disturbances that in 1955 shook this world almost to ruins. Today there are added tents and shops made of cardboard and nailed on laths. Wheeled contractors' huts in a line carry the title "Municipal Offices."

Volos is Greece in microcosm. The Thessaly railway epitomizes its economic problems. United States aid reconstructed its track and rolling stock. Thirteen brand-new diesel cars ($100,000 each) replaced its vintage locomotives and passenger coaches and cut in half the time of the journey to Thessaly's towns and villages. Yet "Jason" still runs, and so do some of his aged relatives. Over two million dollars of United States aid went into this line. Before the war it made a small annual profit. Today passenger traffic has increased, but freight has slightly declined. The "new look" railway made a trading loss last year, including depreciation of over one million dollars, a bill footed by the Greek taxpayer.

Diesel cars in theory provide a substantial cut in labor, since the problems of maintenance are made so much easier. The moderate oil consumption, moreover, results in a marked reduction in operating costs as against coal-consuming units.

Despite this the railway staff has markedly increased, including temporary workers, to around 60 per cent over prewar levels. The main operation of this surplus labor is in the Volos workshop, where time and money are spent in tinkering with the "museum pieces" and the diesel cars. It is generally agreed that the diesel car establishment is at least four and possibly six more than required, so that units are engaged for less than forty thousand miles per year. However a ministerial proposal to transfer surplus to S.P.A.P. was met with a campaign of protest in Thessaly—fomented, it is said, by the railway staff—and was dropped.

The Thessaly line constitutes a serious political embarrassment, since Volos is not only suffering sharply from unemployment and underemployment, but like other ports is a center of "extreme left" agitation. The Thessaly Railway could cut its deficit by wholesale dismissals, but such a solution would arouse difficulties.

In 1955 the cash deficit on operations amounted to some 25 million drachmae ($800,000). This payment is a subsidy, a bribe to keep employed several hundred men whose work is in no way essential to the economy. Though theoretically borne by the Greek taxpayer, it is in a sense really met by the American taxpayer, who subsidizes the Greek state budget.

In a report on the Greek state railways I recommended that the necessary economy measures should be taken, but that funds should be provided to employ discharged workers productively. I suggested that engineers be consulted to determine whether workshops and staff could be used for producing railway equipment at present imported, such as wagons, lifting gear, etc. In another context, the need is for a radical solution to the problem of underemployment in Volos, Patras, and Salonika by the introduction of new industry.

When we examined the problems of S.P.A.P., the Peloponnese-Athens railway which runs an annual deficit of five to six million dollars, we found the position more or less duplicated. The Kalamata "Rocket" and its brethren should have been superseded by the new diesel units imported under the aid projects. In fact, they still functioned to the number of eighty. We calculated that a proper redistribution of the diesel units could eliminate all steam locomotives except a group of modern freight engines imported under the program.

An obvious fuel economy would result. The obstacle was the manpower cuts, which should have occurred earlier, but as in Thessaly had been replaced by an upward creep in personnel. In this case, although workshops were a big factor, the worst element was in the headquarters staff in Athens. Here again was another typical symptom of the Greek or any other developing economy. The growth of education, and consequently the output of clerks, administrative staff, and various types of "technical graduates," exceeds absorption capacity. All sorts of pressures political, and through relations, friends, and associates, were exercised to find a job for "my son" (or daughter or nephew). The result was a steady increase in overhead. During my stay in Greece I received hundreds of requests of this type, ranging from dishwashers upward, to recommend through the Mission or my contacts. Usually they were supported by such pathetic and commonly authentic details as a widowed mother having striven in some arduous employment to educate her child at college.

S.P.A.P. troubles, however, did not arise only from a staff load. With four times the track, and linking the comparatively well-developed Peloponnese with Athens and Piraeus, its total freights were barely double those of Thessaly. Practically speaking, this was due to almost total loss of agricultural freight to the trucks. Argolis, Messenia, Arcadia, Elis are the market gardens and orchards that supply the one and a half million population of the metropolitan area. We calculated that S.P.A.P. handled no more than eighty thousand tons of this traffic per year, and that only because the trucks had to shed a certain amount at peak times.

A more dynamic administration, which can hardly be expected from an undertaking in the hands of a receiver for fifteen years, might do better. There are, however, certain fundamental problems and obstacles. First, the city markets in Athens and Piraeus are long outdated and too far from the railway. A new market, long planned, alongside the rails is needed, but was inexplicably never included in United States aid programs. Secondly, handling and loading charges are doubled on the railways, as against motor truck. Of course this factor normally is offset by the compensating economies of mass rail movement, under which one power unit moves twenty-five to thirty truckloads. In Greece, however, exceptional conditions apply. Loading and unloading is not performed by employees of the railway or trucking company, but by cooperative groups of workers known as labor unions. These parasitic growths are another symptom of chronic underemployment. They have a legal monopoly and charge rates sufficient to pay the wages of members and a pension fund. Normally a union is entrenched in a restricted area. In one small port I found a union that unloaded boats with sails and another which unloaded boats with motors. Less work, higher tariffs. The same pressure forces operate to expand and extend these unions, and their united membership of course provides an organization for political blackmail.

This entrenched power hamstrings the railway in competition with the road. Efforts have been made to chip at sectors of the problem, and recent legislation enabled private employers to reject union service if they employed recognized porters on their staffs.

In our report we suggested a frank facing up to this problem by direct employment of porters selected from the unions, and that the other union staff be progressively absorbed in more productive work.

The problem of alternative employment faced us in the engine sheds and carriage and freight-car depots of S.E.K. and S.P.A.P. The main engine sheds of the two railways adjoined. Both had been partially re-equipped, and major extensions had been made from aid funds. It was quickly manifest that the combined labor force of these two establishments of between one thousand five hundred and two thousand men was far in excess of requirements. Over two hundred locomotives were operated by these railways, but it was quite obvious that many were kept in service just to keep men in employment. An efficient utilization of the diesel cars and the most modern locomotives introduced by the program combined with a few additional coaches, would enable all the vintage models to be withdrawn. It is evident that the labor cost for maintaining an 1890 locomotive in operation is immensely greater than for a modern diesel car. One engineer explained to me as we surveyed a dismantled model dated 1889, "You see, we Greeks are economical. Of course this is not really the original. Probably the name plate only remains, because it has been rebuilt so many times." A foreign engineer with me contributed a terse aside, reflecting discreditably on the economics of the rebuild and the probable astronomic costs of operation.

The technicians of the railway depots could be progressively absorbed in local industry, since labor in this field falls a little below demand, but it is difficult to cut an operation of this type.

We proposed amalgamation of the workshops and the establishment of part of the operation as a car-building establishment.

ACHIEVEMENTS OF THE PROGRAM

Little has been said in the foregoing sections about the actual aid given, and a few comments are necessary. In most cases it is a catalogue of bridges and tunnels rebuilt, embankments made good, and sleepers and track replaced. In western Macedonia the subsidiary line from Salonika to Florina and the Monastir Gap was supplemented by a branch to Pobemais* and Kozane to develop the new lignite and other mines. S.E.K. rails were replaced over large sectors by heavier American rails, and the S.E.K. rails were transferred to S.P.A.P., whose lighter meter-gauge track was improved by the heavier but old standard-gauge lines. Major imports for all railways were sleepers and telecommunication equipment.

A new station and extensive workshops were built at Salonika, and as previously stated the Piraeus depots were partially rebuilt and re-equipped.

Rolling stock was imported to replace lost or aged stock. Present figures of locomotives, carriages, and tank cars are still substantially below prewar strength, but of course the modern diesel car units have replaced many of the older types. In addition, more modern equipment is able to accomplish a considerably greater performance. Consequently passenger traffic is vastly increased—over 50 per cent and still rising. Total freight carried is still below prewar figures, but due to longer hauls, freight in miles shows an increase.

In 1955 the national budget had to provide some three hundred million drachmae (ten million dollars) to meet the cash deficit in operations. We estimated that the annual further sum required to cover depreciation and capital replacement, amounted to nearly as much. (In fact S.E.K. and S.P.A.P. were already asking for capital expenditure in the current year of more than this sum for track and rolling stock.) An annual deficit of around twenty million dollars is being incurred. With American aid, this has progressively increased rather than decreased.

* As we have seen in a previous chapter, the railway arrived several years ago, but the main program is not yet seriously under way.

Greek railways have to face some extremely delicate problems. But it should also be added that they must abandon the nineteenth-century methods under which they have been working and must show a more competitive spirit and provide greater public service. As one bus proprietor said, "Those donkeys could put us out of business if they operated their diesel cars more intensively."

THE FUTURE OF GREEK RAILWAYS

In considering the future of Greek railways it is perhaps better to refer to early Mission reactions. The railways have always been a field of disagreement between government and Mission, which originates in the fundamental difference between European and American approach. In the United States the railway is basically a carrier of long-distance freight and passengers. The network is continental. In Europe the railways are also a continual system, but due to divided national sovereignties checking the free movement of goods, no railway could economically operate on continental traffic but must be largely supported by internal movement.

This divergence is intensified by the much smaller use of the motor vehicle. Again, this is based on simple economic facts. Europe is not an oil producer (excluding Russia and Roumania) and moreover modernization or construction of roads in Europe is not as feasible as in America, due to denser population and entrenched landholdings. A European therefore looks at rail differently. To him it is a machine economically organized for comparatively short hauls of passengers and smaller freight carriage.

When the aid program commenced, this open clash became evident. The need for restoring S.E.K., which was essential to the European system, was recognized. However

Americans freely proposed the total abandonment of the meter-gauge lines of S.P.A.P. and S.B.D.E., or alternatively their use as passenger lines only. This last course is not economic.

We spent some time studying the first course. The original American opinion had been that motor haulage would take the traffic of the Peloponnese and West Greece. This may be feasible at present levels, but will not be so with progressive development.

Enough has been said in the roads section to indicate the major difficulties of terrain, but not enough perhaps to indicate the difficulties of driving straight trunk roads. The narrow corridor of the Scironian path on which road and rail skirt the sea between Athens and the Isthmus is typical. This road and its difficulties are the theme of Greek myth. Indented mountains rise almost sheer from the sea. Road and rail must follow the indented sides in a continuous switchback roundabout. The road is already under maximum pressure. To widen it with sheer steeps rising above is not perhaps technically impossible, but it is just not economically feasible. This is one section. The same comments can be applied to many other sections. It is therefore self-evident that the Greek insistence on maintaining both road and rail is valid for another half-century at least. Luxury "face-lifting" of this type is well beyond the economic capacity of Greece.

The unfortunate consequence of this disagreement, however, was that sound American Mission plans for technical assistance to reorganize the railways were cold-shouldered. In my own contacts with the railways I was told flatly that, though the need for foreign advice was recognized, American assistance in this direction was not acceptable. As one official explained, "We are part of the European network, applying European practices. British, Germans, French, Italians know our problems and can help. Americans can neither understand nor help."

This is an underlying, almost a principal obstacle to putting the Greek railways on a sounder basis. It is the major reason why the Greek taxpayer, and indirectly the United States taxpayer, is meeting an annual deficit of twenty million dollars. To date no one has faced the fundamental need for a broad and balanced plan to meet the transport requirements in Greece, because the problem has not been grasped.

This is a highly difficult and complex field, in which United States aid has failed drastically and dramatically. The problem of the rail is partly excessive staff. Constructive assistance to Greece would have redeployed this staff. It is also a problem of weak administration, which understanding cooperation and decisive reorganization could have provided with a solution. Instead, the problem has been intensified by sustained importation of road transport, without regard to its effect on the rail.

In this type of problem it must be remembered that America's allies have a great deal more experience, and that it is here that their advice should be solicited and welcomed.

CHAPTER 12.

The Housing Program

THE MINISTRY OF RECONSTRUCTION

No project involved so large a United States aid investment as, and none has drawn more criticism than, the Rehousing Program operated by the Ministry of Reconstruction. The faulty operation of the projects, the inefficiency of results, the high costs involved, alleged defalcations and frauds, faulty workmanship, nonexistent or fictitious financial records, graft and corruption in almost every form, have been the allegations hurled at the Ministry concerned by Greeks and foreigners, in words and in print.

The size of the project and the absence of any reliable statistics of performance make this position inevitable. Nearly sixteen million dollars in materials, timber, reinforcing steel, etc., were imported, and almost eight hundred million drachmae were provided from counterpart for local materials and construction costs.

Something has been said in earlier chapters of the devastated villages. Mass destruction of houses is not unknown in many countries since the war. Recently in Greece the earthquakes in Thessaly (1954) and Volos (1955) caused widespread local devastation. The position did not have the same seriousness. The weather was mild, the summer was coming. Sleeping under canvas or even in the open was not a major hardship.

The Communist destruction was almost unique in Greece and in other countries for other reasons. Primarily it affected the towns and villages in the mountains, along the northern frontiers, down the spine of Pindus, and in areas and pockets of the Peloponnese and Peninsular Greece.

Here the villages lie on bleak plateaus or cling to the sides of the great peaks. At the best of times life in these regions is grim and severe, testing the endurance of men and women as they wring the fundamentals of a bare existence out of almost naked rock. I have seen the struggle to grow a little coarse barley on the shallow earth on mountainsides with an inclination of 45 to 60 degrees. Elsewhere shallow terraces are hewn to grow a few square yards of grain. Nearer the sea scraggy olives wage an unending struggle to wring some nutriment from poor soil, or some straggling vines show feeble promise on a southward slope. The main support comes from the sheep and goats searching for grazing among peaks, precipices, and plateaus. In some regions forests yield a return in wood, resin, and other materials. In summer a brassy sun beats down from a cloudless sky, to be thrown back from limestone screes. In winter snow lies deep, and access is virtually impossible.

The Communist guerillas deliberately and efficiently wrecked these clustering mountain villages and the little towns where the shepherds and graziers drew supplies and winter shelter. The people fled or were evacuated in the areas of military and guerilla action, losing all their scanty goods and chattels, livestock, and equipment. If, then, the people were to return to their villages, early provision of homes and shelters was essential.

The reader envisaging a devastated village may think of a flattened mass of rubble. This is rarely the condition. The actual damage varies very greatly with the type of construction, the methods used, and the efficiency of the destroyers. Greek construction varies a great deal with locality and available materials.

In Argolis, for example, most of the houses are of adobe construction. In the mountains, however, the principal material is rough stone and rubble cemented. I have frankly often been puzzled by the wide divergences of Greek construction on a comparatively simple theme of two, three, or four rooms.

There are, too, the astonishing wattle huts that form the winter quarters of the nomad shepherd, the adobe and brick, and the stone. An important factor is the availability of construction timber, which has a marked effect on style.

Another interesting phenomenon is the question of one or two floors. I have seen this vary markedly between neighboring villages. One would consist entirely of one-story buildings. In the next all the buildings would have two floors. The Greek is an individualist, and therefore even wattle huts can demonstrate amazing variety. (I recollect one such establishment proudly equipped with quite large plate-glass windows, and another distinguished by two rows of glass portholes.)

The Greek is also gregarious, with close family ties, and it is not unusual even in sophisticated Athens for several family units to share the same roof. Of course the degree of separation of establishments turns on comparative wealth.

Consequently a Greek house is often built with the idea of progressive expansion. American families in the Athens area have several times found that the house they occupy as a single-story villa grows to two floors with the help of their monthly rent.

With this unusual type of architecture and its generally less amenable materials, construction costs in Greece are high. In the villages and even in the cities there is a good deal of self-help. This is often of a crude type and sometimes has unusual consequences. One unlucky Mission member acquired a newly built house in which his bath taps oddly ran cold, but his water closet flush was boiling.

THE PLANS FOR RECONSTRUCTION

These facts conditioned the plans for restoration. A special agency, the Ministry of Reconstruction, had been established to meet the special needs of the situation, and its branches were established in every affected area.

The work of rebuilding obviously had many forms. In some cases whole villages had been so effectively destroyed that the only practical course was to choose another site and start all over again. In these villages houses were produced to a standard two-room pattern that would give space and opportunity for later expansion. These villages are clearly recognizable as being the only villages in Greece of uniform pattern. Any observant traveler, however, may note an older type of village on similar lines, but now considerably changed by individual modifications. These are the villages in which some of the Asia Minor refugees were established between the wars.

In other towns and villages where wholesale destruction had not occurred the houses totally destroyed might be rebuilt on site or as a little suburb. In some cases contractors moved in to carry out repairs and rebuilding of partly demolished houses. As the program developed, further categories of help were provided. Materials were given to applicants who understood how to carry out their own repairs, and these were often supplemented by cash grants. It is obvious that a program of this magnitude required considerable backing on the supplies side, and the considerable allocation of funds is comprehensible.

Oddly enough, the relative project agreements were subject to a clause that provided that the work carried out and the materials and loans supplied were on a repayable basis. The mountain village was therefore subject to a loan charge on its rebuilt property. I have never been able to understand what was the objective of this clause and how it was hoped to secure repayment. The project agreement also required that the Ministry of Reconstruction maintain full and detailed records that would enable such repayments to be claimed.

THE PROCESS OF RECONSTRUCTION

The Greek government has the reputation of being riddled with graft and corruption. This may have been true at one time, but it is by no means a fair picture today. To my mind, the source is in the Greeks themselves, who are inclined to be indiscriminate in charges of graft in private and in the press. Having had the responsibility of tracking down many of these allegations over several years, I have come to regard them with contempt. In my experience the Greek is a reasonably honest man.

Part of my reason of existence as a professional accountant is the prevention and discovery of misuse of funds. Against what I usually describe as "smash and grab," there is no protection whatever. If a cashier is prepared to grab today's cash and run, there is no way you can prevent him. Against other forms of abuse of trust, the protection depends on the degree and efficiency of supervision. This again turns on how much money you are prepared to spend on supervision. An emergency organization such as UNRRA or the Ministry of Reconstruction is of course especially vulnerable to all kinds of abuse. Firstly, it has no established system and procedures. Secondly, action involving the committing and spending of funds cannot wait until organization and procedures are established. Even when they are, it is a long time before they can catch up with facts. A cold trail is too difficult to follow for the ordinary practitioner. The Ministry of Reconstruction is one of the classic examples of unique opportunities. It not only had no system to start; it never seems to have had any effective controls.

In 1953 I was a member of a little conference that discussed this problem. Three of us were qualified public accountants of mature age and experience. We discussed the possibilities of exhumation. (The Ministry had then been abolished.) Our particular concern was to settle this unpleasant loan clause. To recover the loans, the records would have to be put in order or an alternative method of recovery established.

The Controller's Office had initiated an audit at the Ministry some eighteen months earlier. A preliminary look-around was to be followed by a full-dress audit. The night before this took place the offices fortuitously took fire. Some months before our meeting we had made a brief test and inspection of some of the regional activities.

Our discussion, therefore, centered on what was the next step. I recollect my own statement that I preferred not to do post-mortems for their own sake. If we were to collect evidence for prosecution, then the function properly belonged to the Greek state. I could see no conceivable benefit to the United States taxpayer at this point in simply writing up a review. Others present endorsed this view. Prevention and cure were too late, since events had moved too fast. We should have been on to the job in 1949, and only then could practical steps have been taken. Unfortunately the United States Congress had not at that stage seen fit to equip ECA with effectively manned audit and investigation services.

The meeting closed with the piously expressed hope that the situation would not come to the attention of some tactless congressman, and the instruction to me to examine what practical steps were to be taken on the repugnant clauses. Greek state auditors had neither technique nor staff to undertake detailed investigation of the project, and therefore any charges against the Ministry remain unproven.

THE PRACTICAL ACHIEVEMENTS

Let it be stated fairly and squarely that the Ministry of Reconstruction did achieve a great part of its basic objective. Whole villages were rebuilt, thousands of houses were repaired and reconditioned, and large quantities of material were issued on the self-help schemes. No one can state reliable figures of its accomplishments, but they were very real. The Ministry included a substantial number of sincere and competent men who performed their duty well.

On the other hand it is true that control over contracts and materials was lax. I remember a village near Kilkis near the Bulgarian frontier. Its inhabitants told me of a visit of a Reconstruction official. Materials would be provided for rebuilding if the inhabitants were prepared to pay him. The village was an Asia Minor settlement with the stiffness and rectitude in administration that often characterized those mature communities. They made a formal report. The official was dismissed. No more Reconstruction materials were ever offered the village. The village president and his council sat with us taking *ouzo* and *meze*. They were a little tired and discouraged, they said. They had had homes in Asia Minor. The Turks had driven them out. They had settled here and started a new life. Then the war and the Communists. Last year they had finished rebuilding and getting the land into condition. This year (1953) they were tired. Next year they might get Mechanical Cultivation Service to drain that marsh at the bottom of the hill. They had thought of it this year, but some of them felt that with the Iron Curtain just over the hills there, the same old round would start all over again.

One village in Crete had been rebuilt, but no one would occupy it. The villagers had "repaired" their old homes without help and preferred to stay there. They had told Reconstruction that the new site was impossible owing to the direction of the prevailing winds. We found one or two who had tried to live up there. They had been driven out, they explained, because the village was exposed and open, so that in winter it was not possible to keep warm. Their old village lay snug in a protected hollow. Another rebuilt village was also unoccupied. The local explanation was that it had been built on someone's land without legal steps being taken to acquire it. The villagers were not prepared to test the law.

The materials and grants program appeared to have been fairly well administered. Of course we did find one odd case. One old gentleman had been allocated wood to build a house. He had instead built himself a boat. He explained that the Germans had taken his boat and his house. With his boat he could earn enough to build a house, but no one had ever earned enough to build a boat with a house. This action was completely improper according to the legal terms of the project, but reason seemed to be on his side.

The importation of materials often had some curious effects. I remember being fascinated by the gleaming and flashing roofs of one Pindus village. Closer approach revealed that these were galvanized sheets, which had been used to reroof damaged houses. Internal inspection revealed that the houses were intolerably hot.

Reference has already been made to the training program organized by the Extension Service in self-repair, which did good work in the mountain areas.

It is very difficut to make a fair assessment of a project of this type. Personally I consider it impossible to say, or even to ascertain now, the extent and amount of waste and loss involved. The urgency of the program made some losses inevitable. In such circumstances it is impossible to avoid the consequences of relaxed controls. These emergency situations call for special techniques, which are not always available on call. The Greek government could not reasonably be expected to have staff of the necessary caliber available and free from other duties.

In my opinion better planning in the beginning would have saved large amounts of funds and secured better organization. The Greek contention was that the American Mission "rushed" the position more than was necessary, and that the Reconstruction Ministry got completely out of control through American failure to appreciate that administration could not cope with more than a certain demand. Foreign procurements should, for example, have been wider spread and better controlled. Local procurements and local contractors should have been better supervised. The story is told of a Reconstruction village that was later affected by earthquakes. The houses destroyed were the new "Reconstruction" ones.

THE "REPAYMENT CLAUSE"

To my mind, the puzzle about the whole project is that, despite the confused state of the mountain areas, the urgency of the work, and the emergency planning, someone inserted the peculiar clause requiring repayment of the project costs from the beneficiaries. As mentioned earlier, our office was later asked to consider feasibility. Apart from the fact that many records were nonexistent, our inquiries revealed that no one of the beneficiaries had ever heard of this provision.

We pointed out that the majority of people concerned were living on subsistence level anyway, and the probability of substantial recoveries was therefore very low. The administrative problems require no emphasis, and the political repercussions were summarily described by one nomarch as equivalent to inciting revolution.

ASSISTANCE TO FARMERS OF DEVASTATED VILLAGES

Apart from rehousing, the mountain peoples had to be assisted to re-establish their way of life. They had suffered very severely through losses of livestock. I recall one shepherd from Andritsena among the mountains of Arcadia. Before the war he ran nearly a thousand sheep. Four hundred went during the war, and six hundred during the guerilla war. Now he worked as a hired shepherd.

As a whole, though, the larger flocks did not suffer as much because these were generally nomadic. The village flocks, particularly in the frontier areas, suffered the most severely. Even more important than the loss of sheep was the loss of the mule, the tractor of the mountains, ready to plough or move to market. Many of the refugees had lost even the simplest instruments of cultivation: spade and mattock. An American aid project provided some thirteen million dollars in foreign exchange to procure mules, oxen, sheep, and either tools or metal for local fabrication.

This project too contained a repayment clause, usually providing that around 50 per cent of the market value of the items supplied should be reimbursed. This was fair and equitable in that project funds could meet only the more desperate cases. Others had to replace their own stock and tools. The loan note provided that the repayments should be made to a special fund with the Agricultural Bank for the benefit of construction works in the receiving village. We made a fairly thorough check of the project, starting in Mount Taygetus in Laconia and working through the mountains north to the frontiers. As I recollect, only one village in around a hundred visited had any complaint about the distribution.

We were able to obtain an excellent impression of the mountains and of the sturdiness of the mountaineers who make the hard core of Greece. The sad impression that we unfortunately obtained was the small degree in which we had been able to restore the necessities of life. The mules had, of course, been almost totally lost during the war and the Communist war, but UNRRA, the project, and bank loans had largely restored the position.

Sheep, however, had been more difficult to restore. The clearest statement came from one village on the Albanian border. Before the war this village had owned some five thousand head, which they grazed on some excellent range. This was a Macedonian village.* In those remote Balkan mountain areas it is possible to meet all sorts of isolated odds and ends of nations. One friend of mine, a Highland Scot, on a walking tour in Yugoslavia found an isolated villager with whom he could converse in Gaelic.

These villagers explained that they were grateful for the American aid which had given them five sheep each, or around three hundred altogether, but they faced a difficulty. They had the pasturage for ten times the number. However at present they had little or no hope of increasing the flock. With five sheep only, a man must kill the lambs to eat or sell. They wanted to buy another five hundred. They had no cash, but as a security they had offered two thousand acres of standing oak. It was good security, but the banks had no money to advance.

Another village facing the same problem suggested that

---

* In Greek Macedonia a village may be Vlach, that is Romanian-speaking, or Greek, mostly the new settlers from Asia Minor, or Macedonian, that is dating back in the area and speaking a dialect. Formerly there were also Bulgarian and Albanian villages. Opinions differ as to whether there is a Macedonian nationality, or whether Macedonia is just a language of communities. There is a Macedonian nationalist movement, centered in Yugoslavia, which claims part of Greek territory.

the loan repayments be deposited into a revolving fund to finance flock expansion.

This brings up the one unfortunate aspect of this project. Arrangements had not been made to collect installments on the bank notes, although the bank told us many of these mountaineers were in fact making repayments. The problem lay in the terms of the project. The loan notes were widely dispersed through hundreds of villages. The repayable capital was some three million dollars, but under the project provisions it was being split into so many small packets for the benefit of individual villagers that it was improbable that it could be used constructively. The villages were in favor of its establishment as a nomos county fund, either revolving to finance flock expansion, etc., or for some general works of public good.

WATER SUPPLY FOR DEVASTATED VILLAGES

Another excellent special project was one designed to improve public amenities in the devastated villages by providing an improved water supply. Pipes were provided to a value of nearly a million dollars, and an installation program was financed in drachmae. This was in general an excellent and beneficial program.

CHAPTER 13.

Mountain and Sea

The mountains look on Marathon—
And Marathon looks on the sea . . .

Byron knew his Greece, and this well-known quotation conveys a true picture. Greece is a land of mountains from whose heights and peaks the sea is almost always visible. The sea, in turn, is peppered with islands which are also mountains, of which the intervening valleys and gorges have sunk under the sea.

Is the mountaineer a different man from the plainsman? Or the islander from the mainlander? There is good reason for believing that the direct clash with nature does bring out the higher qualities in man. It is said that the late Archbishop Damaskenos, Regent of Greece during the period immediately after liberation, used to claim that the mountaineers were the very soul of Greece. There are others who claim that the islanders who have sailed the seas for untold generations are the truest of all Greeks. Whichever claim is true, both groups might be described as forgotten men.

The mountaineers suffered most bitterly during the German war and the guerilla war. The islanders, essentially seafarers, bore the worst burdens of the occupation. The first efforts of UNRRA were to replace the mules and the boats lost in World War II. We have already seen something of American aid to the devastated villages.

The mountaineers and the islanders, however, face fundamental economic problems. The islands are constantly declining in population due to progressive deterioration in conditions. The mountains suffer acutely from the progressive destruction of cover. In the past, mountains and islands were dense with forest. Its destruction has opened the way to extensive erosion. The Greek mountains are late formations (Tertiary), predominantly limestone in various forms with other intruding rock. They are consequently particularly exposed to the effects of torrential rains. Overgrazing of plateaus and slopes intensifies the problem.

Of the Greek land area of 51,000 square miles, approximately 14,000 is taken up by the cultivated landholdings. Part of this is in the mountains. Almost all the remaining area is mountain country, divided into 8,000 square miles of forest, 19,000 of open range, and 9,000 or rock and barren land. Of the total area, the islands (excluding Euboea) account for some 7,700 square miles, of which 2,100 are cultivated land.

FORESTS

The five million acres of Greek forest are, of course, small compared to those of some other lands, but they are not inconsiderable. The rangelands are exceedingly extensive proportionately, and the forage crop and valley pastures must be added. Yet, despite the possession of these natural assets, around one-tenth of the imports of Greece, to a value of over twenty-five million dollars, was made up of livestock and wood products in 1953.

My first interest in the mountain areas arose rather oddly. Visiting M.C.S. depot in Kalamata, I was invited to visit some special works in progress. The lovely Messinia Valley ("smiling Messinus," Homer called it) is a Garden of Eden lush with fruit. As in Laconia, the sources of this fertility are the springs rising in Mount Taygetus, which lifts its seven-thousand-foot hulk between these two valleys. We turned past the old castle, relic of crusading knights, and started the climb of Taygetus. Beyond a deep-cut gorge we passed into a different world. Small patches of cultivated corn and olives scattered the sides of a large basin. Around the rim were clustered masses of tall pines. We spiraled up a series of roads to top the ridge. There our jeep rocketed through forest paths to emerge ultimately on a high peak above the forest level.

There we settled down with the forest warden to enjoy stewed chicken and the hard cheese made from sheep's milk. Below us lay the smaller peaks and ridges of Taygetus, crowned with pine and fir. Our meal extended to a conversation on forest development and utilization. The forest chief of the area explained the present levels of timber production and the financial and economic problems of the service. Finally: "Our friends in M.C.S. tell us of the good advice you have given them. Is it possible for the Controller's Office to make a study of our problems? It would mean a good deal to the mountain people." We returned to Kalamata. We never saw any special work. M.C.S. and forest officials had conspired to lure me to that mountaintop from which one could see the serried ranks of fir and pine spread below like a marching army.

I returned to Athens and secured the approval of the Controller for an investigation of the Mission forestry projects. Five million dollars, mostly in counterpart, had been invested. The biggest allocation had been made to Macedonia. Houlis and I took a trip in October, 1953, through Macedonia with Loucopoulos, the YPEM forest chief.

Our first stop was in the Laela forest, on the Bulgarian frontier north of Serrai. A road had been driven over rolling hills. As we approached the forest we had to change over from station wagon to jeep. The change-over was marked by some disturbance. Congress had been rather slow that year in approving the budget. Aid allocation had not been available in time, and determination of counterpart releases was affected. These factors in turn had delayed the Greek budget, which cannot be prepared until aid figures are known. As a result, none of the road workers engaged in a United States aid project had received any pay since July 1, and they were understandably upset.

Laela had never previously had any access road, and was consequently mainly virgin forest, mixed deciduous, with a great growth of saplings and small trees. In the forest were the skeletons of villages destroyed by the Bulgarians. The scattered inhabitants had not returned to their homes. This was understandable, as through the trees the blockhouses that marked the Iron Curtain could be clearly seen on the next ridge.

We stayed the night in the YPEM guest house, and traveled the following day through the hills. A major cause of rapid runoff of water is the stripping of cover from the mountain slopes. Rain rushing down in torrents quickly reaches the rivers and floods the valley lands. The Forestry Service, YPEM, and M.C.S. strongly maintain that works of limited extent in the hills can often save more substantial protective works in the lower lands. These works may consist of a series of small mortared stone or concrete check dams in the torrent beds, or loose dams with wire mesh, which checks the speed and amount of the water. An alternative technique is to plant trees along the torrent beds. These techniques retard water flow, so that the flood peak in the valley is delayed and spread, thereby often obviating the need for retaining walls. Slowing of its velocity of flow also reduces erosion. Plantations of trees along the slopes, apart from future harvest value, have also a retarding effect, since leaves and roots hold and retain water as well as binding the soil.

On the high range, experimental seeding and fertilizing had been developed. This again had the dual purpose of acting as an antierosion measure and improving feed facilities on the range. Water tanks and reservoirs had also been established at various points to prevent long cattle treks.

Loucopoulos also showed us the measures taken at Philippi. The reader may remember from Chapter 6 that this ancient city where Saint Paul first preached the gospel in Europe had become a malarial swamp. Beside the ruins of the ancient walls flows a stream, at which Saint Paul spoke to the dyer, Lydia, when he arrived in the city. This stream had been the main feed of the marsh. Drainage farther down and technical works in the hills had been supplemented by dense plantation of poplars along both banks of the stream to provide additional absorption of the water.

One of our company expressed the opinion that the good saint, being an essentially practical man, would be properly appreciative of the work done to make his favorite area habitable. We passed to a view of the broken remains of his basilica and prison, once a major pilgrimage center for Christianity. The shattered ruins of a temple inscription referring to the "God, Julius Caesar" reminded us that this place had been the scene of the two great battles in which his assassination was avenged. As a consequence Philippi had enjoyed special privileges. Today the new village whose inhabitants are once more making the fertile plain bloom is a collection of single-story two-room hovels made of loose stones, not a few of which come from the ruins of the ancient city. We proceeded through the pass to Kavalla, where the conifers planted on the slopes above the town by Loucopoulos before the war developed into dense plantations and effectively checked any heavy rainfalls from sweeping down the steep streets. Above the conifers rises the tall cross that commemorates the landing of Paul here nineteen centuries earlier, with his message to the gentiles.

Kavalla is a tobacco entrepôt where the main warehouses for this primary product of Macedonia and Thrace exist. This is a seasonal occupation, and today Kavalla presents almost as difficult an economic problem as Volos. After our return from Macedonia and the impressions of field work, we made a further survey of the project operating in other districts.

Another trip through Thessaly revealed further extensive erosion and flood-control works, and all our tests indicated that these were effective and useful. However this had been only one aspect of the project. The work on the rangeland in reseeding, controlling, and improving facilities was in the experimental stages and would take time to bear fruit. A very important field had been the development of nurseries. Lousopoulos had already told us that his nurseries contained literally millions of seedlings that he was unable to plant for lack of funds. The same position prevailed in other areas. Trees were given away, but there were not enough takers. The initial Mission program had provided funds for tree planting, but these had now been exhausted. However, forestry is a revenue-earning operation, and funds should be generated from felling mature timber.

To achieve this purpose the Mission project had provided funds for forest roads, for rebuilding certain state sawmills destroyed by the guerrillas, and for importing new equipment. The funds had been expended, but no substantial revenue return had been realized.

We made a preliminary report which was discussed with Minister Apostolidis and Mace and Packard of the Mission. It was agreed that we should go ahead to examine in detail what was wrong with the exploitation side. We reached a preliminary conclusion that a technical service team on similar lines to the M.C.S. group seemed the best course.

Our examination of the sawmill and lumbering operations was carried out very systematically. We were fortunate to have on our staff a former timber merchant. Initially, he told us that Greek lumber was not of comparable quality with foreign, and that it was impossible to eliminate the Greek dependence on importation. Of Taygetus pine he spoke in harsh terms as fit only for village construction. About the fir of Arcadia he was kinder. It was comparable with Scandinavian "as fallen," with 5 per cent to 10 per cent better grades, but as our inspector passed up through Pindus reports became more optimistic. In Chalkidiki the stands of oak were surpassed only by the best Appalachian, the beech was better than imported Turkish, and the chestnut would meet any local needs.

Examination of costs and of records of cutting and maturities indicated that the State sawmills were operating only to a fraction of their possiblities. At this stage Congress saw fit to ax more than half our staff and effectively wrecked every investigation in process. When we were able to sort ourselves out from the debris and complete our report some ten months later, the favorable opportunity had gone.

We presented definite conclusions. The Forest Service, while well-intentioned, was experienced only in conservation and highland water control. The exploitation operation was starved for lack of capital, authority and commercial organization. Local production outside the state services was limited to firewood and village needs, as the operators were small and unskilled in the special techniques of lumber preparation. Certain of the American imported machinery, including a fully equipped sawmill, had never been unpacked.

We proposed that a separate exploitation service under the guidance of outside specialists should develop standards of lumber preparation in three or four state mills to compete with imported lumber. These pilot operations should set an example to private enterprise which would encourage establishment of private mills in other main forest areas.

This plan unfortunately remains stillborn, so that Greece is still importing timber, because the local timber merchants are convinced that Greek qualities cannot compete with foreign. Our staff, by the way, had explained this in two ways. First, they said, it was Forest Service policy to conserve trees, and as a general rule only poor qualities were cut; second, of course, poor felling and preparation could not produce the best quality of timber. A practical policy of selection combined with proper training in sawmill techniques would soon convert the timber merchants.

To the obvious question as to why the timber merchants do not know better, the reply is that the best Greek forests are in the central mountain areas, while the timber merchant lives in Athens or Salonika. He has never had cause to travel to Karpenision, and in fact could not easily do so until the road was there. Forests like Laela are untouched because only recently has anyone been able to reach them except by mule, and some are still in that state. And funds for exploitation have carried us to this stage: that the timber is now accessible, but it is not yet exploited. Working capital is needed to expand and develop.

The conservation section of the service is primarily concerned with preventing further denuding of the mountain area; consequently trees die of old age, dry rot, or fire, instead of being cut under constructive management policy. Informed public opinion has been so impressed with the conservation view that recently an outcry was raised and an YPEM-M.C.S. scheme to clear a derelict forest in a plains area of ideal farm land was stopped.

THE RANGE

The range presents another type of problem. The shepherds as we have seen have progressively destroyed the forest by burning. Earliest records speak of the innumerable cattle and sheep. Currently there are eight and one-half million head of sheep in Greece, about the same number as there are people. There are also four and one-half million goats whose destructive capacity to range and forest prompted the prewar dictator, General Metaxas, to introduce legislation for their total extermination.

There are also some 900,000 cattle but a large portion of these are draught animals. In Macedonia and Thrace the ox-driven plough and wagon are still characteristic. Not more than one-third of the total are milk producers, and beef production is small. The cattle live almost exclusively in the plains areas. American Mission specialists and forward-looking Greeks consider that there is considerable scope for an industry, as in the Alps and Scandinavia, where cattle graze in the mountain tops in summer, and in the winter are fed on forage crops.

The plateaus of Olympus and the border mountains are reputed to be ideal. Not long ago I was talking to one of the farm school graduates. He and some other enterprising young men in Kilkis were buying the nucleus of a herd for beef production. Their trouble, as usual, was shortage of capital to secure good basic stock and to tide them over the development period. This village had its own range but most of the mountain pasture is in theory state-owned and, therefore, free and uncontrolled.

As mentioned in earlier chapters, the settled villages lost a large proportion of their livestock, but in postwar years these have been replaced by a growth in the nomadic herds.

The principal group of nomadic herders, known as Vlachs, are foreign immigrants who speak a corrupted Latin language* and are said to have emigrated from Romania in the disturbed fourteenth and fifteenth centuries. They claim direct descent from the legionaries of ancient Rome who were settled nearly two thousand years ago on the Danube to provide the

* They are now bilingual and enjoy political equality with the Greek-speaking peoples.

defense against the "Iron Curtain invasions" of those times as the predecessors of the European garrison troops of America and Britain.

In the discipline, order, and steady progress of a Vlach column on the march, one can find this claim believable. In the winter their herds shelter in the valleys, but with melting snow, millions of sheep and thousands of men, women, and children start the annual trek. In the late spring of 1953, we made a long trip in Pindus and the Albanian border country, and my companion from the American Embassy took a unique series of photographs. Ahead moves an advance party, then perhaps five hundred or one thousand sheep and lambs with boys herding; next come pack mules loaded with bedding, pots, utensils, dry goods, etc. Perched on top of such a burden will be the domestic hens, surveying the changing scene with apparent interest and maintaining a steady "cluck cluck" with their neighbors. Sometimes a grandmother will be asaddle, but more often she with her daughter will be driving the mule train. Next comes a convoy of scraggy goats, the domestic milk and meat supply, and again more mules. Another large sheep herd follows with the great dogs scouting its flanks. Herding this are the teen-age girls, laughing and talking. The Vlach women have a traditional dress, voluminous, gay, and colorful with embroidery, in marked contrast to the drab Greek peasants. We stop the car, as we have done several times before for photographs. The girls are shy, however. The next section arrives—mules and donkeys, guarded by another grandmother. She laughs and sets an example to the girls by posing in front of a mule piled high with multicolored blankets, topped by another hen.

Another herd of sheep, and behind it some older men. Houlis speaks to them in Romanian. The column is one family, including brothers, cousins, and in-laws. There are over ten thousand sheep. This is the main party. A day ahead is the advance guard to establish the route and lay out the camp. With it are the animals that can move fastest. Perhaps a day's march behind now is the rear guard, with the very young lambs and the sheep shortly due to drop. They are going into high Pindus by progressive stages, and will return in the autumn.

They live in one of the Vlach towns. Others live in the wattle huts, and some of these are incredibly de luxe, with gay-colored textiles and imported amenities. These people are not poor; some are even wealthy. This is the way of life that they have lived for perhaps ten centuries. There are no signs of arms, but in earlier times these people were trained soldiers, and at one time established their private empire across a good proportion of Central Greece. In the Communist war their losses were small, since their mobility enabled them to concentrate in the "safe areas."

Oddly enough, one Vlach base is a collection of wattle huts and sheep pens lying just near Pharsalla. I have often wondered whether these descendants of the men who followed Caesar's eagles are aware that their sheep graze the battlefield where Caesar defeated Pompey to establish the unity of Imperial Rome.

Admirable as is their organization and discipline, the Vlachs, and the Greek shepherds who follow their ways, are destructive like all free sheep rangers. They have no immediate interest in maintaining an area of pasture, and consequently they inevitably overgraze before moving on to the next section. As a result the mountain pasture is uncontrolled, has been progressively reduced and debilitated through the centuries, and continues to deteriorate. This is a vicious circle, which has resulted in the deliberate burning of forest cover. The Forest Service has closed some areas scheduled for reforestation or erosion control to access, but its work is obstructed by the bitter opposition of many shepherds to the trees. One village president, a returned American immigrant, told me that three times he had planted trees that in no way affected grazing in and around his village, but they had been deliberately destroyed by the shepherds. The fourth time he had replanted he had to establish guards and protective fencing.

The American Mission has recommended to the Greek state that the first essential is to develop a rangeland service that will gain the shepherds' confidence. The next step is to establish shepherds' associations to govern and direct the range, and to attempt serious management and improvement. YPEM has submitted a plan for the practical organization of five scheduled territories along the Macedonian border as a model demonstration. This plan suggests controlled grazing, fertilizing, and introduction of a range of more nutritive grasses selected in the Service experimental station. A Mission productivity demonstration involving ploughing, fertilizing, and reseeding has attracted the attention of villages owning their own range, but no one is at present taking practical steps on the free range. The principal obstacles, as usual, are financial. Meantime almost the entire United States aid investment in forest and range stagnates.

THE SEA

In the immediate past a large proportion of internal traffic moved by sea. The caïque, the traditional boat of the Aegean, still carries many cargoes. Movement to the islands, of course, must always use these means.

For external trade, Piraeus. after twenty centuries of decay, has recently been restored as one of the world's major ports. In 1953 unloading in Greek ports from international trade and coastwise traffic had returned to 1939 figures, but loadings for export had not yet reached two-thirds of prewar volume. However, rather striking change had taken place in traffic distribution. Entrance of vessels into Greek ports, by gross registered tons, had increased slightly. The proportionate share of Piraeus had risen from 39 per cent to 45 per cent in 1950, to decline to 31 per cent in 1953.

The shares of the next most important ports, Patras, Salonika, and Volos, had been halved. Of the major ports only Heracleion had increased its share. The utilization of other ports has risen by 50 per cent. These figures are in fact somewhat deceptive, since 60 per cent of the total relates to passenger ships. The acquisition of the Dodecanese and an improvement in services to the islands for tourist and other purposes are important factors in swelling the proportion of other ports. The serious factor, however, is the catastrophic fall in the traffic of all kinds passing through the three principal ports and the progressive centralization in Piraeus.

The retreating German armies thoroughly wrecked installations at Piraeus itself and in most of the other ports. Piraeus was put into working order by the British Army, was later worked on by the Army Corps of Engineers, and received considerable equipment from ECA.

Later programs initiated reconstruction works in Patras, Kalamata and other ports, but the lion's share of this secondary aid fell to Alexandroupolis and Irakleion, on which around a million dollars each has been expended. Salonika, most severely damaged, and of considerable significance as the entry port to south-central Europe, received some 800,000 dollars. Total expenditure accounted for fifteen million dollars, of which five million was in imported equipment.

The policy of concentration on Piraeus has raised acute problems in the second line of ports. Labor cooperatives handle loadings and progressive decline in trade has been countered by commensurate increase in tariffs, in the same vicious circle that characterizes the railway labor unions. Port administration is government-controlled. Shipping management rests with the Ministry of Marine, and the construction, maintenance, and technical works with the Ministry of Public Works through entities known as Port Funds. This ridiculous arrangement generally allows no scope for local control.

Heracleion has a more dynamic local board, which led them into the ice and cold-storage problems mentioned in our discussion of industrial loans, but has nevertheless increased the trade. However most port administrations are sinecures for retired officials of the Ministry of Public Works. We made a tentative study of port problems, an investigation unfortunately truncated by our staff cuts. We recorded that most port works have been satisfactorily undertaken, although in 1951-1952 program reduction had resulted in many unfinished works, but considered that effective benefits could not be expected unless some more constructive governmental and Mission policy was applied. We believed the catastrophic fall in Patras traffic resulted from this neglect. Patras is actually an excellently protected port, which can take the biggest modern vessels with some slight improvements, but it is virtually neglected, with inevitable economic and political consequences. A plan to establish a fish market and cold-storage plant petered out in the 1951–1952 cut after clearance of the site and completion of the quay. A comparatively small expenditure on the port would make it capable of berthing all but the very largest liners.

THE ISLANDS OF GREECE

An examination of Greek statistics in 1951 shows a marked decline in the populations of the mountain areas, which was an inevitable aftermath of the Communist war. An even more marked decline in the population of the Ionian and Aegean Isles is part of a long-term trend. These islands were and still are densely populated. The national average per square mile of 148 is fairly generally applicable, apart from Athens and Salonika. Of the Isles, Corfu has 429, Zante 241, Chios, Lesbos, Samos between 180 and 210. In the past, seafaring, fishing, and so on gave an occupation to these populations. Unfortunately there is no new industry and no constructive policy of development. Works in Cephalonia and Zante since the earthquake have been confined to reconstruction, but no attempt has been made to develop new productive capacities. It has been said many times of the American Mission that they looked first to Athens, second to Macedonia, but never to the islands. Personally, I am not sure whether a great deal can be done, but a serious try is at least necessary. I remember a discussion on earthquake relief with some members of a relief committee. It was unofficial. One government official recommended that instead of any considerable help being given to Zante, the money be provided for a drainage and irrigation project costing around a hundred thousand dollars. This, it was claimed, would enormously increase island income and place the people in a position to undertake all their own reconstruction. Unfortunately neither private nor official charity would recognize this as the sort of project that could be undertaken from reconstruction funds. Consequently immensely greater expenditure has been devoted to rebuilding houses, churches, and public buildings, and the inhabitants have received a charity dole of food and pharmaceutical products. At the end they are no better off than in 1953, whereas a little elasticity in programming, achieved by the charity dole, would have then achieved results a million times greater.

This misguided type of help is astonishingly common. I remember eating a prime meal of lobster in Volos two days after the earthquake, while the world was busy sending vitamin pills. This futile kindness rather irritated some of my Volos friends. Melias' parting words that day were, "Tell people not to send any more meat extract or dried milk." Volos, of course, is the port of a rich agricultural area and has an excellent modern milk-processing plant. Earthquakes do not affect crops or disturb the production of cows. Yet for quite inexplicable reasons, part of the charity of the American people consisted of food parcels.

The islands have considerable tourist attractions, but apart from Mission finance to hotels in Rhodes, Mykonos, and Corfu, little constructive work has been done.

In a report I suggested that specific island development authorities should be established, and projects developed to make the most of natural advantages and resources. The enterprising M.C.S. spread itself into the islands and in conjunction with Hydraulic Construction developed reclamation projects in Corfu and Crete. On its own initiative, M.C.S. has tried hard in the Dodecanese and Zante. Unfortunately, funds have not been available to finance numerous small-scale land improvement projects that its surveyors developed. It must be remembered that during World War II the Greek islands had considerable military importance. It is therefore surprising that American aid projects have not been developed in regions where established friendship is of vital significance in certain circumstances.

CHAPTER 14.

Miscellaneous Programs

EXPENDITURE TO SUPPORT THE STATE BUDGET

A program of reconstruction and development involves a complex of activities that cannot be readily described in one book.

First of all, it must be recognized that in a position of economic and budgetary instability, such as affected Greece during the early aid period, much expenditure must be concentrated on securing budgetary and monetary stability. As against the expenditure on individual projects already discussed, one hundred million dollars was absorbed by the state budget to meet the relief operations of and during the Communist war, and a nearly equivalent sum has since been contributed to support the defense budgets, which are straining the fiscal resources.

In addition, there are numerous smaller projects, which each have a value and a purpose. Only a brief review of these can be given.

TOURISM

Under the Marshall Plan, nearly five million dollars was invested in tourism projects. These included the improvement of the hotels in Rhodes, and the construction of three small hotels at Delphi, Mykonos, and Nafplion. There was also work on pavilions, museums, teahouses, archaeological

243

sites, and similar activities. Hotel furnishings and sanitary fittings were imported. In 1952, we used to condemn this program as a misuse of aid funds. In retrospect, it was not bad in its ultimate affects. In 1953 tourists provided a revenue of twenty-three million dollars. This figure must have more than doubled in 1955. The "tourist popularity" of Greece has now become a significant feature of the national economy.

There were some serio-comic incidents and some tragedies in the program. The Tourist Hotel at Delphi was unused for two years because a source of water supply had been omitted from the original construction. The three small de luxe hotels, with about twenty-five bedrooms each, are not economic, due to their big public rooms. Oddly, too, they were never planned for expansion. It is now well recognized that simpler establishments with more accommodations would have been better. Personally, and this applies to most of my acqaint- ances, I find the Kastalea at Delphi with its simple rooms, good food, and glorious view, immensely preferable to the de luxe built-in cupboards, telephones, and foam rubber pillows of the Tourist at Delphi.

The great inspiration of one small project was to attract visitors to the famous battlefield of Thermopylae. It was de- cided to plant three hundred cypress trees around the mound to commemorate the Spartan dead. The site was duly fenced and the trees planted. Unfortunately, no one bothered to pro- vide maintenance and regular irrigation. When I last visited the site, the cypresses were as dead as the three hundred heroes they commemorated.

Other projects provided for the re-equipment and re- establishment of the museums. When war broke out, most of the exhibits were cautiously hidden: many of the most precious still rest in the vaults of the national bank. For some unknown reason restoration has proceeded at a snail's pace. The Museum of Heracleion, where most of the finds of Knossos are located, is, however, in excellent order and well catalogued.

One project planned to signpost the main archaeological sites in English; I have yet to see any results of its work and suspect the markers are in some storeroom. Regrettably, all Greek sites are almost unmarked. As a consequence the unsuspecting traveler misses a very great many objects of interest.

DOMESTIC WATER SUPPLIES

An improvement in water supplies was required before tourists could be attracted to Greece. Personally, I still stick to bottled mineral water outside Athens, Patras, and Salonika. The aid program imported some five million dollars worth of pipes and equipment apart from the village program, and expended four million dollars from counterpart. A large part of this was used for the repair and improvement of the Athens water supply. This undertaking had been financed by American investors in the 1920's, but its main storage dam at Lake Marathon had suffered during the war, and in 1950 the water supply of Athens gave such genuine cause for anxiety that supplementary sources were tapped, including deep wells in adjacent areas. Important improvements were also made in the sewerage system.

In a number of towns obsolete lead water pipes were replaced by steel. On my last visit, Sparta (twelve thousand population) enjoyed the unique position of having two complete pipe-line installations—the new and the old. However, they were still using the old, as more than half of the householders would not agree to pay the cost of connection to the new system. Argos has constructed a new main line and pumping station above the town, but the distribution pipes were still piled up in the town square, as they could not find the funds to dig in and provide pipes and faucets to every house. (Argos at present draws water from standpipes in the streets). These cases were not unique, and a number of other systems were still not in operation, although material was provided as early as 1950.

COMMUNITY PROJECTS

The various community projects have been referred to elsewhere. They showed almost invariably excellent results. One community claimed that in four successive years they had provided a new domestic water system, built a public lavatory, drained a small swamp, and beautified their village square. They explained this last improvement as being intended to develop a small tourist business from a neighboring town. It was partly for this trade also that the public toilet had been built, although the mayor explained that the building had domestic value as well.

The roads program and water are the basic benefits of the community works programs, but power and light have been other activities.

SCHOOLS

School construction was initiated in many areas, and a program of equipment manufacture was also developed, which absorbed nearly four million dollars from counterpart. The problem in Greece, of course, is the rural school, where a single teacher must try to cope with an age range of seven years simultaneously. However, Greece is not an illiterate country. One of the amusing, if pathetic, sights in the more remote areas is to turn the corner of a mountain road and see a string of eight or ten boys, a scouting party from a mountain village, calling on all passing cars for newspapers.

It is difficult, if not impossible, to measure the results of any program to assist education. American Aid Funds were directed principally to the construction of classrooms and the supplying of desks for primary schools. After some early difficulties, the program controlled by the nomarchs, through grants-in-aid to school management committees, was well administered.

Reference has already been made in the appropriate chapters to the aid to technical and agricultural education. The Departments of Agriculture and Veterinary Science at the University of Salonika, and the School of Agriculture in Athens, have also been the subject of comment.

In general, the field of higher education received little assistance. The outstanding exception was the American College in Athens. This college is a long-established American philanthropic institution, to which entry is widely sought, and based largely on competitive examination. The assistance given was in the form of scholarships provided by T.C.A. (Point 4 Program).

TECHNICAL ASSISTANCE

Expenditure on technical assistance falls into many categories and may often not be so described in the program. The work of EBASCO and Pierce in the power program, and of Knappen-Tippets-Abbett-McCarthy on the reclamation program, have already been described. The work of the American extension officers and other Mission specialists may also be classed as technical assistance.

Under the old program considerable flexibility was exercised, and specialists of various types were recruited from Europe as well as America. Under current procedure an excessive rigidity is exercised, which effectively limits use of technical assistance funds to Americans only, while other specialists must be employed by the Greek government at its own discretion and from its own funds. During the aid period technical assistance was provided in many fields. Government departments or public corporations were the principal beneficiaries. To these aspects, reference is made in the following chapters.

It is universally recognized that an absolute essential to the development of the less advanced countries is the provision of experts for long periods, to develop industry, administration, and techniques. Unfortunately these programs suffer from two major disadvantages. The first is a failure to recognize that very long periods are required. Everyone refuses to face this—UN, advanced countries, and beneficiary countries alike. This is plain moral cowardice. On being asked on one occasion how long, given technical assistance, it would require to produce a Greek of corresponding capacity and experience to myself, I replied twenty-five to fifty years. On this being contested, I replied simply that it was then twenty-six years since my training had commenced, and that I was still learning and did not believe that I had failed to develop rapidly. A Greek would be fortunate to enjoy my opportunities. The second disadvantage is the failure in the United States to recognize the type of expert that is required. It must be recognized that Greeks, Persians, and Hindus are peoples with high culture and quick pride. A top expert is not essential, a good teacher in the best sense is. Even more important is a sympathetic mind, which can grasp the virtues of the world, and the great glories of the Creator in the diversity of man. To attempt to create another little America in every country is driving flatly against man and God. Unfortunately it is repeatedly and continuously attempted, with a consequent enormous wastage in technical assistance funds. The only compensating fact is that the little seed that does bear fruit becomes a rich harvest.

The other aspect of technical assistance, the provision of short and long courses in the United States, suffers from reverse defects. Often the student becomes antagonized by the excessive Americanism. At other times he acquires a veneer that antag- onizes his own people. It is an undoubted fact that the more tolerant and experienced countries such as Austria, England, and France provide a far better background for a foreign student. In short courses especially, there is a very real diffi- culty in reconciling American culture and techniques with those of underdeveloped countries.

AGRICULTURAL SURPLUSES

A very brief reference to the recently developed pro- gram for disposition of agricultural surpluses is necessary. In part, this is merely aid in disguise, where products are provided to the country for disposal in place of cash grant. In actual fact, a main use of aid funds in the past was for procurement of wheat and sugar, the proceeds of sale of which were utilized for capital construction within the country. The reduction in aid grants partly created the surplus, and the present procedure is merely a different form.

However, one new procedure has been developed. Sub- stantial contributions in kind are made to leading American charitable organizations such as Church World Service, Na- tional Catholic Welfare Conference, and CARE. These agen- cies develop programs of free distribution of flour, sugar, cheese, and fats to underprivileged groups.

In Greece NCWC, in conjunction with the Ministry of Education and the Greek Red Cross, provided noon meals for school children. CWS, through the World Council of Churches and the Greek Orthodox Church, provided food parcels to the destitute and to refugees. CARE assisted in earth- quake relief in the Ionian Islands and contributed to various institutes for the aged, sick, lepers, and so forth. In the American Mission we thoroughly examined this program, and it must be recorded that it is of high value, well administered, and undoubtedly beneficial.

In a program involving something like one million people, in a country where little organized relief exists, some errors and abuses are inevitable. It is impossible to prevent some old lady's selling a tin of dried milk or exchanging it for potatoes or bread. It is doubtful whether one should. In practice, however, few complaints were ever made against the scheme, and undoubtedly it was much appreciated by the recipients.

CHAPTER 15.

Administration and Government

LOCAL GOVERNMENT

At one time it used to be claimed that the American Mission's greatest achievement had been the firm establishment of local government in Greece.

This is an extraordinary paradox, since Greek supremacy in this field goes back three thousand years. In fact the most curious feature of all their political history has been that, unlike every other great nation, the Greeks have always possessed a community loyalty stronger than national patriotism. The Greek national tie as far back as the tenth century B.C. has taken second place to the local bond. Athens, Sparta, Corinth, Thebes, were not kingdoms or nationalities, but cities. Their colonies, Syracuse, Marseilles, Naples, were free cities enjoying only a filial relationship with the parent. The great centralized power of Persia was defeated at Plataea and Salamis by a union of free cities. Even in our era the Roman Empire in both its earlier and later forms left considerable independence to the constituent cities.

Greeks attribute the survival after the Turkish conquest to this community spirit, so that each city and village managed to maintain the seeds of liberty and to be a little "Greece." Smyrna and Chios are probably the outstanding examples of the maintenance of a communal spirit and progressive local government in most difficult circumstances.

251

The original War of Independence was a revolt of communities and clans. In Chapter 3 we have already stressed that this was a revolt of the most backward areas. This accounts in part for the astonishing fact that the modern Greek state since 1833 has pursued a policy of destruction of communal rights and substitution of a highly centralized state. The originally German court and the Athens oligarchs consistently followed this policy. The long liberation struggle with Turkey probably caused its acceptance. Its last stages were reached during the prewar Metaxas dictatorship, when community rights were virtually abolished.

Greece is at present divided into fifty nomarchies, properly counties or prefectures. Each ministry has its own office at the county seat; police, agriculture, public works, social welfare, et al. Every action is dependent on national direction. Each nomos is headed by a nomarch, an official of the Ministry of the Interior, who is responsible for general supervision and coordination. His county council consists of the representatives of the other ministries. There is no democratically elected county council, and no elected officials. Community action of any sort is so stifled as to be nonexistent. Mayors of towns and presidents of communities are appointed. Such a system, of course, is characteristic of most underdeveloped countries dominated by small educated oligarchies, but it is odd that it should have been imposed on the liberty-loving Greeks. The passionate Greek love of freedom is no more vividly expressed than in the national anthem, whose opening word is "Eleutheria" (Liberty).

Until 1948 the nomarchs were political appointees whose prime concern was to watch the interests of party members. In "New Greece" (Crete, Macedonia, Epirus, Thrace) a governor general presided over the nomarchs of the provinces.

American pressure, backed by a growing Greek resistance to centralization, secured a reorganization of local govern-

ment. Town and community elections were held, and village
and town councils elected. A new law made the nomarch's
office a career appointment instead of a political favor. Certain
revenues were guaranteed to local authorities, and they were
empowered to use these for works and undertakings of various
kinds. It was these initial steps that made possible the communal road programs and self-help projects to which we have
referred. This position continued until the success of the right-
wing Papagos party in December of 1952. The preceding governments had been coalitions of the moderate center.

This development coincided with a progressive withdrawal of American intervention. The immediate effect was
the assumption by the Minister of the Interior of powers
to replace unsatisfactory mayors and community officials by
appointees.

The second stage was an attack on the career nomarchs
established on American advice, as no longer subject to political intervention. The government started moderately by an
attempt to remove a small number as "unsatisfactory." The
independent tribunal that, under the law, was charged with
the responsibility of reviewing such cases rejected the applications. It is generally accepted that the Ministry had legitimate
grounds in one or two cases. As a general principle, however,
the "career nomarchs," freed from political pressure, had done
excellent work. Like other Mission field officers, I was personally acquainted with many of them, and I have often discussed
the situation existing prior to the nomarchy law and the tremendous improvement in local government that followed. The
success of the community projects, of extension, of the small
works, and of the rural road activities was largely due to the
new conditions of cooperation between the nomarch, the communities, and the agricultural services.

In late 1952 we made a review of state activities and
local government in Crete. It was clear that in areas such as

housing and school construction, the increased authority and prestige of the nomarch had resulted in elimination of the major faults evident in the earlier stages of the project. The most obvious benefit had been the destruction of political patronage in the distribution of aid and similar funds, and the elimination of "vote-buying tactics" by the deputies.*

Despite this, the Minister of the Interior proceeded in early March, 1954 to rescind the "career nomarch legislation," and immediately dismissed one-third of the nomarchs. The odd characteristics about these dismissals was that they were not necessarily based on political opinions nor on efficiency. Several strongly pro-government nomarchs were dismissed despite known efficiency. Apparently this arose through internal dissensions within the government group, which were to break out a week or two later on the replacement of the Minister of the Interior among others and the secession of the Markezines group. It was a question of removal of antipatronage elements. The dismissals were legally contested, and subsequently several of the career nomarchs were restored to office. In late 1955 the reorganized government party introduced legislature again re-establishing the career nomarchs.

The generally muddled policy on local government by what was regarded as an American-established administration has accelerated the leftist trend since 1952. The Mission has been blamed freely for not intervening to protect measures that have always been regarded as essentially American-sponsored.

CENTRAL GOVERNMENT

The postwar Greek government machine had a peculiar inheritance. Immediately before the war, Metaxas' dictatorship policy had concentrated administrative initiative at the center.

---

* We had recommended a further extension of local government by the transfer of local offices of certain ministries to local government status.

An excessively centralized machine may be extremely effective under a dictatorship, where continuity of policy is theoretically assured without consideration of day-to-day political advantages, and is based on ministerial initiative. Under conditions subsisting after the war, when due to political instability ministers have been playing "all change" or "musical chairs" at six-months' intervals, the machinery is liable to clog.

Apart from this it must be remembered that Greek administrative procedures as at present operated have not been developed over a long period. The United States as a nation-state is only fifty years older than Greece, but the basis of American democracy goes back in continuity with its parent roots in England. The War of Independence did not represent the liberation from a foreign yoke, but the setting up by a full-grown man of his own household in resentment against excessive parental restrictions. In Greece the old laws and customs had been torn up by the roots, and replaced by an inconsistent and inefficient foreign code that was completely alien to national sentiment.

In 1833, therefore, it was necessary to build the whole system of legislation and procedures anew. The German monarchy accomplished this very largely by the introduction of laws and systems based on eighteenth-century models in Germany and France.

In Britain, the United States, and other long-established countries, governmental activities are usually so much of the essence of the tradition and in accordance with ways of thinking that a public servant does not need to spend his time with a library of lawbooks. In Greece, law being imposed from other conditions and not built up on tradition and common sense, if he does not do so he may well land in jail. Mechanical Cultivation Service, that most dynamic of Greek services, manages to keep itself out of trouble by an extraordinary process. One official occupies proudly and successfully the position of "tame stumbling block." It is his responsibility to find anything illegal or dubious in M.C.S.-proposed action or policy. A "tame lawyer" is also retained to solve these illegalities or dubieties by some technical device.

It is not easy to picture the obstacles that Greek legislation sets in the path of the unwary. At the time of the Volos earthquakes, emergency measures taken by military and civil authorities were said to have rendered a number of officials liable to astronomic terms of imprisonment.

United States aid in the period 1948–1952 could not be administered effectively with this complexity, and the applicability of regular state procedures was suspended. An example, perhaps extreme, of Greek administrative problems is seen in the case of Hopkins, the financial adviser to M.C.S. Hopkins is a chartered accountant employed by the British Ministry of Agriculture who was loaned to M.C.S. in February, 1954, with the proviso that the Greek government should pay to the British government his basic salary, pension rights, etc., and to Hopkins a supplementary salary and living allowance.

In November, 1954, the Greek cabinet formally decided to retain his services for another year. Necessary proceedings were set on foot, and have at date of writing taken more than seventeen months. Hopkins is still unpaid.* The British government claim was settled in February, 1956, after frequent diplomatic representations. M.C.S. "evasion experts" did manage to keep Hopkins fed and housed during the period by authorizing excessive advances for travel expenses.

Hopkins and other British and American advisers have amused themselves by various calculations of Greek administrative time problems. The registry and postal processes were the easiest targets. Hopkins claimed that between Nikaea (M.C.S. Athens office) and the Ministry of Agriculture, a fifteen-minute journey, regular mail channels took seven days.

* Now settled.

Restrictions on powers and authority of responsible officials and necessary reference of trivial day-to-day matters to ministerial level and above are characteristic. To employ two interpreters at eighty dollars per month for Hopkins and his colleagues required the personal signature of Marshal Papagos.

Despite these restrictive measures, the Greek financial system is as full of holes as a sieve. On one occasion I defined it as established to catch all gnats and give complete freedom to camels. The Audit Court, for example, concentrate their entire efforts on such trivialities as checking and rechecking travel claims, without any attempt to investigate major frauds or wastage. Audit is merely a check that certain legal requirements have been met. Any frauds, evasions, or wastes will escape unnoticed so long as legal formalities are observed. This greatly facilitated the irregularities that took place in the Ministries of Reconstruction, Public Works, and similar agencies. The absence of any local government, such as county council, higher than commune or town councils makes the public check on waste difficult.

Apart from these weaknesses, the general administrative structure of the various ministries has remained unchanged during the aid period, and requires a complete overhaul to meet modern conditions. In 1948 AMAG officials conducted a survey and based plans for reorganization of certain ministries. The plan of reorganization for the Ministry of Agriculture was based on prior surveys by UNRRA and FAO.

TECHNICAL ASSISTANCE TO IMPROVE GOVERNMENT SERVICES

The most important application of the plans to overhaul and improve general administrative machinery was the work conducted by Public Advisory Service Inc. of Chicago. This well-known American agency was primarily concerned with the

Ministry of Finance and with plans to improve the working of tax collection, disbursements, budgets, and accounting. Its conclusions were contained in voluminous reports on the procedures and techniques to be followed. These reports were started in 1951 and reached their final form in 1954.

Parallel to this activity a British expert, later succeeded by an American, was loaned to the Greek government to establish an "Organization and Methods" unit and to improve the machinery of civil government. Training visits to the United States were arranged for selected Greek staff.

A special effort was made to solve the problem of jurisdiction between Public Works, Agriculture, and other interested parties over reclamation, flood protection, and similar problems. Initially a coordination committee was established, but after some years of futile negotiations, a more positive step was taken in early 1953, and a draft law was prepared under guidance of the Adviser on Land and Water Resources Development (Walter Packard). Spasmodically this law or some alternative draft was due to be submitted to Parliament, but to date action is still untaken. Meanwhile the whole organization of the ministries, subject to minor improvements, remains the same.

With very minor exceptions, this has been the general fate of all reorganizations. In the fiscal year 1955–1956, agreement was secured in principle to the formulation of a contract with an American university (Pennsylvania State, I believe), and funds were provided. Negotiations broke down at the last moment.

Similarly it has long been recognized by both Mission and Greek state that a management audit bureau was imperative to obtain maximum benefits from aid. Negotiations in 1952 petered out. The Mission accordingly strengthened its audit division, and over nearly four years we were responsible for preparing a series of reports on aid utilization, which have formed the basis of this book. The reports have been translated into Greek and have enjoyed a wide circulation. It is generally accepted that this independent criticism is of constructive value. Greek officials, even those criticized, have spoken highly in their favor.

In mid-1955 negotiations to transfer this section, in entirety, to the Greek state, and to strengthen it by the addition of further Greek and foreign staff and by American certified accountants, progressed also to an advanced stage. This in turn petered out. One Greek explanation is that the Mission had originally implied a willingness to meet salaries from T. A. funds, but subsequently insisted that the Greek state should itself pay my salary and the salaries of the Greek staff from budget funds. This introduced legal and technical difficulties.

Reference has already been made to the expiration of the M.C.S. project. Its abandonment at a stage when development was well advanced is also attributed to "concealed" Mission opposition. The ultimate result in these and other cases is the same. Little is accomplished, and the practical possibility of modernizing Greek administrative procedures fades farther into the future.

MINISTERIAL RESPONSIBILITY AND LACK OF DELEGATION

It is well known that a major cause of the failures to reorganize government administration is excessive authority being vested in the minister. Under American and European procedures considerable authority rests with the permanent state employees. In the not-too-distant past a change of government in Greece often meant a change of staff. Recent measures to improve the position of civil servants have in fact much strengthened their position, and very few changes followed the right-wing victory after the 1952 election. Nevertheless all senior civil servants feel a basic instability, which limits their field of activity.

Ministers in recent years hold office for so comparatively short a time that only an administrator of first rank could be expected to grasp the situation and apply remedies. The minister, following a traditional pattern, will concentrate on patronage and benefits to his own supporters and favored areas. If, for example, a Minister of Agriculture hails from Thessaly, a rash of local schemes may be expected. When a minister follows a constructive policy, on the other hand, it may be expected to be expressed in spectacular schemes that will attract some attention. The more tedious work, which attracts little publicity, of passing through such technical legislation as internal reorganization or such essential legislation as drainage authorities, will be shelved. Each minister in turn will be brought to recognize the need, and will even initiate steps; but he will be out of office before accomplishing anything.

Similarly, anything of a major policy nature such as requires approval of several ministers or the cabinet will be squeezed out by the changes.

A classical example of these difficulties is the well-drilling story in Chapter 9. Three Ministers of Agriculture in succession have been convinced of the need to develop this project. The first stage is legislation to incorporate the service in Mechanical Cultivation. The second is the policy question of persuading the cabinet and the Ministers of Finance and Coordination to back the scheme with funds.

The lack of initiative in the higher civil servants is held by some to be attributable to low caliber. Actually this claim is not justified to the degree that could be expected in view of the very low salaries received. Christides, YPEM chief, and many officials of similar caliber earn around $100 per month. A very top civil servant will carry little more than $150. Some accounting and similar grades run between $30 and $60.

The lacks are mostly felt in the technical categories. A senior mechanical engineer with a degree might reach $120 with M.C.S. on the special scale applicable, but the same man could earn $400 a month with a Greek cargo boat.

In the Greek Civil Service, as in any other national civil service, there is quite a lot of dead wood, men who take an easy path, and in such circumstances there are inevitably men who are malcontents and idlers, and some who are ready to turn any dishonest penny. On the other hand, one of the facts most astonishing to a fair-minded observer is the amazing proportion of conscientious, high-minded men who are sincerely concerned with trying to do an honest and thorough job for the benefit of their country. Some of them have private means; some have not. I recollect Packard's private comment to me after introducing John Palaeologos—that he was one of the most upright and sincere men and truest patriots that any country could produce. That tribute could be extended to scores, even hundreds, of Greek state employees. A patriotic Greek has 3,500 years of tradition behind him, and his education is full of models from the past on which to pattern his conduct.

The tragedy of this section is that so much of their effort is stultified and rendered abortive by an inefficient and archaic government machine. Inevitably many become impatient or frustrated by the unfulfilled promises, and leave or move towards the left. Dr. Frixos Letsas,* a highly experienced German-trained engineer, worked with UNRRA and the American Mission for nearly ten years in a selfless effort to benefit his country. Finally economic pressure compelled his move to commerce, where he can at last enjoy income enough to keep his wife and himself. Letsas had been marked for years to take

---

* He may be personally known to British readers from visits to the United Kingdom and to American readers as having appeared on TV.

a principal part in the new reclamation bureau, but the legislation never came.

CREDIT AND CURRENCY

No field of Greek reconstruction has been so hotly contested as the credit and currency problems. It is not necessary to recapitulate here the difficulties that have arisen in banking and credit policy as outlined in earlier chapters. As has been shown, there are fundamental difficulties in developing adequate credit in undeveloped economies.

There are also fundamental defects in organization. The banks are almost invariably overstaffed. One manager with foreign experience assured me that he had computed the excess as compared to British banks as being something of the order of eight to one. This is partly due to the power of the employee groups, and partly due to inefficient and complicated methods: the old typical story of the man to watch the man to watch . . . the cashier.

Recently the Mission fetched over a specialist to report on the Agricultural Bank. The report, I am advised, raised strong resistance, recommending (quite rightly in my opinion) the introduction of a technical assistance group to reorganize the bank. To the Greek, already exasperated by the Mission credit squeeze, this merely implied a further tightening of the screw. Personally, I consider that it was an exceedingly tactless move. Over fifteen months earlier, reporting on the bank when this project was in view, I stressed that in my opinion the Mission should call in European specialists. Nothing could be really accomplished without securing the confidence of the Bank and the cooperative movement. Any American report would be suspect, and European specialists were in fact far more competent to advise on local problems, which they had encountered elsewhere, than Americans.

A special problem arises at the Agricultural Bank through the large trading inventories carried. The Bank has become a general merchant as much as a bank, through its efforts to coordinate and supply the needs of a multitude of small farmers.

In the commercial banking field, the Papagos government intervened in 1953 with directives to amalgamate certain banks. The National Bank of Greece and the Bank of Athens have in fact been integrated. By virtue of complete dependence on central bank loans, the government is able to exercise complete domination. Frequent changes have consequently been made in bank executives. The usual disputes are over the difficulties in "unfreezing" past credits and over allegations of preference to certain individuals or groups.

MARKETING AND COOPERATIVES

Closely bound up with the Agricultural Bank and its credit problems is the cooperative movement. This is a highly complex subject, warranting a very detailed account that it is impossible to give in these pages.

Most Greek farmers are united in village cooperatives, which federate at county and national levels. The intention of the movement initially was to provide the small Greek farmer with the advantages of large-scale buying and selling. In practice the cooperatives have lost their initial purpose in a close tie-up with the bank. For obvious reasons the Bank prefers to make production and crop loans to the cooperative, and leave to the officials and committee the responsibility for individual allocation and collection. This has become their prime purpose, and there is no cooperation in selling general farm products.

The government carries out bulk purchases of the wheat harvest, and responsibility for collection and warehousing is exercised by the bank and the cooperatives. M.C.S. tried to encourage a policy of operation of farm machinery through cooperatives but found this to be a failure. Enterprising farmers buying tractors and hiring out to neighbors were far more successful.

Cooperatives have entered various specialized fields. Eleourgiki, an agency of the olive growers' cooperatives, stores, refines, and sells olive oil and olives. Two cooperatives of dairy farmers, one in Attica, one in Volos, were started to operate pasteurization plants. A cooperative canning plant was initiated in Argolis. Wine growers' cooperatives function, and so do some odd packing plants. There is, however, no real impulse behind the movement, which has been imposed and has not grown. In the result, the dairy farmers of Attica and Volos and the tomato growers of Argolis in the main take their products to private merchants, without regard to their contracts with their own cooperatives, if the slightest improvement in terms is offered. (Usually the cooperatives offer, say, 70 per cent cash down, the balance in three months or at season end, in order to maintain working capital. The private merchant can usually break the cooperative by offering 90 per cent of the price down.)

On the marketing side, the abortive efforts of the cooperative have unfortunate repercussions. There is no grading of product; transport and distribution costs are enormously increased because production is bought up in small packets by an immense multitude of local dealers. (There are around a thousand wholesalers in the Athens-Piraeus general vegetable markets, supplied by these local dealers.) This disorganized marketing creates a parasitic class and effectively inhibits schemes for export markets.

The clear need for taking some action in this very complex field was met only within the last two years by provision of a Marketing Technical Assistance Group. This group is currently headed by a dynamic Midwesterner, Ned Mason, whose forte is common sense, not specialized knowledge. He is assisted by three or four European specialists. All have been enthusiastically working on a complex of projects—a new central market in Athens, packing and grading stations, etc. However, Ned is the first to admit that to date they have touched only the fringe of the problem. The "high policy level" in Mission and government seemed unable to grasp the imperative need for this work and for a full and thorough survey and reorganization of the whole field of cooperation and marketing and of the processing and packing industries.

At lower levels, the dangerous position that might arise through expanding production with no organized outlets is clearly perceived, but the capacity or opportunity to pass the realization "up" is missing in this as in other fields.

THE NEED FOR IMPROVED ADMINISTRATION

To convey to anyone the dangers of poor administration, or the lack of any administration, is exceedingly difficult. Anyone is prepared to recognize the need for "specialists," but as one of the shrewdest officials of the American Mission remarked, "There are too —— many specialists and not enough generalists in Greece." This is characteristic of the development of any country.

Administration is an imperative need in these countries, because so often the enthusiasm of the specialist creates imbalance. To coordinate, plan, and administer is a technique that is acquired by example and experience rather than theoretical bookwork. The special capacities required can be built in most people of intelligence, and we all feel that we possess them already. It is extremely difficult to disabuse people of this impression without causing offense. The only solution in facing this problem is to give the maximum opportunity to "administrators" to visit abroad to acquire wider experience, and to ensure that technical assistance personnel have broad general and administrative backgrounds as well as specialized knowledge.

CHAPTER 16.

Sentiment and Sympathy

This chapter has presented more difficulties in writing than any other; its objective is to draw some profitable conclusions from what has been written of individual projects. No one can feel satisfied that one hundred cents of benefit has been derived from every American dollar spent on Greece. In fact, I have heard pessimists (Greek and American) hazard that perhaps five cents was the exchange rate.

In the review of individual projects, it has been impossible to refer in detail to the administration of the aid program. That would require a volume on its own account. Something may be said of the difficulties that encompass it and that may cause a catastrophic loss in the exchange of dollars for benefits.

Undoubtedly the prime requisite for aid administration is sympathy. The word is used in its Italian or Greek meaning, rather than in the more sentimental interpretation that English usage has attached. It means the capacity to feel for a fellow human being as one member of the family for another. It does not mean, however, that intellectual appraisal should be swept away. Sentiment gives a beggar a dime or a dollar. True sympathy requires the more difficult approach of trying to set him on the right track again as a fellow man.

Americans are, as every one knows, generous-hearted and kindly people. On the other hand, they are not very patient in trying to understand the complexities of human problems, particularly where these are rooted in the history of man.

As members of a new society whose structure has changed rapidly in a short time, they cannot easily grasp why the same revolution that has lifted them from poverty to wealth in a little more than a hundred years cannot be applied as a cure-all recipe everywhere. This lack of complete understanding is a factor that has caused much difficulty between America and its friends and beneficiaries, British, European, and Asiatic alike. The impression exists that Americans neither understand, nor try to understand, the real problems of the twentieth century, and it is a constant irritant in all relations with other countries. On the American side there is disappointment that their efforts for others are not sufficiently appreciated.

CONFLICT IN AID ADMINISTRATION

In aid administration this sense of conflict has become a cause of wastage. In the case of well-drilling referred to in an earlier chapter, I have no doubt that a principal cause of failure was lack of understanding. The initial American insistence on private enterprise is typical. The basis of thinking is simple. Private enterprise built America; therefore private enterprise can solve all the problems of Greece. Because the Greeks do not accept this, they are obviously stupid or unintelligent. If anyone, Greek or foreign, tries to explain why private enterprise will not work in particular circumstances, he meets a blank wall. There is no possibility of convincing or explaining. However, all this is generalization. Not all Americans involved are stubborn or unreceptive, and not all Europeans and Asiatics are deep-thinking. The real, radical trouble is that so often Americans engaged in aid administration are not of the intellectual level of the men they meet.

The men who are charged with the administration of nations, with the solution of economic problems, and with leadership in other spheres, represent the cream of the country. In the Old World they are mature men, deeply read in the past and present, possessed of outstanding ability. They are human and not infallible, but the cream of Europe or Asia is in no way inferior to the cream of America.

Unfortunately, America has limits to the quantities of men of approximately equal caliber it can produce. As a consequence, in general, the level of employees of the United States government is below the standards of the people with whom they have to deal. This, inevitably, produces conflict. The Greek or English or Indian is unable to make contact. He is talking to someone who does not possess his ability or experience, but that person is determined to impose his own ideas, and is neither willing nor able to comprehend his associate.

SELECTION OF PERSONNEL

It must be remembered that, let us say, the Director of Agriculture of the United States Mission to Greece has to discuss and decide on an aid program in conjunction with the Minister of Agriculture, the Minister of Economic Development, and the general directors of these ministries and other high officials. He is himself, in a sense, a minister and top-ranking public servant of Greece. In this particular instance, the man who held this post for some years, Mr. Bryce Mace, was an excellent selection. He typified some of the best qualities of America, sociable and friendly, shrewd, deep-thinking, and full of human understanding.

The Greeks with whom he had to deal also typified some of the best traditions of their country. Messrs. Apostolidis, Papaligouras, Kalinsky, Christodoulou, and Palaeologos, all men of outstanding ability, were genuine patriots, determined to accomplish something good and constructive. It is, perhaps, the

combination that made possible the real achievements of the
agricultural program.

However, a good chief alone is not sufficient. The department as a whole must be well staffed. Again, the chief of the
Land Reclamation Service, Mr. Walter Packard, was a man of
outstanding ability and sympathy. The achievements of M.C.S.,
alkali land reclamation, Macedonia, and the Arta project were
largely due to that fact, combined with the characters and
ability of such persons as Messrs. Palaeologos, Letsas, and
Christides, the personalities of several of the American extension agents were admirably suited to the needs. The tireless
work of such men as Charles Yale has really achieved miracles.

Some other selections were not always so fortunate, and
sometimes the failure to make a selection (as in research) was
even more disastrous. All in all, however, the Agricultural
Division was singularly lucky. Its failures were due to other
causes. Selections elsewhere were not always so lucky. It is
preferable not to stress these failures.

The problem of selection is conditioned by limitations.
First, the pay levels are not adequate. A top-ranking pay of,
say, $14,000 per year may draw a good man. The conse-
quence further down the line at working levels is obvious.
To men of ability and technical skill, $6,000 or $8,000 per
year is no inducement. The economies secured by these low
salaries have been outweighed a thousand times by the disastrous waste of aid funds. If America wishes to send men to
supervise the program properly, the payment must be comparable. The alternative is low-caliber staff, enormous waste,
black marketing of commissary and PX supplies, and loss of
respect abroad. Given adequate pay scales, it may be possible
to attract staff with the right qualities. Technical skill is not
so important. Capacity to face and solve new problems, willingness to try to understand the other man's point of view, and
real experience of the job are the significant qualities. Person-

ality and integrity are imperative. Interest in and sympathy with the ways and traditions of other people are a great help. In all it must be remembered that the selection, to quite low levels, is of people who have to make decisions that seriously affect the lives of many thousands of human beings.

Apart from the inducement of pay scales, the question of long-term employment is important. The aid administration was recruited on a short-term basis. The staff consisted partly of long-service employees loaned from other government agencies, institutions, etc. It is clear and obvious that, as a general rule, staff of the right caliber look for permanent employment. If aid is to attract staff in competition with regular state employment or industry, it must offer a career. The failure to face a long-term, continuing program entails the employment of poor-caliber staff indefinitely.

In sharp contrast, American employees of commercial and industrial firms abroad are people of high caliber and possess the qualities indicated above to a marked degree.

RELATIONS WITH OTHER NATIONS

Given the best selection possible, weakness and difficulties will nevertheless arise. There are faults on the other side as well. Greeks or Indians or anyone else are not perfect. Their national characteristics can be equally irritating to Americans. After recognizing that many of the men occupying responsible positions are men of first-rate ability, this does not necessarily imply that they know what they are talking about all the time. There is a weakness which has been revealed especially within the later years of aid. In the early stages, Americans forced through their opinions and made disastrous mistakes. In the later stages, advice was tendered when asked. The Greeks and others made their own decisions, often without consultation, and made equally bad mistakes. In underdeveloped countries, theoretical training is often not balanced by practical experience. The sources of information may not be accurate or may give a wrong picture. Many misconceptions arise as to what has happened elsewhere. In general, the underdeveloped countries particularly lack experience in such fields as industrialization or economics, and overestimate the value of their book learning.

In aid administration, the local knowledge of the country, its social structure, and conditions, is something that must be obtained largely from a discussion with the responsible officials. On the other hand the local officials, right up to the top level must recognize that in many practical fields their theoretical knowledge and doctrine and information should be tested against the foreigner's experienced and broader views.

The work of developing a country rapidly must depend on a really well-founded understanding between the local officials and the aid administrators. I have said elsewhere, and repeat here, that in this third-nation nationals can be of really great help. This cooperation, however, must be based on new and honest thinking on all sides. Better selection on the American side will help considerably. Recognition is needed on the recipient side that Americans are entitled to express a view on how their money should be spent, and that they can produce intelligent views.

RELATIONS WITH HEADQUARTERS

No matter how good relations may be at the local level, the achievements may be completely vitiated by the intervention of another party.

In the earlier days of aid, the Chief of Mission and his staff had very wide measures of discretion. In the latter stages this authority had been whittled down progressively. The Chiefs of Mission, formerly often distinguished men of affairs, have been replaced by regular government employees, now subordinate to the State Department. The early aid program operated with the intention of building the country economically. Now the emphasis is on State Department factors rather than economics.

Locally, the power of action is extremely limited, and constant reference to Washington is required. The reference may, and does, provide a useful buffer against local pressure. In practice, it is notoriously difficult to obtain replies to cables from the Washington bureaucracy. This is well known to officials of other governments and indeed was a subject of jest in Greek circles.

If in fact replies are received, they can be most embarrassing. It must be borne in mind that, with the best will in the world, there is a big difference in outlook between the local group and a desk in Washington. This is reduced where the Washington incumbent has been an experienced field man or makes regular visits. The nearer the project, the closer the appreciation of realities.

As a general principle, therefore, local aid missions should be staffed well and should have the maximum possible autonomy. Their decisions should not be subject to change or reversal through political factors.

CONGRESSIONAL REACTIONS

It is of the essence of democratic government that the people, through their elected representatives, should have the right to a say. The degree and extent of that say constitute a bone of contention. A program of economic aid is a long-term commitment, which should be interfered with as little as possible. Congress has so far reacted strongly against any suggestion of interference with its right of annual review. Something has been said already of the problems this creates. Long-time planning is imperative. Some solution under which Congressional committees could review country programs by stages must be developed to displace the uncertainties of present annual aid.

RELATIONS WITH POLITICAL ISSUES

The confusion of economic and political issues has been sharply underlined by the Suez crises since this book was originally written.

Economic aid should not be a price for political support. It is either justified or not justified on its own grounds alone. Once it becomes a purely political decision, it loses any economic justification. Control on economic grounds becomes impossible, since it is regarded as a payment for services.

CHAPTER 17.

Program Evaluation

DIFFICULTIES OF EVALUATION

Before proceeding to draw conclusions from the aid program in the light of difficulties experienced, it is first necessary to consider the degree of success attained. The aid program had not the single clear purpose of economic development. Its objectives were complex, and achievements and failures must be measured against the various aims. Moreover, the economic aid was in fact associated with military aid, and the two programs cannot be entirely separated.

The initial AMAG program sought to end the state of war along the southwest fringe of the Iron Curtain. If Greece had not received both military and economic aid in 1947, it is virtually certain that, like China and Czechoslovakia, it would have been absorbed by the Soviet bloc.

Military aid ended the civil war. Without economic aid to feed the victims of that war and to maintain the economy of the country, internal collapse would have been inevitable. The supply of basic necessities, wheat, sugar, fuel, etc., through 1948 and 1949 was an essential military requirement.

In view of what has been written in early chapters about the strategic consequences of Western defeat in Greece, the expenditure of aid cannot be questioned. The Greek peninsula and isles were absolutely vital. The West had to make absolutely sure of their security. Viewed in this light, the entire economic aid program to Greece of nearly two billion

275

dollars, was in no way an overexpenditure. There is no need to stress the enormous difficulties that would have beset the Korean war if an unsettled Greece had continually posed another threat.

Given this unquestioned necessity and benefit of the aid program, we are nevertheless entitled to ask whether better value could have been obtained. Excluding immediate strategic considerations, we have to consider political and economic benefits sought and attained.

In this field we encounter doubt. Recent developments have caused acute political problems in Greece and neighboring countries.

POLITICAL ACHIEVEMENTS

Apart from its significance in the military field, Greece has special political features. It is the immediate neighbor of two Iron Curtain countries, Albania and Bulgaria, and of a principal "neutral," Yugoslavia. It is therefore a "Western shop window." In prewar days more than 25 per cent of its trade was with countries now engulfed in the Russian economic sphere. The Macedonian ports of Salonika, Kavalla, and Alexandroupolis are natural trade gates to southeast Europe, although the access through the Black Sea ports is now mainly used.

Even more important perhaps, and liable to be underestimated by Americans, is the profound psychological influence of the past. Western philosophy, art, and politics are predominantly of Greek origin. Its loss to an opposing ideology would be a shrewd blow to the West and would have sharp repercussions in the East, where Western-educated Asiatics are well aware of the profound influence Greece has exercised on European thought.

fortunately justification in a few cases is applied to the whole. Belonging to neither party but being regarded as a friend of both, I have had a unique experience of hearing both sides. More than once I have been treated on the same day to a Greek's views of a certain American and the American's view of that Greek. Normally this would tend to expand into a view of the whole American and Greek people. The American has his side. He feels the bite of ingratitude, and unfortunately but understandably reacts unfavorably to certain Greek characteristics. The Romans twenty centuries ago spoke unkindly of the Greeks' truthfulness. Unfortunately, Greeks are to this day still inclined to lie. More often than not it is a polite lie, an optimistic lie, told to please the listener and usually so palpably untrue that it could not deceive a child. This makes it all the more exasperating. It is unnecessary to make clear that men of the caliber of Kalinsky, Palaeologos, Samaras, Letsas, and others do not lie. The characteristic is with servants, landlords, shopkeepers, waiters, office staff. Although not a few of these are persons of real integrity, there is a far greater proportion of liars than in the United States or Britain.* Even the Greek of the highest integrity is subtle, and in a game of wits the American is no match.

Our classic story in this connection was of a clash between Miller and Palaeologos, both sincere and honest men. M.C.S. was importing 150 new tractors and had undertaken to surrender an equivalent number of old, uneconomic units. At a meeting, Miller announced that the new tractors would be held under his instructions at Piraeus and released as Paleologos handed over the old units. J. P. left the meeting without comment and quietly diverted the landing instructions to Patras. Some weeks later I chanced to walk in accidentally on

* This is also true of many other "aid" countries.

Moreover, Greece, through force of circumstances, is th least-developed of the European nations. It has a standard c living below FAO standards of basic requirements, but a popu lation which is almost wholly literate and has no submerge classes. This population shares fully with its Western allies th individualist outlook that we characterize as democracy. I political reactions to America and Britain and to our policie therefore, is a test case in which the scales are weighted in ou favor.

This preamble is necessary to give proper significance t the reactions to the aid program. Therefore I quote a Gree opinion to which I attach the utmost significance: "I am mo: deeply disturbed by present trends of opinion. Despite th Cyprus issue the feeling in Greece is more anti-American tha anti-British. There is a deep discontent with the West, whic goes beyond present issues. In part it is the result of left-win propaganda, but that does not account for the strong sentimer in other classes."

The last election, fought on a foreign policy issu returned a pro-Western government to power with a minorit of votes. That minority position must not be exaggerated, b cause the anti-government forces included those who voted fc the opposition for other reasons, but the position is not sati factory. It is a setback.

Initially, the restoration of stability and the first ec nomic aid did secure a considerable amount of goodwill f the West. There were, however, certain underlying grievanc A large American Mission, civilian and military, moved i House rents and servants' wages moved up. Even sergeants h cars, refrigerators, electric cookers, and other luxuries alm unknown to Greece. Legal selling at high profit and bla market operations followed. The comparative American wea provoked unpleasant comparison. I have already remarked the previous chapter on the problems of recruitment, and the unloading operation. I challenged J. P., who explained that it was most inconvenient to withdraw before replacement. He had given his word to surrender certain units, and as an honorable man he would do so. He had carefully avoided committing himself to time and conditions, and, knowing Mr. Miller, had let him talk on and assume his concurrence while scrupulously avoiding saying any word of agreement. Actually he did surrender the units later, but Miller, not appreciating the subtlety of distinction, took a rather dim view of the event.

These clashes in national temperament create as much of a problem in prolonged relations as do frauds. Contrary to general European opinion I would like to record that there are Americans of outstanding capacity in sustaining foreign relations. When they are good, they are the best, because there is genuine warmth in their relationships. But if bad they are impossible. Oddly enough, the first class are usually of Irish origin, and the second of German.

Apart from personal reactions, there was and is deliberate misrepresentation and anti-Western propaganda by the left-wing press, which makes the best possible use of all cases of personal friction. If an American car knocks down and kills or injures someone, it becomes a major event. All these, however, are family squabbles which are inevitable with closer acquantance and proximity.

The real root cause is an economic grievance. The original impetus of the program of American aid, whatever its defects, carried Greece back to prewar standards and better, but the world has changed much since 1939. Radio and films bring the highest material comforts within the sight of the least developed. When a mountain shepherd goes down to town he can see Hollywood's latest productions. When his wife and daughter go to town, the trouble really begins. It is, in a sense, extremely unfortunate that a major stress in United States propaganda in the cold war has been to emphasize the material prosperity of Western democracy. The logical sequence is to expect a share, as a friend and ally.

It is an extraordinary human characteristic that man can stay content indefinitely with a certain state of life, but becomes quickly dissatisfied with his speed of progress once improvement commences. This is the fundamental Greek difficulty at the moment. Improvement has been tasted. The village girl in the Peloponnese has now changed her dark homespun dress for a gay cotton frock, but she wants nylon underwear. This is not figurative speech; it is factual and fundamental in the areas above subsistence level. In less prosperous areas it is more basic. Men who lived on black bread and olives for centuries without question are now wanting milk and meat. This again is factual. One experienced welfare worker asked, some three or four years ago, why villagers did not eat their chickens. They replied in the Greek idiom that this was too high for them, "flesh meat was for city people." This long-standing tradition is now breaking down, and the lower strata are demanding more and better from life. One of my colleagues visited some villages that had received "United States agricultural surpluses." They liked the new "cow cheese," which they had never tasted before, and wanted more. This is the fundamental of economic progress. New demands are produced.

An announcement on the radio that a scheme has been instituted to irrigate 100,000 stremmata in Macedonia provokes demands for similar progress for every area of Greece. Now, everyone knows that irrigation schemes do not come without capital, and the only possible source of capital is the Western Allies, especially America. Every cut in the aid program since 1952 has set up an accumulative disapproval. The restrictive credit policy that freezes heavy tractors and drilling rigs, and that checks the upward progress, becomes an American expedient to rob the honest, hard-working farmer of his hopes of meat once a week. Such ground becomes fruitful to hostile propaganda. *Avghi* (the left-wing paper) announces that Russia would help. The right-wing papers grumble that Turkey (the traditional enemy) is getting x times as much as Greece.

The initial fault lay in the sharp cutoff in 1952, which laid emphasis on the changed policy and slashed projects indiscriminately without regard to priorities. A second major failure at this stage was the omission of insistence on the operation of the revolving fund repayments.

The elections in December, 1952, returned the right-wing parties to power instead of the center group. Greek opinion, impressed by the parallel swing in the United States, anticipated sympathetic backing. The Economics Minister approached the Mission and later visited the States and other Western countries to press for a five-year plan.

The importance of a term program to Greece is due to the fact that a large part of investment must go into programs where expenditure is necessarily spread over several years. Major land improvement projects to be carried over five years cannot be initiated on this year's vote if there is no security for funds to complete the project. The request for assured support over the period of construction is reasonable. As it is, no continuous program of development has been possible since January, 1952. This uncertainty has resulted in periodic crises and regular shutdowns of work.

Now obviously the Government has to sell itself to the electors. Faced with a hand-to-mouth budget, the need for United States aid is evident. The only answer is to get more aid. As gentle words and friendly appeals do not succeed, the alternative is "blackmail."

The press starts some campaign. There are not sufficient funds for more investment works, they say. The only course is to break the NATO commitments and reduce the army by a division. As soon as sufficient pressure is worked up, the United

States produces an extra ten million dollars. As a consequence, aid is no longer assistance to an ally, it is a payment for a service, to stay within NATO another few months, extorted by threats.

Each year as budget time approaches the same course is followed. First friendly appeals, the statement of needs, and polite hopes are expressed in the press; then grumbles and growls; and finally threats. Attention is drawn to the significant strategic position of Greece. Mention is made of the profits Egypt makes through sitting on the fence. Suggestions appear that neutralists like Tito and Nehru do better. The left openly repeats that the United States is concerned to give the very minimum to Greece. The American capitalist will wreck any proposal to finance sugar beets. He is determined to keep Greece open for his wheat or coal. Russia would give a fair deal. Finally, of course, Washington announces a little more, dribble by dribble.

Public opinion should be better informed. At one time the Mission had its own publicity service. Now it is handled by USIA. Regular releases are made to the Greek press and conscientiously printed. Since 1952 it has not been the practice to mark works as provided by aid funds. It is still the practice to mark imported goods. No publicity campaign to inform people on the mechanics of aid has even been undertaken. Now this has peculiar repercussions. Dried milk with aid markings might be imported by a private importer if the Bank of Greece decided, as explained in Chapter 2, to allocate his purchase against aid funds. On the other hand, direct gifts out of agricultural surpluses to the needy groups also carry aid markings, different in type. However a peasant not speaking English can hardly be expected to grasp this subtle distinction without explanation. As a result, many loose accusations are circulated concerning sale of aid supplies. At present the theory of counterpart operations is not publicly grasped. (I believe this is true in almost every country.) As a result many people say that aid is not given, it is sold. There is great need for public information on this point.

What then can we say about the public impression concerning aid? Greeks recognize the work on the roads and other rehabilitation. They know something or other about the other programs, but have no real picture of what aid has accomplished. Most Greeks will admit some of these benefits, but then complain that nothing is being done to settle the fundamental economic problems of the country. As a consequence Western influence is steadily losing ground, because the ordinary Greek peasant or worker feels that it promises far more than it fulfills, and that only under pressure.

ECONOMIC GAINS

Aid succeeded in its first purpose of establishing stability. As we have seen, the friendship and respect this gained has been blunted with the years. How far it has enabled Greece to progress on the economic side is an open question. Substantially, it did in fact restore the lost capital assets: rail, road, bridges, ports, dams, schools, houses. There are gaps still unfilled but on the other hand there are works accomplished that did not previously exist. We may therefore say that the scars of war have been healed. There is another consideration. The United States for example has been undisturbed in its economic expansion by the war and its aftermath. Seventeen years have given ample time to increase the nation's assets. For Greece, ten of those years represented the negation of progress, and some of the others have been devoted to reconstruction. Allowing for the extra impetus given by American aid, it is still not unreasonable to say that, in relation to the United States and many other countries, Greece has fallen farther behind, perhaps by five or six years, in development as a result of its war losses. This is a generalization, but it is borne out by statistics. This leads us to the question of whether aid has been not enough or whether it has been ill spent. The previous chapters have evaluated the program in different fields.

One of the most frequent questions to me over the last few years has been to give a valuation of the percentage benefit from aid. This is an impossible question to answer. With a sufficient army of staff, it might be possible to compute. Nevertheless, I have developed an answer: less than 10 per cent. One Greek official challenged this and claimed 40 per cent. We argued that both figures were completely arbitrary, but we both of us possessed very considerable data, and these were our respective impressions. We were limiting our consideration to the investment program as distinct from relief activities, which cannot be evaluated in monetary terms.

My own low estimate has to be, and is, always qualified. There are many projects that can still be salvaged, such as the well-drilling or the Phiniki irrigation project. Other projects, such as Mechanical Cultivation Service or railways, have shown only partial benefit. In time it is still possible to develop a much greater value for past aid.

Nevertheless the fact must be faced that a large proportion of aid funds have been wasted. The primary object of this book is to ascertain causes. The initial cause lies in the people who originally voted the aid. With the appropriation voted yearly, the beneficiary countries and the Mission planners have always been faced with the problem of committing it before the financial year's end. Failure to do so might result in loss of the funds, and almost certainly in a cut in next year's allocation.

It is possible to work to deadlines in an advanced, developed industrial country, where all relevant information is available as required. It is not possible to do so where conditions are unstable, organization is poor, and administration and information limited. As an inevitable consequence, blind guesses were often the substitute for plans. It is a definite fact that some of the worst mistakes arose in the last rush of payments made before the fiscal year's end. At that stage almost any request would be accepted, provided funds were available in the particular budget code. Often many such approvals would go through as "temporary filling" with the intention of later cancellation.

The next most important cause of loss is the failure to appreciate the consequences of a certain course. A major plan of development of any kind has certain inevitable results, which should be realized at the planning stage. No major industrial company would build and install a new plant without providing the working capital, the executive staff, and the key personnel to run it. Obviously the construction of even a small irrigation scheme requires advance plans for its future maintenance and administration. It is clear, too, that the cultivation pattern should be studied, arrangements made for training of farmers, and possible consequences, such as processing plant for new products or new varieties, studied and cattle selected. This equally applies to hospitals, ports and factories, or almost any other enterprise. In the majority of cases planners did not even consider these aspects. The aim seems to have been to build and then to face the problems.

On the Greek side this is partly comprehensible. They definitely lacked experience in many of the fields involved. On the American side it is less explicable. In fact, in many issues it is clear that the need was recognized by some people. All projects for reclamation include references to the requirements of project maintenance and administration. Very few of theses references and conditions passed beyond this stage.

The cause of this rests partly in the staffing of the Mission. As one colleague used to express it, "too many men with big ideas and no patience with the next stage." A fairer viewpoint would be that the Mission staff were primarily planners and construction men. It was considered that all other functions would be handled by the Greeks or by later American specialists. However, it must be remembered that if you are undertaking a program, say to build highways, there is little point in doing so if you do not see that the technique and administrative machinery exist to keep those highways maintained. This applies to almost every aspect of the program. Research equipment cannot be used fruitfully unless staff exist and funds are available to conduct research and to circularize and publish results.

As we have seen, the aid agreements in some cases contained provisions that the government was to take steps alone or in association with the Mission to meet these needs. These provisions have in almost all cases become completely inoperative. They are not worth the paper on which they are written. Since 1952, emphasis has been laid on the rights of sovereign governments to manage their own affairs. This has been asserted by Greek ministers and accepted by the Mission. The Mission relationship is advisory only. No one would or could dispute the sovereign rights of governments to rule within their own territories.

Equally, no one can dispute the right of a donor to attach conditions to his gift. If the recipient does not like the conditions, he can reject the gift. If he accepts the gift, he accepts a condition. That is the position of an aid project. If the conditions are good and valid, then their enforcement should be secured. If, therefore, an irrigation scheme was provided from aid funds, with the condition that a plan of administration and utilization be developed, and it be found as at Phiniki that the scheme is inoperative, United States Mission in no way intervenes in the sovereign authority of Greece by requesting an amendment in this state of affairs. If the sanatoria of Avestochori, Sparta, and Knossos stayed unoccupied, it is clearly the business of the Mission to ask the Greek government for an explanation.

As the aid program is a relationship between friends, it is obviously the correct policy for the United States Mission to discuss these problems of undigested aid on a practical basis and to see how a solution can be obtained. As at present practiced, a completely negative policy is followed.

In June, 1955, the Deputy Chief of Mission remarked to me that he thought our well-drilling report excellent and hoped that the Greek government would do something about it. Two or three days later I was approached about this report by government officials. They pointed out that to get the program under way required initial capitalization. As budget preparation at present stood, to introduce provision for funds would require cutting back other programs. They suggested that the Mission could cooperate with an additional release of counterpart, or an additional approval by the Currency Committee for part of the amount. This fell on deaf ears in the Mission. Any positive offer of this kind constitutes intervention in the affairs of a sovereign state.

I have already mentioned the Greek viewpoint that the Mission could greatly help the present civil servants by raising these issues at ministerial level. A little thought will make one realize why this is so. How many times have readers endeavored to raise questions with their chief or higher level and been postponed or brushed off. To be in a position to maintain continuous liaison over a wide range of projects, a mission must have continuity and a staff of high caliber. This, as we have seen earlier, is what the Mission in fact lacks. Constant turnover of staff necessarily breaks contact with the past. Only higher-caliber men can pick up and grasp a multitude of problems.

The argument over the years has been that aid is a temporary feature, and that aid to Greece was clearly a short-term program. Since 1945 I have heard with continuity of this constant short-term nature of aid. I recollect affirming over ten years ago that anyone who did not recognize that we were committed to fifty years of aid programs had not begun to recognize our basic dilemma.

PRIVATE INITIATIVE AID

I recall that at the time I was answered by the statement that private capital investment would take over. Now I am by profession a public accountant, and therefore it is part of my training and my business to advise on such matters as balance sheets and investments. I am not in any way a Socialist, and I believe that state intervention should be restricted to the minimum, but I know the limits of private enterprise. If I were asked today by a client for advice on investment of, say, a million dollars in Greece, my attitude at the best would be one of cautious reserve. Let us take some typical investments.

In the 1890's British and French capital formed the company to drain Lake Copais in Boeotia. In 1952 the lands of the company were expropriated and a final payment made to the shareholders in compensation by the Greek state.

There are ample opportunities for similar schemes in Greece, but no substantial private enterprise syndicate is prepared to undertake them.

An obvious project of this type is the Achelous plan of Knappen-Tippetts-Abbett-McCarthy. This involves the reclamation of the lagoon area and delta near Missolonghi by construction of levees and pumps, and an irrigation dam upstream. In practical business terms this means that initial capital investment of twenty to thirty million dollars would have to be produced over a period of seven to ten years, as a result of which the whole cultivation pattern of the area would be completely changed. From this point the investment might be amortized and a reasonable interest returned on capital over, say, thirty years. It is obvious that no investment house could sink its funds in such an investment, nor successfully float an appeal to the public.

First of all, what security could any investor feel as to the ultimate return of his capital? Prior to World War I the British, German, and French investor was prepared to face risks of this kind (as in the Copais) because he felt confident that his rights would in the last resort be enforced by his country's naval and military strength. No one can feel that such methods will be employed in present circumstances, and how can the investor be sure that Greece will not follow Czechoslovakia or Romania behind the Iron Curtain?

Apart from this angle, in present circumstances private capital is sensitive that such investments attract the political attack of "colonialism" or "economic exploitation." The modern investor regards seven to ten years as a long-term loan, but major agricultural developments require thirty-to-fifty-year commitments.

In the industrial field quicker returns might be expected. French and German capital has been offered for the Megdovas power scheme and for the Ptolemais thermal (lignite) plant. The terms are not overclear, but this was apparently on a ten-year basis. This is simply a credit deal for sale of plant and equipment by installment, and not a true investment, since it is not financially possible to amortize the costs of these schemes within the narrow time limits, without levying astronomical rates for power. These credits are in any case underwritten by the governments concerned.

A field where the private investor should in theory be able to find opportunities is the establishment of new industry. During the period of my stay in Greece rumors have been constantly raised of new American private capital. Greek-American interests have been involved in various negotiations. A sugar refinery, with development of beet sugar, was suggested but abandoned under pressure.

On several occasions I have discussed projects with representatives of these groups. Invariably almost all proposals have been rejected as outside the field of the particular group. Businessmen are fundamentally conservative in their approach. The man whose business experience is in cinema circuits becomes ultracautious in such foreign fields as logging and papermaking, or milk pasteurization and canning.

The establishment of branch factories or assembly plants tied up with leading British and American producers is an obvious hope to absorb the surplus labor of Patras and Piraeus. In India this is happening to some degree, but the large potential Indian market justifies the risk. Greece of itself is a limited market and does not justify the investment involved. It is the natural center for factories producing or assembling to supply the Near East or southeastern Europe, but political uncertainties within the region fail to attract capital in competition with safer areas. Israel is, of course, developing industrially but here other impulses are involved.

Private capital is ready to invest where the inducement is commensurate with the risk. In Greece and in most other underdeveloped countries there is not and cannot be an adequate inducement within a reasonable time. There are certain fields, like mining or oil drilling, where highly speculative investments are made. Even in this field it is to be noticed that the only mines that have surpassed prewar production in Greece are those to which "stockpiling loans" were made by the United States government, as bauxite and chrome. Nickel ore exports in 1938 aggregated fifty thousand tons, but none has been mined since the war. Canada is a safer and more reliable producer.

It has been frequently suggested that the United States government should guarantee foreign investments. This immediately places them as equivalent to government stock, yet with a return in terms of profits which would be ridiculous. The opportunities for corruption need no emphasis. If, on the other hand, these investments be made by private groups, supported by government guarantees of capital and interest at government bond interest rates, there is no difference at all from direct government loans, made from capital subscribed to meet national budget deficits as at present.

CHAPTER 18.

Planning Aid in Underdeveloped Countries

AID PROGRAMS IN THE LIGHT OF THE GREEK EXPERIMENT

The purpose of this chapter is to present a constructive approach to the aid problem generally, against a background of experience in Greece.

Conditions vary in each country affected. In general, however, the Greek picture is typical except for local modifications. The writer possesses a considerable background of information on conditions elsewhere. Program results and local reactions appear to be much the same as in Greece.

The reader can feel no better pleased with these results than are experienced aid personnel. We have achieved something, but it is not good enough to make for a feeling of satisfaction. Mistakes are inevitable in any walk of life. No business enterprise has ever enjoyed unalloyed success, and no experienced investor has not met losses. All human actions are fallible, and we learn from mistakes. Any value in this book depends on this constructive outlook.

A lot of mistakes occurred in Greece through total lack of experience in handling a program of capital development. It was a "nursery" effort, but its greatest benefit cannot be obtained unless we recognize this and examine it critically.

NECESSITY OF AID PROGRAMS

Let us face hard facts. Aid programs are just as essential as social welfare programs. Half a century ago, or even twenty-five years ago, many intelligent people remained unconvinced of the need of social welfare, collective bargaining, and state intervention in economic life. We now recognize, in Britain and America and almost throughout the world, that these activities are essential to the lubrication of our economic system. A wider distribution of economic benefits and the introduction of progressive welfare activities have helped the system rather than inflicted severe handicaps. The threat of a society split between "haves" and "have-nots" is progressively disappearing with rising wages, stable employment, and protection against old age and the catastrophes of life. Productivity continues to rise, and capital expands.

Aid is the application of the same intelligent self-interest outside the immediate family circle of our own economy. Charity begins at home, but it spreads out to a widening circle of neighbors. Just as the destitute unemployed of 1930–1931 presented a threat to our whole political and economic system, so today do the destitute peasants of India and Greece.

The moral law recognizes the right of a starving man to steal, provided his legitimate request for bread has been ignored. Ostentatious display of wealth is offensive to poverty. The radio, the press, the cinema every day taunt the submerged masses of Asia, Africa, Latin America with the wealth of the United States or Western Europe. Others besides the writer have doubted whether the best propaganda against Communism is to emphasize the material advantages gained by "democracy." Unless this propaganda is accompanied by a helping hand, the hostile demagogue simply presents the logical solution of taking from the "haves" to give to the "have-nots." This means inevitable war, with a consequent loss of wealth. We have already seen that economic gains are naturally the prelude to further economic demands. Development of any economy must be sustained. To hold a cup of water to the lips of a thirsting man, and to snatch it away after one sip, is torture, not help.

The economic liberal is inclined to argue that, as we helped ourselves, so should others. There is some justice in this claim, which we should recognize. It is not our obligation to provide nylon underwear for every girl in Asia. Economic aid is required to give a hand to the beneficiary to help him to his feet, not to provide a stretcher and an ambulance. It is quite evident that where a country is already possessed of the power to get on its own feet (e.g. the oil-rich countries) no assistance in capital schemes is necessary. The countries that do require assistance are those in which income is relatively low in relation to population, and consequently there is little or no surplus available for development. These are mainly agricultural countries with few exceptional resources and almost no industrial development. These are chronically short of capital, largely because an agricultural economy is tied to the harvest cycle, which absorbs the existing resources. Further development is absolutely dependent on further investment in the land and some degree of industrialization.

PRIVATE RISK CAPITAL

Many people who recognize the need for capital investment press the slogans of "Trade Not Aid" and "Private Risk Capital." These contentions again are valid in certain circumstances. On one occasion a certain distinguished senator visited Greece and emphasized these two aspects. On being told this by a colleague I inquired whether anyone had bluntly asked this gentleman what the United States proposed to buy from Greece and whether my colleague was prepared to make any personal investment or to recommend that anyone else do so. Undoubtedly, as the reader will have gathered, the Greek economy is ultimately capable of self-support and of exporting products abroad. To do this, however, its agricultural production must be increased by the land improvements studied in Chapters 5, 6, 7, and 9. If this is done, Greece can become the fruit producer of the Near East. If new industries are developed with outside capital, it may become a substantial exporter of manufactured goods.

However, no sane private investors would contemplate lending Greece, say, the capital to undertake the dam program, to be repaid in fifty years. This type of investment is essentially marginal, if the claims of the landowner and cultivator are given priority, as they must be. Political insecurity requires no stress, and investments that create a "land charge" for interest and capital are particularly open to the attacks of demagogues as "exploitation of the toiling peasant."

Investments in utilities, rail, ports, telecommunications, and power in undeveloped countries were undertaken successfully in the past. However it is extremely doubtful whether the modern investor is likely to follow this example. Many losses have been suffered, since the outcome usually depends on an increase in production, which may be deferred through extraneous circumstances. Furthermore, past investments have skimmed off the cream. Power in Greece is typical. The Athens projects financed by British capital thirty years ago were a reasonable commercial proposition. The nationwide network of power, the prosperity of which is dependent on the development of rural demand, is immensely more speculative, and the capital required is beyond the normal capacity of finance houses. Moreover, the foreign investor has found an obvious difficulty in extricating his funds from large-scale utility investments. This field is also susceptible to political pressures and threats of expropriation.

Investments in industry and commerce are more attractive than those in agriculture and utilities. Individual investments are smaller, more easily liquidated, and less vulnerable to political pressures and threats of expropriation. The main difficulties faced by the investor is the conversion of his local currency profits into pounds or dollars, and, of course, the eventual repatriation of his capital. This conversion involves the foreign exchange position of the country.

In reviewing the position of industry in Greece, we have already seen the difficulties in handling industrial expansion through state activities. This is a natural field for private capital if present handicaps can be overcome.

INDUCEMENTS FOR PRIVATE CAPITAL IN INDUSTRIAL DEVELOPMENT

The full use of private risk capital in industrial development is handicapped by socialist tendencies among political leaders in the countries concerned and by nationalist trends. The industrial enterprise contemplating such investment must recognize that full scope must be given to develop a local managerial and administrative class. The rising middle classes of the countries are extremely sensitive. Understandably, they do not want an industry that employs local labor as factory hands or clerks but reserves all supervisory posts to foreigners. There is a necessary period of establishment, followed by a transitional training period, as local management gradually takes hold.

The United States government has already initiated a program of investment treaties with developing countries, aimed to guarantee fair compensation against expropriation and to avoid difficulties in "repatriation." In certain fields guarantees have been offered against loss of investment and interest. These are usually limited to short term, five to ten years, and it is manifest that the building up of an industry able to liquidate initial capital and charges during so short a period is impossible in practice.

So far, results have been negligible. The possibility of further inducements and guarantees to encourage the private investor requires thorough study and exploration. Moreover, effective propaganda is required at home and in the countries concerned.

Certain governmental steps to assist private investors can be taken. The foreign investor could be guaranteed, or preferably insured, against loss through appropriation, war, or civil disturbance, and this guarantee or insurance fund could also assist repatriation of profits and capital through exchange difficulties. Recognizing that the investment incentive must necessarily be a high rate of return on capital, and appreciating that excessive profits attract the accusation of "exploitation," the home state of the investor could help enormously by concessions such as tax rebates on income received from "classified types of overseas investment."

The whole field of private investment requires careful study and continuous investigation by some established bodies of representative industrialists and financiers in the principal investing countries, working in cooperation with one another, and with the encouragement and support of their respective governments.

This is an opportunity for constructive private enterprise to make the best use of its resources.

INTERNATIONAL AID

There are still Britishers and Americans who have not yet learned the value of international cooperation and who persist in the outmoded notion that their national policies should be evolved separately and independently, without regard to neighboring or friendly nations. The problem of aid is international, yet many problems arise through its administration on an international basis. Britain, through colonial and Commonwealth arrangements, is able to keep most of its development program out of the strict field of international affairs. The United States is to some degree able to apply a family policy to Latin American affairs.

No one can legitimately challenge either of these arrangements. There are other countries also interested in foreign development whose individual contributions may not be significant, but which cumulatively are helpful. In the future it is to be hoped that, as nations move forward, these smaller contributions will progressively expand. The pooling of resources must therefore be encouraged at this stage. The "mite" of a developing country may extend and expand to a worthwhile effort later. If capital cannot be provided, technical assistance can sometimes be given. We are concerned in our own interest to develop mutual cooperation everywhere.

Nevertheless, we must recognize that in the UN aid agencies the burden must primarily be borne by America and Britain. The International Bank, FAO, UN Technical Assistance, and other agencies do useful and constructive work, which could be considerably expanded. Most members are receivers, not givers. There is obviously a tendency to "deals" and "share-outs" of availabilities, but this must not be exaggerated. Apart from the additional help developed and the outlook which becomes important in the future, the UN agencies can approach certain problems that could not be handled easily by single states.

Certain countries more favorably placed are able to generate substantial capital, particularly the oil group. These countries do not always manage these resources to best effect, but it is obviously impossible to dictate their internal affairs and the use or misuse of their own funds. Technical assistance schemes, involving employment of foreign experts, can be encouraged through international agencies, with the legitimate expectation that friendly advice, without strings, may be accepted. Ultimately constructive development of these countries will provide worthwhile foreign markets to developed and underdeveloped countries.

There is also a further group to which international aid is acceptable. Certain nations, through geographical position, internal politics, or other special cause, find difficulty in accepting direct aid that might have or might appear to have "strings." Ultimately we hope to attract some of these countries more closely, but at the present stage international aid, through either capital or technical assistance, maintains some measure of goodwill and assures these countries of genuine friendly intentions.

It is also to be recalled that certain agencies do establish a definite bridge between the two blocs into which the world is divided. Unless we believe in an inevitable armed clash, the maintenance of some constructive cooperation is ultimately beneficial to a more stabilized relationship. Despite all these advantages, we must realize that to operate aid programs on an entirely, or even predominantly, international basis is an ideal that is not easily attained.

There are certain halfway steps which to date have not been fully developed. OEEC (Organization for European Economic Cooperation), initiated in association with Marshall Plan aid, is an important medium for cooperation between members of the NATO group. The recent Baghdad Pact between Britain, Pakistan, Iran, Iraq, and Turkey incorporates significant provisions for economic development, with which the United States is now associated. This group has particular importance since it includes countries of widely different type. Britain is a developed economy. Iraq is oil-rich and is utilizing its new capital in constructive development. Iran, after setbacks, is again on the way to constructive self-support from its expanding oil revenues. Pakistan is a fairly stable, developing economy, which has some capital and some private investment support. Turkey is at present an acute problem, with an unstable currency and development problems similar to those of Greece. This type of limited international agreement may be ultimately very constructive.

So far, although there is fair measure of cooperation between the United States and Great Britain, the principal "aiders," agreements between prospective associates in the aid program do not exist. There are several economies capable of doing something useful in this field. Germany, Japan, and Canada are the most important, but France, Switzerland, Italy, Benelux, and the Scandinavian countries are not to be disregarded. The labor potential of Italy could be put to fuller use in expanding production of investment goods. There is unlimited market to absorb the full production of the developed economies if we can only establish the machinery.

DIRECT UNITED STATES AID

Despite the possible help from other countries, the United States must continue to carry the main burden and responsibility, as enjoying the greatest wealth and production potential.

Understandably, Congress wishes to protect the American taxpayer from unnecessary or wasteful expenditure, and for this purpose it wishes to retain the established right of annual review. No democratic body can be expected to sign a blank check on the future. Yet no other single cause has contributed more to the waste of aid funds than the annual basis on which they have been voted.

The major investment projects in agriculture and utilities require progressive, sustained investment over several years. The importation of heavy construction machinery requires a program of progressive utilization.

Customarily, funds for aid are not voted before July. National investment programs cannot be prepared until the aid allocation to the country is known, perhaps in September or later. Then must follow detailed programing for foreign exchange and local currency proceeds. All the procedures of quotations, amendments, contracts, and commitments must take place. Any funds not committed before the end of May must lapse. Congress members who are businessmen must realize that they could not operate their own enterprises on this alternating cycle of uncertainty, lull, and rush. They must also recognize that aid funds mainly involve construction works. Construction work in any country is dependent on season. In Greece, for example, the best working period for earth-moving machinery is July to September, but this period is over before aid credits are known. One year's funds are therefore usable only during the next year. In the meantime they have been partially committed to some other project, since the country is operating from hand to mouth.

A definite level of aid established for three years in advance would make possible orderly planning and performance—making best use of funds and securing all commercial and climatic advantages practicable.

It is not necessary to emphasize further the detailed advantages of term aid, nor the disadvantages of fluctuating, uncertain annual aid. One has heard it claimed that the annual basis of aid is a sort of check on the good behavior of aided countries. If this opinion is sincerely held by any man, let me disabuse him at once of this belief. The temporary nature of aid in fact imposes more pressure on good relations, as it has come to be recognized that a certain amount of recalcitrance will secure a larger contribution.

Longer-term aid with an assured program of development several years in advance is the surest guarantee of stable relations. Undoubtedly beneficiary countries will continue to

ask for more, but they have ample time to discuss and negotiate before applying pressures. The donor can always withhold
his gift, and the recipient is not so foolish as to risk the loss
of certain aid for a speculative benefit. At present, United
States aid is as speculative as Russian, but a guaranteed annual
contribution places it on an entirely different basis.

Term aid as distinct from annual aid would also make
it possible to specify clearly the objectives for which it was to
be used. At present, political factors become confused with
economic factors. The result is seen in the regular breach of
project agreements in Greece and elsewhere.

Longer-term aid could and should be labeled as to des-
tination and conditions. It is clear that a constructive American
aid program for Greece should carry fairly definite tags. So
many million dollars for well-drilling, so much for land improvement, so much for Axios dam. The people would be well
aware of what the United States was doing for them. They
should also be made aware of the conditions attached, such
as organized administration, repayment over so many years,
and so forth. Non-compliance should be bluntly recorded.

I recollect visiting a certain project in which a condition
of payment of maintenance dues had not been observed. I
visited two villages, predominantly growing rice. I said: "The
money for these works was given you by American taxpayers.
Many of them grow rice like yourselves. Those American rice
growers paid their own dues and gave the money for your
works out of their profits. What will they think if I tell them
that you allowed the irrigation canals they gave you to fill up?"
Immediately a farmer fresh from the paddy, legs bare and
trousers rolled up above the knees, stood up. "I am ashamed.
Tell our American brothers that we did not know that they
had given us this project. We withheld our dues because we
thought this was a government project, and we were dissatisfied
with the delay in completing works." (This was one of the

projects shut down in 1952 in a partially completed stage.) Numerous speakers who followed begged me to address a meeting of the ten villages involved, to explain the project and its conditions. The local government officials endorsed this request, but the Mission would not approve.

The aid issue is not a matter between diplomats and governments. It is, and should be recognized as, the neighborly helping hand given by one man to another. Plain, honest, hardworking men throughout the world understand how others feel. In Greece I used this type of approach time and again with the same instantaneous reaction.

AID ADMINISTRATION

This paragraph brings me to the end of this book, and to a repetition of what I regard as one of its most important lessons.

I am most bitterly opposed to the present integration of diplomacy and aid, foreign service and aid administration. First, if you integrate diplomatic and economic issues you lose the whole benefit of goodwill. Aid loans or grants degenerate into "bulls-eyes" for good boys—or into plain blackmail.

Obviously and understandably, you give a helping hand to your friends first, but friendship is not bought. Equally obviously, you give priority to political danger points. These are not day-to-day considerations but long-term trends. We know our established friends, and we know the danger points. Over and above this, we do what we can on a man-to-man basis, and not to buy adherence to pact or policy. This is a clear answer to Russia. If we adopt any other policy, we turn the aid program into a flea circus.

Equally as damaging as the attempt to integrate objectives is the attempt to integrate administration. Diplomacy is a career requiring certain training and characteristics. Normally this field does not require specific technical knowledge, management experience, or commercial training. These qualifications are imperative to aid administration. No one can honestly make recommendations about aid to underdeveloped countries if he does not possess the ability and training to appreciate fundamental business and technical problems. A United States military mission is only theoretically under the control of the ambassador. Until June, 1955, the Economic Aid Administration had the same status. Currently, it is a part of the State Department. This is equivalent to placing the management of a bank in the hands of a schoolteacher. Diplomacy and aid administration are widely divergent fields. The aid administration, apart from the requirement of possessing the ordinary courtesy and tact necessary to any social relation, depends not on capacity to present a viewpoint in an attractive manner, but on capacity to assess and present business and technical problems.

This again does not mean that any businessman or technician will do. An aid administrator must be endowed by nature with a broad outlook, capacity to grasp a problem involving technicalities as well as any competent administrator, and sympathy and understanding of fundamental human problems and relations, not carried to sentimental excess.

As far as possible, all technical staff working on aid programs must possess the same qualities. Sometimes people talk about international spirit and other virtues. Really all one needs to deal with the members of any other nation on a friendly basis is a recognition of the facts that men everywhere have much the same hopes, aspirations, ideals, outlook, and intellectual and moral characteristics, but that there are certain national and environmental modifications that must be studied and learned.

In the future, when we recognize the inevitability of aid, someone will no doubt evolve a course of training. For the present the only school is experience, which inevitably means mistakes. Mistakes are expensive. It is all the more necessary to retain the services of those who have learned from experience. For the last ten years, to our cost, we have pursued quite the contrary policy.

Aid salaries are not, I repeat not, adequate to attract the right type of men. A country program of, say, fifty to a hundred million dollars per year is a substantial and complex operation, as this book will have shown. It must be adequately staffed with competent people, not clerks. The Controller's Office of the United States Mission to Greece never had more than one man with a salary above $10,000. Few aid salaries were much above that figure. This is hardly attractive in its prospects.

Personally, I would also like to say with deference that an extension of the policy of employing "third-nation nationals" as practised in the Greek Mission would be beneficial and useful. At the time that it was initiated, extension was contemplated. It would secure that introduction of a different view that is so beneficial to the international agencies, and break down the "front-to-front" relationship between recipient and beneficiary, which tends to embarrass direct aid. Close cooperation with international agencies is imperative.

In the technical assistance field under direct aid, introduction of other nationals is important. In the first place it is much cheaper. In the second, most candidates from other nations already have excellent experience in the problems involved. Thirdly, it avoids giving the impression of creating an American colony or dependency.

That is perhaps the most important consideration in all aid administration. One must recognize that every nation or group of men has its particular pride, often when it is least noticeable. Western democracy recognizes the fundamental equality of man and his rights to liberty. Economic aid must not, therefore, be associated with any expressed or implied threats to freedom.

This does not mean that the other man's view should be accepted. It does mean that you should answer him fully and fairly with reasons for your own view, and not secure results by bullying.

Local administration should be given considerable autonomy as there is nothing more exasperating than a fiat from headquarters given without reason or explanation, and with no way of presenting a reasonable case.

It must be recognized that in human affairs perfection is unattainable. It is impossible to eradicate all waste and all errors. However, the progress of man to his present standards of civilization has been made possible through a continuous willingness to learn from mistakes. The object of this book, as stated from the beginning was not to criticize, or to raise scandals. I have sought to explain where mistakes have arisen and to indicate for the benefit of all—for Americans, for British, for Greeks and for all the other peoples of the modern world— the ways in which I personally think those mistakes may be avoided in the future.

I would like to close this book with what I think to be the fairest view of the Aid Program. Since 1945, the American people have faced a responsibility and carried a burden which have been exceedingly heavy. The fact that the burden and responsibility have been faced to the utmost of their ability is itself a great achievement. Mistakes were inevitable and fully excusable by the novelty of the situation and by the fact that experience can only be gained in practice.

I recall my father's advice: "Remember that only the man who never acted, never made a mistake. Never be afraid to act and never be afraid to admit mistakes."